Dancing

with

MRS. DALLOWAY

DANCING
with
MRS. DALLOWAY

STORIES OF THE INSPIRATION
BEHIND GREAT WORKS OF LITERATURE

CELIA BLUE JOHNSON

A PERIGEE BOOK

A PERIGEE BOOK
Published by the Penguin Group
Penguin Group (USA) Inc.
375 Hudson Street, New York, New York 10014, USA
Penguin Group (Canada), 90 Eglinton Avenue East, Suite 700, Toronto, Ontario M4P 2Y3, Canada
(a division of Pearson Penguin Canada Inc.)
Penguin Books Ltd., 80 Strand, London WC2R 0RL, England
Penguin Group Ireland, 25 St. Stephen's Green, Dublin 2, Ireland (a division of Penguin Books Ltd.)
Penguin Group (Australia), 250 Camberwell Road, Camberwell, Victoria 3124, Australia
(a division of Pearson Australia Group Pty. Ltd.)
Penguin Books India Pvt. Ltd., 11 Community Centre, Panchsheel Park, New Delhi—110 017, India
Penguin Group (NZ), 67 Apollo Drive, Rosedale, Auckland 0632, New Zealand
(a division of Pearson New Zealand Ltd.)
Penguin Books (South Africa) (Pty.) Ltd., 24 Sturdee Avenue, Rosebank, Johannesburg 2196,
South Africa

Penguin Books Ltd., Registered Offices: 80 Strand, London WC2R 0RL, England

While the author has made every effort to provide accurate telephone numbers and Internet addresses at the time of publication, neither the publisher nor the author assumes any responsibility for errors or for changes that occur after publication. Further, the publisher does not have any control over and does not assume any responsibility for author or third-party websites or their content.

First edition: October 2011

Library of Congress Cataloging-in-Publication Data

Johnson, Celia.
    Dancing with Mrs. Dalloway : stories of the inspiration behind great works of literature / Celia Blue
Johnson.—1st ed.
        p.   cm.
    Includes bibliographical references.
    ISBN 978-0-399-53692-2
    1. Fiction—Authorship.   I. Title.
    PN3355.J55 2011
    809.3—dc22   2011015555

PRINTED IN THE UNITED STATES OF AMERICA

10 9 8 7 6 5 4 3 2 1

Most Perigee books are available at special quantity discounts for bulk purchases for sales promotions, premiums, fund-raising, or educational use. Special books, or book excerpts, can also be created to fit specific needs. For details, write: Special Markets, Penguin Group (USA) Inc., 375 Hudson Street, New York, New York 10014.

To Mum and Dad,
for encouraging me to be inspired

CONTENTS

INTRODUCTION

I HAVE ALWAYS BEEN A WILLING PARTICIPANT IN THE ART OF fiction, eagerly following a trail of words wherever they might lead, and I often wonder how a writer arrived there before me. There was no path carefully etched for them. Instead they had to forage through the vast possibilities in their imagination to arrive at one specific idea, a concept they chased with fierce determination from the beginning of a story to its end.

One cold winter day, I finished reading *Mrs. Dalloway* for the third or fourth time and decided to investigate what happened before page one. I traced the steps that Virginia Woolf took to create her polished socialite and soon discovered that there was a real-life Mrs. Dalloway, a woman just as complex as her fictional counterpart. Then I began to speculate about the origins of all my favorite books. So I set out to track down the bright sparks of inspiration that prompted great writers to pen their famous works of literature—and this book is the result of that quest.

None of the writers I studied share the same road to creative genius. Each book is drawn from the intricate fabric of imagination, experience, and, often, pure chance. What these authors do have in common, though, is an intense desire to seize inspiration the moment it appears. And it usually arrives when least expected, whether it is at a surprise meeting with a stranger, while daydreaming during a lull in the day, or in the middle of reading a fairy tale aloud. Ideas can turn up anytime, and they are as unique as the stories they inspire.

The essays in this book are all based on rigorous research, but I would hesitate to assert that any of them defines precisely what spurred an author to write. After all, it is impossible to place ourselves within the minds that produced these literary fireworks. We have to settle for witnessing the display from a distance, through first- and secondhand accounts. And it is important to remember that the same writers who tell us about their inspiration are also master storytellers. They know exactly how to take a simple tale and add a twist to make it a little more interesting. Oftentimes, authors and their friends and family members have conflicting memories of definitive moments in literary history. There is no way to tell which version is correct, and perhaps they all are. It is very difficult to pinpoint the exact truth behind any of these books. What we can do, though, is study the events that led to each novel and appreciate the stories that have been told about their composition.

These accounts may amount to literary myths, but they capture the spirit of creativity. They also reveal that inspiration could be lurking around any corner. Ideas are often fleeting, overwhelming one moment and forgotten the next. But if you are ready, you might be able to grab hold of lightning when it strikes.

Dancing
with
MRS. DALLOWAY

When Lightning Strikes

The difference between the almost right word and the right word is really a large matter—'tis the difference between the lightning bug and the lightning.

—MARK TWAIN, IN A LETTER TO GEORGE BAINTON

COUNTLESS MEDIOCRE IDEAS HAVE BEEN SCRUNCHED UP AND tossed into wastepaper baskets over time. Every writer knows the agony of waiting for inspiration to arrive. It is possible to sit at a desk for eternity, head burrowed into hands, with no guarantee that lightning will strike. Yet sometimes, out of the darkness, there is a big, bright burst. It might be a concept, a simple image, a line of text . . . whatever form it takes, it is enough to propel a writer to action. And it might just be the flint for an enduring novel.

Strangely enough, many literary treasures were born suddenly out of mundane tasks. Gabriel García Márquez was driving his car, J. R. R. Tolkien was grading papers at school, and E. B. White was carrying a pail of pig slop. These duties would have been forgotten without a second thought if inspiration had not struck with great force. Instead, they became literary milestones.

In the following pages, some book concepts erupted after simmering in the back of an author's mind, and others seemed to arrive out of nowhere. What they share in common is that magical moment, a snippet in time that altered a writer's career forever.

Anna Karenina

1875

LEO TOLSTOY

LEO Tolstoy sat back on a sofa in the grand home he had lived in since childhood. The estate was called Yasnaya Polyana, and it lay about 125 miles away from Moscow. It was twilight and the birch trees that lined the dirt roads were barely illuminated in the dying light. Tolstoy had just finished dinner and his full stomach had a somnolent effect. As he drifted toward sleep, he was struck by a vision. It was "a bared female elbow," and Tolstoy found that he could not look away. He watched a figure grow around the elbow. She stood before him in a stylish ball gown, and despite the party attire, there was sorrow on her beautiful face. The vision haunted Tolstoy and he felt compelled to tell the story behind his fleeting daydream. Tolstoy never mentioned when he received this fateful visit, which lingered in his mind until he finally began to write a novel in the spring of 1873. The book that evolved from his twilight muse was *Anna Karenina*, the tale of an ill-fated adulteress.

Tolstoy only saw one person in the after-dinner mirage, but before commencing work on the novel he encountered a couple of women who may have contributed to the character of Anna Karenina. One of these ladies appeared during a party at General Tulubyev's home in Tula. Tolstoy was captivated by the stunning woman with dark curly hair and a "smooth gait." He asked his sister-in-law Tanya for the name of the beauty, and she told him that it was Maria Hartung, daughter of the poet Aleksandr Pushkin. It is not clear whether Tolstoy saw Hartung when he was relaxing on his sofa, but many believe that she is the physical model for Anna Karenina. In fact, Tolstoy named Anna's family Pushkin in an early draft of the novel.

Another woman may have sparked Tolstoy's imagination. In 1872, Anna Stepanova Pirogova committed suicide by jumping in front of a train at a station near Tolstoy's house. She had been having an affair with one of Tolstoy's neighbors and was devastated when he left her for another woman. It is often said that this bereft lover inspired Tolstoy and that he used her name for his protagonist. But Tolstoy never acknowledged that the awful event influenced his book; in fact, he said he had been pondering a story about an adulteress for some time before Pirogova's death. In February 1870, Tolstoy's wife, Sofia, noted in her diary that he planned to write about an elite woman in the midst of an affair, who was "not guilty but merely pitiful." Perhaps his vision of the elbow occurred around the time of the diary entry.

Aleksandr Pushkin played arguably the most important part in the creation of the novel—he inspired Tolstoy to sit down and write. In the spring of 1873, Tolstoy read Pushkin's *Tales of Belkin* for about the seventh time. It was a series of five interconnected stories and the poet's first work of prose. Tolstoy admired the brilliance of the simple opening in "Loose Leaves": "The guests were arriving at the country house. . . ." Pushkin did not bother to offer a lengthy introduction or waste too much time setting the scene. The story began with the action already in full swing. Tolstoy fixated on the impact of that one line.

In March 1873, Tolstoy wrote a letter to his friend Nikolaj Strakhov that he never sent. In it, he recalled how *Anna Karenina* came to life right after reading Pushkin. Tolstoy noted, "Involuntarily, unwittingly, not knowing why and what would come of it, I thought up characters and events, began to go with it, then of course changed it, and suddenly all threads became so well and truly tied up that the result was a novel." Before this point, Tolstoy had only pondered his novel in theory. Now he barely paused to take a break from writing the saga of an upper-class woman.

Tolstoy almost finished a draft of *Anna Karenina* within three weeks. But upon revising, the story expanded, and it took much longer to complete than he anticipated. Along the way, Tolstoy began to doubt the worth of a novel about people in the midst of affairs. He struggled, and once lamented, "If only someone could finish *Anna Karenina* for me." The book was published as serial installments in the literary magazine *Ruskii Vestnik* beginning in 1875 and the author was surprised by the positive response from readers. He still insisted that it was "ordinary and insignificant" in 1877, the same year he finished the book. Yet, after his first flurry of writing, Tolstoy had expressed, "This novel—I mean a novel, the first in my life—is very close to my heart." It is possible that this original affection helped him stick with *Anna Karenina* to its conclusion.

Around the World in Eighty Days

1873

JULES VERNE

JULES Verne sat in a Parisian café and flipped through the newspaper. A prolific writer, Verne knew ideas could strike at any moment so he always read with a pencil and a notebook nearby, ready to catch a concept before it evaporated into a hazy memory. As he turned the pages, a travel advertisement in one of the columns caught his eye. It beckoned tourists to circumnavigate the globe in just eighty days. This was an impressive deadline for the 1870s, when the standard method of long-distance travel was by train or boat. Verne's imagination began to fire. He recalled, "It immediately struck me that I could profit by a difference of a meridian and make my traveller gain or lose a day in his journey. There was my dénouement ready found." It was not long before Verne set to work on a rollicking escapade featuring Phileas Fogg, a man who wagers a large sum of money that he can travel around the world within that relatively short time frame. Fogg takes only a couple of changes of clothes, basic travel necessities, and a passport, in which each new stamp will offer proof that he followed the agreed-upon course to circle the globe.

As he wrote in 1872, Verne felt as though he was traveling right alongside his protagonist, racing to win the bet. In a letter to his editor, Verne enthused, "If you could imagine how amused I am with my journey around the world in eighty days. I dream about it! Let's hope our readers are equally amused. I must be a bit cracked; I let myself get involved with all my heroes' extravagances."

Around the World in Eighty Days was a story perfectly suited to Verne. From a young age, he had a great love of adventure, particularly on the water. He and his brother, Paul, often set out on expeditions in a leaky boat on the River Loire. When he was a child, Verne also spent hours watching machines clank, spin, and whir during long visits to a government factory called Indret, which was located near his family's summer house in Chantenay. He never lost his fascination for machinery. Even after he grew up, Verne had "as much pleasure in watching a steam-engine of a fine locomotive at work as . . . in contemplating a picture by Raphael or Correggio." Verne's new novel combined both of his youthful obsessions. Fogg's expedition involved just about every method of transportation you might imagine over land and sea, from modern machines like boats and trains to the more unusual sleigh and elephant rides.

Following his first publication, *Five Weeks in a Balloon*, in 1863, Verne often produced two or more books a year, including *Journey to the Center of the Earth* and *Twenty Thousand Leagues Under the Sea*. Verne received little critical acclaim for his books, but they were popular among readers. Despite his impressive output, he was typically a methodical writer, revising each manuscript so extensively that the finished product rarely resembled the first draft. Verne observed, "I work very slowly and with greatest care, writing and rewriting until each sentence takes the form that I desire." But *Around the World in Eighty Days* was written with unusual speed, begun in the spring of 1872 and finished by early October the same year. It seems that the manuscript needed little revision. It was in such great shape in June that Verne read a few chapters aloud to the Amiens Academy of Sciences, Letters, and Arts.

Almost fifteen years after the publication of *Around the World in Eighty Days*, a young American woman paid Verne a visit at his home in Amiens, France. Nellie Bly, an intrepid journalist, had taken on an assignment to travel around the world as Fogg did in under eighty days. Bly had a lot of pluck for a young woman in the late nineteenth century. A man had first been selected for the piece and Bly told her boss that if he did not give her the job, she would pitch the same story to another paper, beat his man around the world, and then write all about it.

Verne was thrilled that Bly planned to follow in the footsteps of his hero. He said, "My principal thought was—*Dieu!* How I wish I were free and young again! I would have been enchanted to do the same trip, even under the same conditions—rushing around the globe without seeing much."

While she was in Amiens, Bly received a tour of Verne's house, including his study, but it was not the ornate workplace that she had expected. His writing room was small and bare, with a simple pile of paper (his latest manuscript) on the desk, accompanied only by an ink bottle and a pen holder. Clearly he needed nothing more than a vast imagination once he set to work on a manuscript. When they left the study, Verne pulled out a map of Fogg's journey and added Bly's itinerary so that he could follow her progress. Bly reached her destination in just seventy-two days, six hours, and eleven minutes—and during that time, Verne would daily point out to his wife where he thought the traveler might be and mark the spot with a little flag on the map.

Treasure Island

1883

ROBERT LOUIS STEVENSON

OBERT Louis Stevenson dipped his brush into the watercolor paint and added the finishing touch to a remote island. He stepped back to admire his handiwork. It was a beautiful map, carefully rendered and exquisitely colored. And then he saw them, a series of characters looking up through the newly painted woods. They were equipped with weapons and, as Stevenson recalled, "They passed to and fro, fighting, and hunting treasure, on these few square inches of a flat projection." Soon a great adventure story began to take shape in Stevenson's mind. He promptly dropped the paintbrush, picked up a stack of papers, and wrote a chapter outline for *Treasure Island*.

The map was the product of a dreary vacation. In August

1880, Stevenson, his father, Thomas, his wife, Fanny, and his twelve-year-old stepson, Samuel Lloyd Osbourne, all traveled to Braemar, a village tucked away in the Scottish Highlands. It was an ideal holiday setting, surrounded by impressive mountains that were perfect for hiking. Stevenson hoped the elevated climate would help cure his sickness. He had been coughing up blood and, though he was never officially diagnosed, it is believed he suffered from tuberculosis. Unfortunately, it rained constantly in Braemar that season, so Stevenson rarely had a chance to breathe in the mountain air and his activities were limited to the confines of his cottage. Though Stevenson never considered painting one of his hobbies, it was a favorite pastime for Sam. Since there were few options for entertainment, Stevenson sometimes picked up a brush and painted alongside him. Despite Stevenson's lukewarm interest, the watercolor map led him to his first successful work of fiction.

The aspiring writer had tried to write a novel at least ten times, only to stop once under way. There was something different about the tale evoked by the map. Stevenson began writing *Treasure Island* on a cold September morning in Braemar while sitting by the fire. His pen zipped along, filling page after page. Each afternoon Stevenson read the latest installment to his family. Sam and Thomas were particularly invested in the pirate story. Thomas spent half a day compiling a list of the contents of Billy Bones's sea chest, which Stevenson loyally replicated in the book.

Treasure Island's cunning pirate Long John Silver was inspired by poet William Ernest Henley, a friend of Stevenson's. After contracting tuberculosis of the bone, Henley had suffered the amputation of a lower leg, but he dealt with the loss courageously. Sam remembered Henley as "a great, glowing, massive-shouldered fellow with a big red beard and a crutch; jovial, astoundingly clever, and with a laugh that rolled like music." Stevenson removed all of Henley's refined traits to carve out a tough seafaring man, though he carefully left in some of his most admirable qualities. As a result, Silver is not simply a cutthroat pirate; he also displays Henley's trademark warmth and charisma.

Stevenson wrote with great gusto until he reached the beginning of chapter 16, and then he stopped. He suddenly lost steam and could not think of another word to add to the book. As time passed, this failure caused Stevenson to question himself completely. He observed, "I was thirty-one; I was the head of a family; I had lost my health; I had never yet paid my way." But in October 1881, just over a year after Stevenson traveled to Braemar, the book was being serialized in a children's publication called *Young Folks*. The paper had already played an important role in shaping the story, with editor James Henderson changing the title, originally *The Sea Cook*, to *Treasure Island*. Henderson, along with many readers, would have been severely disappointed if the tale was left unfinished.

With a deadline looming, Stevenson traveled to Davos, Switzerland, for the winter, but he resolved not to worry about his swashbuckling adventure. He would immerse himself in reading and cast aside the stress of writing. To Stevenson's surprise, the moment he stopped fixating on his writer's block, his creativity flowed freely once again. Stevenson wrote a chapter a day, hurtling toward two words that he had never written before in a novel: "The End."

In November 1883, *Treasure Island* was published in book form by Cassell and Company. The novel included a map, but it was not the same image from Braemar. Stevenson's precious painting was lost en route to the publisher. He tried to replicate the original version, calling upon his father to remind him of specific details. Yet, as Stevenson recalled, "Somehow it was never 'Treasure Island' to me." The lost map had acted as a guide for the author's imagination, sending him across new terrain and right into the middle of bloody battles. Rugged characters did not peek through the trees in the new topography, but luckily that original spark had already been transferred onto the pages of *Treasure Island*, where pirates, sailors, and a young boy all raced to find buried treasure.

The Sound and the Fury

1929

WILLIAM FAULKNER

IN October 1927, William Faulkner sent the finished manuscript of *Flags of Dust* to his publisher and included an enthusiastic note: "I have written THE book, of which those other things were but foals. I believe it is the damdest best book you'll look at this year, and any other publisher." He could not have anticipated the reply that arrived two months later: Boni and Liveright rejected the novel. Publisher Horace Liveright wrote a detailed description of its flaws, culminating in the following criticism: "My chief objection is that you don't seem to have any story to tell and I contend that a novel should tell a story and tell it well." Dejected, Faulkner waited a few months before he began another piece, but as he settled down to work, he did so with new focus. With his professional career at a standstill, Faulkner wrote for himself. He recalled, "One day I seemed to shut a door between me and all publishers' addresses and book lists. I said to myself, Now I can write." Free from the constraints of catering to a commercial audience, Faulkner drew inspiration from his childhood.

On June 2, 1907, nine-year-old Faulkner attended the funeral of his maternal grandmother, Lelia Swift Butler. While the adults mourned the loss of their loved one, the children were sent outside to play, too young to understand the gravity of the event. Twenty years later, Faulkner had a vision inspired by this memory. A bold young girl climbed a tree to peek through a window after being cast out of a funeral, while her brothers looked up at her "muddy drawers" from below. Faulkner decided to write a short story based on the scene. He thought it would last ten pages, but as he worked, the tale expanded far beyond his expectations.

Caddy, the girl who climbed the tree, turned out to be much more than a mere child in a story. Faulkner recalled, "So I, who had never had a sister and was fated to lose my daughter in infancy, set out to make myself a beautiful and tragic little girl." Caddy's life quickly took shape in Faulkner's imagination; she had three brothers almost before he had a chance to write down her name. The first sibling was Benjy, a mentally challenged boy who symbolizes true innocence in the novel. Faulkner alluded to Benjy in the title of the book, which is taken from William Shakespeare's *Macbeth*: "It is a tale / Told by an idiot, full of sound and fury." After Benjy, Faulkner added two more boys to the family and by that time it was clear that he had begun a novel.

The Sound and the Fury is told in four parts, and three are from the perspectives of Caddy's brothers. Faulkner described these sections as a series of failures to capture a story perfectly. After telling the story from one viewpoint, Faulkner would realize that another one needed to be added—and so the novel grew. Benjy's perspective is particularly complex, with sudden movements between multiple time frames. At one point, Faulkner hoped that this portion of the narrative would be printed in different-colored inks to help readers recognize each shift, but the production costs would have been astronomical. Instead, Faulkner used italics and simplified the narrative as much as possible so that readers would not become lost as they tried to follow his character's unusual thought processes.

Faulkner did not stray from his childhood memories to create the backdrop for *The Sound and the Fury*. The novel is set in Yoknapatawpha County, which is based on Lafayette County, Mississippi, where Faulkner grew up. The name may sound like a mouthful, but it is based on real Native American words. The Chickasaw tribe lived in Lafayette County until around 1800, when the land was transformed into plantations. "Yoknapatawpha" is a combination of Chickasaw words that translate to "water flowing slow through the flatland." Faulkner wrote many stories set in this fictional place, and years later he was asked whether he would ever return to Yoknapatawpha County. He answered that he had never left.

While Faulkner was writing *The Sound and the Fury*, he found a publisher for *Flags of Dust*. Editor Hal Smith from Harcourt accepted the manuscript, though not in its original form. He stipulated that Faulkner must drastically reduce the word count. This was accomplished with the help of Ben Wasson, Faulkner's friend and agent at the time. Smith then turned down *The Sound and the Fury* after he was unable to garner enough enthusiasm for the book from his colleagues. But this turned out to be another fateful rejection for Faulkner. Smith left Harcourt to start his own publishing company with Jonathan Cape. He snatched up Faulkner's new novel for Jonathan Cape and Harrison Smith in February 1929. *The Sound and the Fury* was published to high critical acclaim and even though it did not immediately become a huge bestseller, it was destined to live on as a literary giant for years to come.

The Hobbit, or There and Back Again

1937

J. R. R. TOLKIEN

J. R. R. Tolkien sat at his desk to grade a stack of exam papers. A professor at Oxford, Tolkien was used to the mundane task of reviewing his students' work, but it must have felt particularly tedious on this summer day in the early 1930s. As Tolkien turned from one page to the next, he came upon a blank piece of paper that had somehow slipped into the pile. The gloriously empty space inspired him to pick up his pen and write the first sentence that came to mind: "In a hole in the ground there lived a hobbit." Tolkien had no idea what a hobbit was or why its home was underground. With that simple line, he set up a mystery to unravel. As he recalled, "Names always generate a story in my mind. Eventually I thought I'd better find out what hobbits were like. But that's only the beginning." Tolkien later filled in sheets of blank paper while sitting at the same desk by the window on Northmoor Road, and with each page, he got to know more about his little rotund character.

Tolkien did not have to reach far, as it turned out that hobbits were quite similar to him. Despite a successful career in academia, he was not mired in research and scholarly pursuits. In October 1958, Tolkien wrote a letter to scholar Deborah Webster Rogers, observing, "I am in fact a hobbit in all but size. I like gardens, trees, and unmechanized farmlands, I smoke a pipe, and like good plain food (unrefrigerated). . . . I like, and even dare to wear in these dull days, ornamental waistcoats."

Since hobbits took on many of Tolkien's characteristics, it was natural that their charming Shire resembled his favorite setting. Tolkien had cultivated a love of the outdoors ever since he moved to the small town of Sarehole, England, when he was five years old. Sarehole was in Worcestershire, a county whose lush fields and rolling hills felt more like home to Tolkien than any other place in the world. So he placed the hobbits' houses beneath hills that were just like the ones he explored as a child. Tolkien even named Bilbo Baggins's underground dwelling "Bag End" after a Worcestershire farm that belonged to his aunt.

The Hobbit did not evolve in Tolkien's mind with the speed and spontaneity of his first sentence. He once noted, "My stories seem to germinate like a snowflake around a piece of dust." This tale grew over time, layer upon layer, and it was a few years before Tolkien actually picked up where he left off on that summer day. In the meantime, the only details he recorded were in the form of Thror's Map, which captured part of the world beyond the Shire. Yet Tolkien must have been shaping the story in his mind all along, because when he did resume writing, it flowed almost seamlessly onto the page. He finally finished the book in 1936, almost six years after he first jotted down the enigmatic opening sentence.

During the composition of the book, in cold winter months, Tolkien's children would gather around every evening after dinner to listen to the latest installment. According to Tolkien, his eldest son, John, was the only one who enjoyed hearing about the hobbit's quest. His other children were less eager to listen, and they did not appreciate the marvelous tale until years later, after they had grown up. There are claims that Tolkien wrote the book purely for the enjoyment of his children, and he may have started this rumor himself. In 1967, during an interview for the *New York Times*, he admitted, "If you're a youngish man and you don't want to be made fun of, you say you're writing stories for children." Still, Tolkien must have secretly hoped that he would reach an audience far beyond his home, one that included both adults and children.

When Tolkien completed *The Hobbit*, he typed up a clean version of the manuscript but did not bother to include the final chapters. He merely recited the ending to his children to wrap up the saga and then let the pages lie dormant. Tolkien did not share the book with many people beyond his literary club, a group called the Inklings, which was founded by

C. S. Lewis. While the book was still in draft form, he read portions to these fellow scholars during meetings at a pub called the Eagle and Child.

Elaine Griffiths, an old student of Tolkien's, was one of the few friends outside the Inklings he allowed to read *The Hobbit*, and she immediately sensed its commercial potential. At the time, Griffiths was working on a translation of *Beowulf* for the London-based publishing house George Allen and Unwin. When editor Susan Dagnall visited Griffiths in Oxford, she heard all about the epic tale. Dagnall reached out to Tolkien, who allowed her to pack up the unfinished manuscript and take it back to London. After soaring through the story, Dagnall asked Tolkien to add the final chapters so that she could submit the full book for publication. Her boss, Stanley Unwin, agreed to accept *The Hobbit*, but only after he received a positive reader's report from his ten-year-old son, whom he often called on to review new children's books.

Unwin's son probably deserved more than one shilling (his standard fee) for the report. Tolkien's novel enthralled an unprecedented number of readers. It was published in September 1937 and had sold out by December the same year. Unwin was confident that readers would eagerly buy a sequel. Tolkien did not share Unwin's enthusiasm for another work featuring the little hobbit. He had already covered vast terrain in the book. What else could possibly lie beyond the Shire? So Tolkien submitted *The Silmarillion* instead. It was set in the same world that hobbits inhabited, but it did not feature these charming characters. Unwin did not waver. He turned down the book and again requested a story about hobbits.

Tolkien resolved to at least try to fulfill his publisher's request. More than a decade later, after many stops and starts, including a writer's block that he finally overcame after encouragement from C. S. Lewis, Tolkien finished what he called "the new Hobbit." Despite his reluctance to begin, Tolkien found that this tale was full of surprises. After he wrote the book, he recalled, "I met a lot of things on the way that astonished me." It was a very long saga, much grander in scope than *The Hobbit*. Unwin decided to publish the huge tome as a trilogy, and the first book was renamed *The Fellowship of the Ring*, followed by *The Two Towers* and *The Return of the King*.

Animal Farm

1945

George Orwell

A YOUNG boy raised his arm, whip in hand. The massive cart horse by his side had begun to wander off. The whip flew down and directed the horse back onto the path. George Orwell watched as the diminutive figure took charge of an animal that towered over him, and an idea struck. What if animals realized how much stronger they are than humans? A whip would be no match for a horse. Our power would completely diminish. The relationship between humans and animals reminded Orwell of the dynamic between the rich or powerful and the poor.

Orwell had been looking for a metaphor for Soviet Russia for some time. He wanted to write a story that exposed the country's political system as a failed model for socialism.

Orwell was an advocate for socialism, but only if it meant true equality for the lower classes. He explained his view of Russia: "Since 1930 I had seen little evidence that the USSR was progressing towards anything that one could truly call Socialism. On the contrary, I was struck by clear signs of its transformation into a hierarchical society, in which the rulers have no more reason to give up their power than any other ruling class." So Orwell created an allegorical tale about animals taking over a farm, declaring equality, and then falling into disrepair, in which greedy, lazy pigs represented the Russian rulers.

Orwell had never been to Russia, but he had witnessed the powerful arm of the Soviet government as it destroyed the lives of innocent people. In 1936, civil war broke out in Spain and Orwell rushed to the front lines as quickly as possible. The young writer's wartime experiences proved pivotal to his writing career. He later noted, "Every line of serious work that I have written since 1936 has been written, directly or indirectly, *against* totalitarianism and *for* democratic socialism, as I understand it." Before that time, he had sold two novels and one autobiographical work, all in quick succession. After the war, he continued to write a book a year, both fiction and nonfiction, but with a newly honed political focus.

As an English citizen, Orwell had no official affiliation with Spain, but he was determined to contribute to a worthwhile cause. Orwell met other international volunteers as he traveled through France to Spain in 1936, but he went his own way once he arrived in Barcelona. He wasted no time in visiting the Independent Labor Party's building, striding into supervisor John McNair's office and declaring, "I have come to Spain to join the militia and fight against Fascism." McNair led Orwell to a left-wing militia group called POUM, the United Marxist Workers' Party. Orwell was looked upon as an outsider until his fellow soldiers sat down with him and a large supply of strong wine. They had expected to drink the quiet Englishman under the table, but by the end of the night, Orwell was one of the last men standing, and thus gained their respect. The next morning, Orwell had everyone running drills under his orders. He was a fearless and passionate fighter, surviving many brushes with death, including a shot to his throat.

In 1937, Communists gained partial control of the Spanish government, and among them were representatives from the Soviet NKVD, the People's Commissariat for Internal Affairs. This group accused many people of consorting with fascists, including members of POUM. Soldiers and activists were questioned and then subjected to imprisonment, and in some cases they just disappeared. Orwell and his wife, Eileen, who had joined him in Spain, were lucky to get back to England alive. Orwell recalled, "To experience all this was a valuable object lesson: it taught me how easily totalitarian propaganda can control the opinion of enlightened people in democratic countries." He was then determined to dispel any illusions about Soviet Russia and socialism, and when he saw the boy with the cart horse, he finally had a metaphor for his cautionary message.

Orwell first conceived the idea for *Animal Farm* in 1937, but he did not begin working on the manuscript until the winter of 1943. Every night, he read the day's work to Eileen while they were huddled up in bed, since their apartment was so cold. Eileen must have been thrilled, as this was the only book that Orwell allowed her to see midcomposition. When the book was completed, Orwell sent it from one publisher to the next, and rejections began to mount. Most publishers were reluctant to print a book that offered such a negative critique of Russia, particularly when Russia was fighting Germany, a common enemy of England. One publisher almost accepted the book but then declined. He included the following note in his letter to Orwell: "I think the choice of pigs as the ruling caste will no doubt give offense to many people, and particularly to anyone who is a bit touchy, as undoubtedly the Russians are." Orwell became desperate and, at one point, he entertained the idea of self-publishing the book.

In one last effort, Orwell tracked down Fredric Warburg of Secker and Warburg, a small independent press that had published two of his previous books. Orwell had tried bigger publishing houses, perhaps with the hope of developing his literary career, but Secker and Warburg now seemed like the only viable option. Warburg had just finished lunch and was walking out of a pub when Orwell hurried in and pulled him over to sit by the bar. Disheveled and nervous, Orwell handed him a thin and worn manuscript for *Animal Farm*. He acknowledged that the book was probably too anti-Russian for Secker and Warburg, as it had been for so many other houses.

Warburg disagreed. He decided to take a risk and publish the controversial novel, despite his wife's warning that she would leave him if he did. Paper was scarce during wartime, but Warburg managed to print *Animal Farm*, and his wife, however angry she might have been, stuck with her stubborn husband. The book was published in England in August 1945, with a conservative run of 4,500 copies, but it sold out within a few days, prompting the publisher to go back to print right away. *Animal Farm* continued to sell steadily, but it became a huge hit a year later when it came out in the United States, where it was selected as a Book-of-the-Month Club pick, helping propel sales to over a half million.

The Lion, the Witch and the Wardrobe

1950

C. S. LEWIS

ON an otherwise ordinary day, C. S. Lewis was suddenly swept into a daydream that took place far away from the village of Great Bookham, in unfamiliar snow-covered woods. Intricate flakes drifted onto treetops and blended into the smooth, white ground. This faraway land was just as peaceful as the wintry countryside in England—that is, until a frazzled creature hurried past. He was a faun, half man and half goat. Despite his animal features, the faun was strangely gentlemanlike, carrying an umbrella and a bundle of parcels. Sixteen-year-old Lewis had no idea where the faun was heading. He waited until he was forty to find out.

Decades after his daydream, Lewis decided to write a children's book. He recalled, "I am not quite sure what made me, in a particular year of my life, feel that not only a fairy tale, but a fairy tale addressed to children, was exactly what I must write—or burst." As he searched for a concept, his mind slipped back to the peculiar scene from years before. Lewis resolved to follow the faun, but he had no idea where that path would lead. Before he could take off into the woods, he needed to figure out where that land was located. He soon discovered that it actually originated in a country house like his own on the outskirts of Oxford. The entrance to this place could not be found on any map. To get to the imaginary land, his characters simply had to walk through a wardrobe.

Lewis began to conceive his fairy tale when World War II had just begun. With the threat of invasion, millions of children were evacuated to rural areas throughout the country. A group of schoolgirls moved into Lewis's home under the care of Jane Moore, his unconventional housemate. When Lewis served in the army during World War I, he and his friend Paddy Moore had made a pact to take care of the other's family if either of them died. Paddy was lost in battle and Lewis kept his promise, eventually moving in with Jane and her daughter, Maureen. They lived in a quaint house called the Kilns, which was surrounded by eight acres of land.

The wartime evacuees filled Lewis's home, but they were agreeable guests and offered inspiration for his fairy tale. He decided to place his fantastical vision against the real-life backdrop of World War II. Lewis set down a brief description in his notebook. He would write a novel about four children who leave London because of the war and stay with an old professor in the country. In *The Lion, the Witch and the Wardrobe*, the youngest of the four children stumbles across a magical wardrobe in the professor's house. It is a large oak piece with a mirror on front, much like one that Lewis owned. She pushes through a series of coats and, rather than hitting the back of a wardrobe, steps into snowy woods, where she promptly meets a faun.

A faun was the catalyst for *The Lion, the Witch and the Wardrobe*, but according to Lewis, a lion "pulled the whole story together." Lewis found it difficult to continue his story once under way. He was not sure how the adventure would progress until he began to dream about lions. Lewis drew from these nighttime visions, adding a lion to the tale, and the plot immediately picked up again. Aslan, Lewis's "great Lion," was named using the Turkish word for lion. The land beyond the wardrobe was also named after a real-world source. Lewis was scouring through *Murray's Small Classical Atlas* when he stopped to underline a town, Narnia—or *Narni* in Italian— located in central Italy. The word sounded unusual and mythical, perfect for his fictional realm.

When he was writing *The Lion, the Witch and the Wardrobe*, Lewis asked his friend J. R. R. Tolkien what he thought of the first couple of chapters. Tolkien was a fellow member of the Inklings, a group of literary aficionados who first congregated regularly in Lewis's room at Magdalen College at the University of Oxford. Together they drank beer, talked about literature, and read their own work aloud. Later they also met in other settings, including a local pub called the Eagle and

Child. Lewis had been a strong advocate for Tolkien's *Hobbit* years before (see pages 19–23), and he probably hoped for an equally enthusiastic response for his own children's tale. Tolkien respectfully listened to the opening chapters, but he did not offer a positive review. In fact, when candidly discussing the book away from Lewis with fellow Inkling Roger Lancelyn Green, Tolkien exclaimed, "It really won't do, you know!" Lewis was buoyed by encouragement from other Inklings, including Green. Still, Tolkien felt so strongly about the book that he stopped attending meetings when Lewis planned to bring up his Narnia tale. And yet Lewis was undeterred: he went on to find a publisher for the novel. When *The Lion, the Witch and the Wardrobe* was published in 1950, it became a bestseller, and since then, many critics and readers have disagreed with Tolkien's verdict.

Charlotte's Web

1952

E. B. White

E. B. White watched as a large gray spider crept along its intricate web. Many people would have shrieked in terror, but White was fascinated by the elegant creature. He later discovered that she was a barn spider and, like other orb weavers, she would often dismantle and rebuild her web. The spider lived in White's backhouse in North Brooklin, Maine, and she quietly wove her way into his imagination.

One day, while White walked through an orchard on the way to feed a pig, he was struck by an idea. He had recently quit contributing humorous articles to the weekly "Notes and Comment" section in the *New Yorker* so that he could focus on his own work and enjoy life on the farm. White owned many animals and yet he found the relationship between a farmer and his livestock troubling. According to him, "A farm is a peculiar problem for a man who likes animals, because the fate of most livestock is that they are murdered by their bene-factors." Even though White raised and slaughtered his own livestock, he decided to reverse the fate of a doomed farm ani-mal in *Charlotte's Web*. White had been pondering a children's story about saving the life of a pig, but he was not sure who would be up to the heroic task. Then, as slop swished in the pail by his side, White's mind turned to that magnificent barn spider and its web. Perhaps the talented weaver could rescue his fictional pig!

White wrote *Charlotte's Web* in the boathouse behind his farm. He preferred to work on rainy days, because there were too many wonderful distractions when the sun was shining. Chickens clucking and pecking the ground, cows meandering across the grass, pigs rolling around in the dirt—all those sights appealed to the ex–New Yorker. When he did write, White could look out through the mist of rain to the cove where he first saw the farm that would become his beloved home. In 1935, White and his wife, Katharine, were sailing along the coast of Maine when they spotted a barn from the water. The next day, they drove past the same farm only to discover that it was for sale, and they bought it. That barn became the model for the animals' home in *Charlotte's Web*.

During the composition of the book, White often visited his muse in the backhouse, where she spun her impermanent web, and on a cold fall night, an egg sac appeared. A ladder and bright light were promptly brought into the room so White could witness each stage of the baby spiders' growth. While the little spiders were still forming, White embarked on a trip to New York. To avoid missing an important step in their growth, White placed the egg sac and barn spider in a box, carried them all the way to the city, and tucked them in his dresser. He recalled, "Some weeks later I was surprised to find that Charlotte's daughters were emerging from air holes in the cover of my box. They strung tiny lines from my comb to my brush, from my brush to my mirror. . . . We all lived happily for a few weeks, and then someone whose duty it was to dust my dresser balked, and I broke up the show." New Yorkers were simply not attuned to nature in the same way as White. Despite the terror the newly hatched spiders induced in others, White found the experience moving, and it helped inspire a fitting end to his book, with the birth of Charlotte's offspring.

The tale of White's real-life backhouse spider spanned beyond her own life when one of her babies—kindly returned to the farm from New York—took up residence in his barn. In a letter to his editor, Cass Canfield, White described how every time he knocked down the spider's web, which he often accidentally did, she rebuilt it again. Eventually, the savvy creature caught on and wove the web outside his path, avoiding the destruction of her home. She reminded White of the extraordinary weaver in *Charlotte's Web* and he jokingly wrote of the real spider, "Her ingenuity has impressed me, and I am now teaching her to write SOME BOOK, and will let

Brentano [a bookstore] have her for their window." It turned out that no spider feats were necessary. Upon publication the book was an immediate hit, soaring to the top of the *New York Times* bestseller list for three full weeks.

Catch-22

1961

JOSEPH HELLER

JOSEPH Heller was drifting to sleep when a couple of sentences popped into his mind. Inspiration typically arrived at odd hours and mundane moments, whether Heller was walking the dog, brushing his teeth, or simply lying in bed. He explained, "The ideas come to me; I don't produce them at will. They come to me in the course of a sort of controlled daydream, a directed reverie." Often these ideas had very little context, and the sentences that sprang up that night were no exception: "It was love at first sight. The first time he saw the chaplain, Someone fell madly in love with him." Heller was not sure who the "Someone" was or where the chaplain worked, but he would add those details later. Somehow the lines were full of possibility. He jumped out of bed and paced up and down his tiny Upper West Side apartment in New York. As he walked, a story took shape around those two sentences. The next morning, Heller went to his day job at an advertising firm and wrote the first chapter of *Catch-22*.

During his late-night march, Heller discovered that the fictional chaplain was in the army during World War II. Heller had recently discussed the dark humor of war with some friends, one of whom had been injured in battle. The wounded veteran could not appreciate these types of jokes, even though another soldier felt they were fitting. The conversation inspired Heller to use his two sentences to write about war. He noted, "It was after that discussion that the opening of *Catch-22* and many other incidents came to me." His novel would offer a comedic view of the war and all of its absurdities, from senseless violence to inane bureaucracy.

World War II was a familiar setting for Heller. He enlisted in the Army Air Corps in 1942 and went on to become a wing bombardier. Heller thought he was in for an exhilarating experience and was disappointed to see little action when he was first shipped out to the island of Corsica, off the coast of France. Then a gunner was wounded in Heller's plane and he realized, "Good God, they're trying to kill me, too." War lost its glamour after that point. Heller's protagonist, Yossarian, is also a bombardier, but he is not to be mistaken for the author. After writing the novel, Heller clarified, "He is who I might like to have been, had I the knowledge then that I now have."

After Heller wrote the first chapter of *Catch-22*, his agent sold the unwritten book to Robert Gottlieb at Simon and Schuster. It was the first novel Heller had ever attempted, and it took him a long time to write. He recalled, "Working on *Catch*, I'd become furious and despondent that I could only write a page a night. I'd say to myself, 'Christ, I'm a mature adult with a master's degree in English, why can't I work faster?'" But Heller was forced to work at a slow pace, rigorously revising sections before moving forward. Amid the planning and slow evolution of the story, Heller also experienced sudden bursts of inspiration. He carried around three-by-five note cards to scribble down sentences that came to mind, usually during moments of solitude. By the time he had finished the book, he could have filled a shoe box with all of his cards.

Heller called his novel *Catch-18* throughout its composition. It would have remained that way if his publisher had not learned of another book with a similar title. Bestselling author Leon Uris's *Mila 18* was scheduled to come out right around the same time as *Catch-18*. There was a strong chance that readers would mistakenly assume the books were alike and naturally they would pick Uris's novel over an unknown writer's debut. Another number was sought for the title. Heller suggested fourteen, but Gottlieb was hoping for something with more significance. Eleven played nicely into the theme of repetition in the novel, but there was competition for that number in the form of a popular action movie, *Ocean's 11*, which was released in 1960. They finally settled on twenty-two, also a repetitive number, and one that would stand on its own, without confusing the public when the novel hit bookstores.

Heller's closing line for *Catch-22* came to him just as abruptly as the opening sentences. He was riding the bus and his mind had begun to wander, when the ending appeared. It was a simple and yet powerful sentence: "The knife came down, missing him by inches, and he took off." Most likely, Heller pulled out one of his handy note cards to record the line. Typically he could not start writing a novel until he had the closing line. He did manage to compose the first chapter of *Catch-22* after envisioning the opening lines, but he probably had to wait to continue the story until after that bus ride, when he had an end to work toward.

One Hundred Years of Solitude

1967

GABRIEL GARCÍA MÁRQUEZ

GABRIEL García Márquez gripped the steering wheel as he navigated the winding road that led from Mexico City to Acapulco. With the engine humming, suddenly it came to him, the opening sentence to a novel: "Many years later, as he faced the firing squad, Colonel Aureliano Buendía was to remember that distant afternoon when his father took him to discover ice." García Márquez knew immediately that an epic tale lay just beyond that vivid line. Even though he had just set out on a much-needed vacation with his family, García Márquez threw his foot down on the brakes, turned the car around, and cut the trip short so that he could begin work immediately.

There are accounts that conflict with the story above, which was originally told by García Márquez, and some of these variations come from the author himself. It is not surprising that an intricate storyteller spun a myth around his own writing process. Perhaps he did not turn the car around immediately. Maybe it was not the opening line that struck him; it could have been an idea or a concept. But there is no question that García Márquez was hit with a wave of inspiration during that car ride, and upon his arrival home, he began to write fervently.

García Márquez grew up under the care of his grandparents until he was eight years old. They lived in Aracataca, a tropical Colombian town. One day, the boy and his grandfather visited a local business, and they stopped to look at a crate of fish packed in ice. It was the first time García Márquez had ever seen ice and, to his surprise, when he touched the strange substance it burned. He could not believe that something that was supposed to be incredibly cold could feel so hot. Many of García Márquez's ideas come from childhood experiences. Touching ice for the first time stuck with the author and that memory came to him on the way to Acapulco.

It took approximately one year for García Márquez to write his novel. During that time, he quit his job at an advertising agency to focus on his own writing, so he and his wife Mercedes had to become adept at the art of survival. First they sold the car that García Márquez had been driving on their vacation. Then, as months progressed and their money dwindled, they sold more valuable possessions, from the television to the fridge, all to finance what promised to be an enduring novel. Mercedes negotiated extensions on their rent and eventually told the landlord she would not be paying him for eight months. She set up a long line of credit with the local butcher. With her help, the family managed to survive on barely anything while García Márquez toiled away.

García Márquez at first felt daunted by his literary endeavor. He recalled, "I finished the first sentence and asked myself, terrified, what the hell came next." But after about ten pages, the writing began to flow. Words, sentences, and scenes tumbled out of his typewriter; it was unlike anything he had ever experienced before. Even García Márquez's typist, Pera Araiza, was enthralled with the emerging tale. She received typed pages filled with handwritten notes that she would retype, in addition to correcting the spelling errors scattered throughout the manuscript. Then every weekend, unbeknownst to García Márquez, she would host a reading of the material she had worked on that week. *One Hundred Years of Solitude* captivated a local audience during these weekly readings, but no one was more invested in the story than its author. When he reached the inevitable death of Colonel Aureliano Buendía, García Márquez walked upstairs to where Mercedes was sleeping and wept for two hours.

The end of *One Hundred Years of Solitude* hit the novelist with the same force as the opening on the way to Acapulco. García Márquez was visiting Aracataca, the town where he first touched ice, when one evening the final scene appeared to him. He immediately ended the trip and went home, though this time he raced toward a conclusion rather than a beginning. The book was a huge hit upon publication, pulling García Márquez out of poverty and into international literary fame.

In the Telling

This tale grew in the telling.

—J. R. R. TOLKIEN, "FOREWORD," *The Fellowship of the Ring*

BEFORE THEY WERE WRITTEN DOWN, STORIES WERE TOLD, and they were often altered from one generation to the next. It must have been easy to take creative liberty with an old tale, to revamp a lackluster character or offer a happy ending in place of a sad one. Stories were malleable beyond the confines of the written page, and it seems that this flexibility appealed to the authors in the next part.

Whether they picked up an old classic or came up with an original tale, the following writers all stumbled upon ideas while storytelling. Lewis Carroll discovered Wonderland while rowing up the Thames River with three young girls. L. Frank Baum landed in Oz when he was in the middle of telling a completely different story. And A. A. Milne strolled up to the doorstep of the House at Pooh Corner during a bedtime ritual. Each author was inspired—often unexpectedly—through the act of telling a story. Perhaps this tradition will forge ahead; an unsuspecting writer will pick up one of the following books and, while reading it aloud, come up with a new literary treasure.

Frankenstein

1818

MARY SHELLEY

THUNDER rumbled and lightning curled down to touch the Swiss mountaintops. Fierce storms had raged for days, causing the typically idyllic countryside to become muddy and uninviting. These dreary conditions threatened to ruin a perfectly lovely vacation for Mary Godwin and her companions, who had survived an arduous journey through the mountains to Lake Geneva. While rain pattered against the windowpanes, they huddled by the fireplace, searching for a way to entertain themselves.

It was 1816 and the seventeen-year-old Mary had traveled to Switzerland with her illicit lover and soon-to-be husband, Percy Bysshe Shelley, and their four-month-old son, William. Percy had recently left his wife and run away with Mary, whose father strongly disapproved of their affair. Mary's step-sister, Claire Clairmont, accompanied the couple. She had suggested they visit the famous poet Lord Byron while he stayed by Lake Geneva, as she was eager to rekindle a relationship with him following their brief affair earlier that spring.

Not long after they arrived in Geneva, the travelers settled into a quaint lakeside chalet. They were only a ten-minute hike from the impressive villa where Byron was staying with his physician, the twenty-year-old doctor and aspiring writer John Polidori. The two groups spent much of their time together, strolling during the day and sailing across the lake on moonlit nights. And it was not long before they became one of the main attractions in Geneva that season. A famous literary figure, Byron was also known for his unconventional lifestyle, and tourists were eager to catch a glimpse of him in person. One enterprising hotel owner rented a telescope so that guests could spy on Byron and his friends. Sightseers would have been disappointed when the weather took a dismal turn, forcing the group indoors and out of the public eye.

Late one evening the group had convened at Byron's villa and someone discovered a book that was perfect for a stormy night, a collection of German ghost stories translated into French. They gathered by the fire and took turns reading aloud—the hair-raising tales proved to be thoroughly entertaining. When the storytelling was over, quick-thinking Byron decided to pose a challenge to his guests: they were each to write their own scary tale.

According to Mary, she was the only one who struggled to

come up with something right away. Shelley penned a story that was inspired by his youth. Byron, on the other hand, wrote a chilling fragment about a vampire. Polidori's tale did not have the intended effect. He wrote about "a skull-headed lady, who was so punished for peeping through a key-hole," and Mary was not amused. Despite her negative review, the game proved fortuitous for the young doctor. He later used Byron's abandoned, unfinished piece as the basis for "The Vampyre," a popular story that was the first vampire fiction ever published in English.

Mary had high expectations for her work. It would have to "make the reader dread to look round, to curdle the blood, and quicken the beatings of the heart." But none of Mary's ideas seemed terrifying enough to meet these standards. Every morning, Mary was asked about her progress and she consistently replied that there was none. Meanwhile, the group continued to spend time together, often discussing literature and science. One day Mary overheard a conversation between Percy and Byron about groundbreaking studies in galvanism, which involved bringing the dead back to life. An experiment had already been performed on a little worm that supposedly wriggled after death. Galvanism posed troubling questions about mortality. What if human corpses could be reanimated, too?

The discussion haunted Mary late into the night. While struggling to fall asleep, she had a vision of a monster cobbled together with human body parts. Mary recalled: "I saw the pale student of unhallowed arts kneeling beside the thing he had put together. I saw the hideous phantasm of a man stretched out, and then, on the working of some powerful engine, show signs of life, and stir with an uneasy, half-vital motion." As she lay awake, Mary was terrified but also inspired. If this dream overwhelmed her with fear, surely it would have a similar effect on her companions. Finally she had a concept for her story. The next day, when Byron and Shelley left to sail on the lake, Mary stayed behind to write about a troubled doctor and the monster he galvanized to life.

"Rip Van Winkle"

1819

WASHINGTON IRVING

ASHINGTON Irving was suffering from writer's block. Years had passed since the publication of his humorous debut, *The History of New York*, in 1809. At first, he was convinced it would be better to take a break before picking up his pen again. "I wish to proceed as cautiously as possible," he noted, "and if my caution does not enable me to write better, it will at least preserve me from the hazardous error of writing too much." Now, when Irving was finally ready to get back to work, he could not think of a worthwhile story. He was in low spirits when he visited his sister, Sarah Van Wart, in Birmingham, England.

Irving typically enjoyed staying in what he had jokingly dubbed "Castle Van Tromp," but he was preoccupied with the inability to write. His brother-in-law, Henry, tried to pull him out of his gloom by reminiscing about the Hudson Valley. Irving cherished his memories of growing up in New York, where he had explored dark woods and absorbed the local Dutch culture. Their conversation progressed at a steady clip until all of a sudden Irving jumped up, dashed to his room, and sat down to write.

Irving worked in a frenzy, weaving a story that evoked his native country. It was a fitting tale—given the author's sudden burst of creativity—of a man who woke up after falling asleep for years. His protagonist, Rip Van Winkle, lived in the Catskills, an area that Irving vividly recalled from his teenage years. He noted, "[O]f all the scenery of the Hudson, the Kaatskill Mountains had the most witching effect on my boyish imagination." In the morning, when everyone sat down to breakfast, Irving rushed into the room clutching a stack of pages. Even though he had not slept at all, the curly-haired, dark-eyed writer was full of energy. While his companions finished their meal, they listened to him read "Rip Van Winkle."

Nostalgic conversation acted as a catalyst for Irving's late-night writing spree, but his story was also inspired by "Peter Klaus," a German folktale. In this tale, Peter the goatherd is led to a strange place by a mysterious man. Peter then drinks from a tankard of wine and falls asleep. When he wakes up, Peter is in his old field, but his flock is gone, the grass has grown, and his beard is a foot long. To his dismay, he realizes that he slept for twenty years. Rip Van Winkle has a similar shock after an eerily long nap, but Irving reinvented the classic

German tale with his trademark humor and American sensibility.

Around the time he wrote "Rip Van Winkle," Irving received a letter from his brothers about a promising job as a clerk with the navy, but the short story had given him new confidence and he decided to take a less traditional route. He declined, noting, "I do not wish to undertake any situation that must involve me in a routine of duties as to prevent my attending to literary pursuits." He would become a full-time writer. His career depended upon the success of *The Sketch Book of Geoffrey Crayon*, a collection of stories that included "Rip Van Winkle."

Geoffrey Crayon was a pseudonym that Irving assumed for the book. He was accustomed to using a pen name, a practice that had helped build buzz for his debut novel. *The History of New York* was credited to Diedrich Knickerbocker, an old Dutch historian Irving had dreamed up. He and his publisher planted newspaper articles about Knickerbocker before the publication of the book. Headlines such as "Distressing" were followed by an alert, calling readers to look out for a missing "elderly gentleman, dressed in an old black coat and a cocked hat." Little was said to be known about the man, who had left behind nothing but debt and an unusual book, *The History of New York*. The fake news was a clever marketing ploy, and it worked. By the time Irving's historic spoof made its way into print, readers knew all about Knickerbocker, and some even thought he was a real man. Knickerbocker surfaced again in *The Sketch Book of Geoffrey Crayon*. Two of the stories in the anthology were credited to the old historian: "Rip Van Winkle" and "The Legend of Sleepy Hollow." These tales became the most popular ever written by Irving and, coincidentally, he jotted down an outline for "The Legend of Sleepy Hollow" during his pivotal visit to the Van Warts' home.

Alice's Adventures in Wonderland

1865

LEWIS CARROLL

LEWIS Carroll pulled back on a pair of oars and let them skim slowly across the shimmering water. As he rowed, three young girls looked up at him and called out a familiar chorus: "Tell us a story, please!" Carroll, a tall and slender man with wavy hair and light blue-gray eyes, paused for just a moment before he began to conjure a marvelous adventure. Storytelling was not an unusual practice for the young mathematician, but on July 4, 1862, Carroll wove a tale about a girl who followed a white rabbit down a hole that no one would soon forget.

The curious character who landed in Wonderland was named after Alice Liddell, one of the three eager sisters in the rowboat. Even though she was only ten years old, Alice was one of Carroll's best friends at the time. The Liddell family had moved to Oxford several years earlier when their father was elected dean of Christ Church, where Carroll lectured on mathematics. Carroll adored the Liddell children, Harry, Lorina, Alice, and Edith. After meeting Alice and her sisters for the first time, he wrote in his diary, "I mark this day with a white stone," which was reserved for the most special occasions. Though he has been described as a socially awkward man with a nervous speech impediment, Carroll was comfortable in the company of children, and he became very close to the dean's family.

On that clear summer day, Carroll and Reverend Robinson Duckworth took the Liddell sisters to Godstow for a picnic. An expedition up the River Thames was one of Alice's favorite pastimes. She looked forward to the delicious feast they would enjoy at their destination—whether it was cakes and desserts or a full meal of chicken and salad—and she could always rely on Carroll for a good story. Alice must have been enthralled when Carroll cast her as the main character in his impromptu tale, but she was not the only one swept away by his imagination. Duckworth could scarcely believe that the story was made up on the spot. He interrupted his friend to ask, "Is this an extempore romance of yours?" And Carroll replied, "Yes, I'm inventing as we go along."

Twenty-five years after their expedition, Carroll observed that many of his tales had "lived and died, like summer midges, each in its own golden afternoon, until there came a day when, as it chanced, one of my little listeners petitioned that the tale might be written out for her." Immediately after their trip, Alice begged Carroll to transcribe the story on paper and he began to work on it that same night. Still the tale grew through more storytelling, prompted by the Liddell children. After another expedition up the river, Carroll wrote in his diary, "I had to go on with my interminable fairy-tale of 'Alice's Adventures.'"

Carroll drew inspiration for the story from his surroundings, populating Wonderland with characters that were grounded in reality. At the end of the second chapter of *Alice's Adventures in Wonderland*, Carroll invoked the fateful outing when he first dreamed up his story. The fictional Alice grows remarkably large and starts to cry, only to suddenly shrink so that she is forced to swim in a pool of her own tears. Several animals drop into the water and among them is the boating party in the form of birds: Carroll, the dodo (a reference to his real surname, Dodgson); Reverend Duckworth, the duck; Lorina, the lory; and Edith, the eaglet.

About a year after he first sent Alice down the rabbit hole, Carroll finished the book and, spurred on by close friends, set out to find a publisher. In October 1863, he handed his manuscript to Alexander Macmillan, cofounder of an eponymous publishing company. Macmillan accepted the book and published it two years later, in November 1865. Carroll had written articles, short stories, and poetry for years, but this was his debut novel.

A few months after he met with Macmillan, Carroll put the finishing touches on a personally illustrated copy of *Alice's*

Adventures Under Ground, which was the original title of the book. The green leather-bound edition was presented to Alice Liddell with the inscription "A Christmas Gift to a Dear Child in Memory of a Summer Day." By that time, though, Carroll was no longer close with the Liddell family. He had stopped visiting the children regularly in the summer of 1863 after an incident that remains a mystery today. Despite the rift, Carroll held tight to the memory of that delightful outing. *Alice's Adventures in Wonderland* opens with a poem by Carroll, in which he recalls their "golden afternoon" on the river:

> *Thus grew the tale of Wonderland:*
> *Thus slowly, one by one,*
> *Its quaint events were hammered out—*
> *And now the tale is done,*
> *And home we steer, a merry crew,*
> *Beneath the setting sun.*

The Wonderful Wizard of Oz

1900

L. FRANK BAUM

L. FRANK Baum leaned back against the hat rack in his hallway. His children were huddled around, hanging on every word of their father's latest story. But midway through the tale, Baum lost track of the characters and the direction of the plot and became immersed in a completely different story, one that had never been told before. He ushered the children into another room, grabbed a pencil and a piece of paper, and began to write. His hand had to race across the page to keep up with the tale unfolding in his mind. When Baum ran out of paper, he grabbed old envelopes and continued to work. He had been cast into the wondrous land of Oz with the same speed and urgency as Dorothy's house, plucked off the ground by a tornado.

Baum's writing career began in the nonfiction realm with a short pamphlet he composed in his late teens called *Baum's Complete Stamp Dealers' Directory*. Baum then wrote *The Book of the Hamburgs*, a guide to raising chickens, which was published when he was thirty. A decade after the poultry book, Baum turned to his first love: fiction. When his debut short story collection was published, Baum gave a copy to his sister Mary Louise with the following inscription: "When I was young I longed to write a great novel that should win me fame. Now that I am getting old, my first book is written to amuse children." The book, *Mother Goose in Prose*, was published in 1897, and though it was not a bestseller, it did set Baum on the path of becoming a major children's author. Baum subsequently wrote two more children's books, both poetry collections, before his dreams to write a great novel and to amuse children were fused in one extraordinary tale set in Oz.

After his spontaneous writing frenzy in 1898, Baum's story evolved slowly. He observed, "The odd characters are a sort of inspiration, liable to strike at any time, but the plot and plan of adventures takes me considerable time to develop." Baum worked diligently, recording notes on odd scraps of paper whenever a new idea struck. Soon the yellow brick road had been paved, Emerald City had been built, and Baum had the foundation of a modern fairy tale for American children. He once noted, "To write fairy stories for children, to amuse them, to divert restless children, sick children, to keep them out of mischief on rainy days, seems of greater importance than to write grown-up novels." Baum was tired of the Grimm fairy tales with horrific outcomes meant to strike fear in growing minds. He wanted to write a fairy tale without the dark turns of traditional stories, "in which the wonderment and joy are retained and the heart-aches and nightmares are left out." *The Wonderful Wizard of Oz* was unlike any of the sinister stories he grew up with. It was full of hope, and it was geared directly toward American readers.

Baum's characters and faraway setting could not be found in the pages of well-known fables. Since the publication of the book, countless people have speculated about the origins of Baum's tale. There is no way to tell which explanation is true, but at the very least they all reveal insights into his creative process and personal life.

Baum's wife, Maud, insisted that *The Wonderful Wizard of Oz* was the sole product of her husband's imagination, including the name of his magical land. She noted, "The word Oz came out of Mr. Baum's mind, just as did his queer characters." Yet, according to Baum, he found inspiration in his surroundings. He was sitting at his desk, trying to think of a title for his book, when a cabinet caught his attention. The drawers were sectioned off by groups of letters and the last one was labeled "O–Z," which had a decidedly nice ring to it. Frank Joslyn, Baum's eldest child, remembered a different version of the story. Baum was reciting Dorothy's adventure to his sons and their friends when one of them asked for the name of the place where her house landed. In need of a quick answer, Baum searched the room, spied a filing cabinet, and plucked "O–Z" from the last drawer.

Frank Joslyn also said that his father had always wanted a daughter. Instead, he had four sons. With each pregnancy, Baum hoped for a little girl and even began thinking of potential names. Dorothy was one of his top picks, and since he was never able to use it for a real baby, he gave the name to his young heroine from rural Kansas. Despite Frank Joslyn's explanation for the name, there were a few real-life Dorothys that others believe were Baum's inspiration, including a niece his wife adored and who tragically died when she was only five months old. Still, Baum never confirmed that any of these girls inspired his character or the name, so her origin remains a mystery.

The Scarecrow, the Tin Woodman, and the Cowardly Lion each marched into Baum's mind from a different avenue of his life. Scarecrows had enchanted Baum ever since he was a child growing up on a farm. He recalled, "They always seemed to my childish imagination as just about to wave their arms, straighten up and stalk across the field on their long legs." And so Baum picked a scarecrow to wink and strike up a conversation with Dorothy.

The Tin Woodman, on the other hand, may have emerged from an odd job. Baum's son Harry Neal recalled that his father was once assigned the task of decorating a hardware store window. Baum decided that a funny-looking man would catch the attention of passersby, so he assembled a full body out of the store's products, from stovepipe arms to a funnel hat. This may have inspired the Tin Woodman, though Baum offered a simpler explanation. He said that he thought it would be delightfully odd to create a man made out of *tin* who chopped down *wood*.

The Cowardly Lion might be one of the few characters that did not originate in Baum's imagination. According to W. W. Denslow, who illustrated *The Wonderful Wizard of Oz*, he suggested incorporating the character "for another element of fun."

Whether these stories are facts or myths, they all speak to the sense of magic and enchantment that surrounds *The Wonderful Wizard of Oz*. There is, however, physical proof for the final part of the story behind this book. When he finally finished writing his American fairy tale in 1899, Baum took the shortened pencil he had used for the manuscript and hung it on the wall above his desk with the following inscription: "With this pencil I wrote the manuscript of 'The Emerald City.'"

The Tale of Peter Rabbit

1902

BEATRIX POTTER

BEATRIX Potter was vacationing in Dunkeld, Scotland, when she picked up her pen to write a letter to five-year-old Noel Moore. "My dear Noel," she began, "I don't know what to write to you, so I shall tell you a story about four little rabbits whose names were Flopsy, Mopsy, Cottontail and Peter."

Potter wrote the tale in a way that any young child would appreciate, with adorable illustrations to accompany the prose. Noah could probably relate to the naughty rabbit Peter, who disobeys his mother and sneaks into a forbidden garden. Potter's animals were quite similar to humans, but the world looked marvelously different from their perspective; it was grander, larger, and full of possibility.

Potter often wrote to the six children of her ex-governess,

Annie Moore. Her illustrated correspondence was treasured by the recipients. Marjorie Moore, one of the young siblings, carefully tied her collection of letters together with a yellow ribbon. When Potter visited the Moore family, Annie suggested that she write a children's book based on her letter stories. Perhaps her tales would appeal to other readers and not just her pen friends. Potter thought it was worth a shot. She borrowed a stack of old letters and sorted through them before settling on her favorite one, the story she had written to Noel from Scotland in September 1893.

Potter once wrote, "I do not remember a time when I did not try to invent pictures and make for myself a fairyland amongst the wild flowers, the animals, fungi, mosses, woods and streams, all the thousand objects of the countryside." The outdoors had always fascinated the young Potter, and she brought it indoors in the form of rabbits, mice, hedgehogs, snakes, and lizards. Her brother, Bertram, was a fine accomplice, though he preferred catching wild bats and birds. Many of Potter's stories probably began to take shape when she was a little girl carting around an assortment of creatures and wondering what life looked like through their eyes.

Two of Potter's favorite pets were a pair of Belgian rabbits named Peter and Benjamin. Potter wrote in a letter, "Peter lived to be 8 years old, he used to lie before the fire on the hearth rug like a cat. He was clever at learning tricks, he used to jump through a hoop, and ring a bell, and play the tambourine. I saw him once trying to play the tambourine on a straw hat!" It seems only natural that Potter named her fictional rabbit after the talented pet.

Potter expanded the story from her letter, along with a series of black-and-white and a few color illustrations, and then sent the manuscript to six publishers. She soon received just as many negative responses, criticizing the book for being too long, being too short, or lacking colorful drawings. One publisher suggested that she change the narrative from prose to poetry. Potter was exasperated. She wanted the book to be published as it was, and so she decided to print it on her own.

At the same time that she arranged for the first printing, Potter's friend Canon Rawnsley pitched *Peter Rabbit* to Frederick Warne. Warne was one of the six publishers whose company had originally rejected the book, and Rawnsley insisted he reconsider the project. But Warne was concerned about the illustrations. He wanted to know why Potter hadn't used color throughout. The message was conveyed to Potter, who responded, "I did not colour the whole book for two reasons: the great expense of good colour printing—and also the rather uninteresting colour of a good many of the subjects which are most of them rabbit-brown and green." Potter struck a deal with Warne and, despite her initial reservations, she illuminated her charming characters in browns and greens, among many other colors.

The Wind in the Willows

1908

KENNETH GRAHAME

KENNETH Grahame's son, Alastair, threw a fit on his fourth birthday. The little boy, nicknamed Mouse, was still in tears when he went to bed and Grahame sat by his side until after midnight telling stories set on the banks of a river. Through his sniffles, Alastair picked characters for his father to drop into the tales, including a mole and a water rat. Later that month, Grahame's wife, Elspeth, waiting for her husband to get ready for a dinner date, had to ask the maid where he was. They were late, but Grahame was caught up in another activity. The maid told her, "He's with Master Mouse, Madam; he's telling some ditty or other about a Toad."

Grahame's river tale was growing, and he often found that world, filled with gregarious animals, preferable to everyday surroundings. And it was a secret he shared only with Alastair. Others were privy to the tale when they overheard snippets by chance.

Grahame continued his storytelling, both at home and then abroad, when the family traveled to Scotland in August 1905. During their stay, a visitor walked up to the nursery and stood outside the door, listening to Grahame talk about a group of river creatures. It is unlikely that Grahame or Alastair noticed their uninvited guest. Alastair was probably too busy laughing or chiming in to offer his own take on a new twist in the plot. With each telling, the story grew more intricate, but the grand adventure had yet to be cast on paper.

In the summer of 1907, Grahame stayed in London while Elspeth and Alastair were in Cookham Dene. Grahame visited on weekends, and in the meantime he wrote a series of letters to his son. Each envelope contained a description of the escapades of Mr. Toad from their bedtime stories. That same year, Constance Smedley paid Grahame a visit when he was in Cookham Dene. Smedley worked for the American magazine *Everybody's*, and she had been asked to convince Grahame to pen something new.

Grahame worked as secretary of the Bank of England, but he sometimes wrote in his spare time. He had written two short story collections, *The Golden Age* and *Dream Days*, based on his memories of childhood. He had also penned *Pagan Papers*, a book of essays filled with philosophical musings about life. Grahame resisted the idea of another book. Writing was a painstaking process, he explained to Smedley. But the savvy woman noticed that Grahame took pure delight in telling one particular story to Alastair every night. She recalled, "The story was known to him and Mouse alone and was related in a bed-time visit of extreme secrecy. . . . Mouse's own tendency to exult in his exploits was gently satirized in Mr. Toad, a favourite character who gave the juvenile audience occasion for some slightly self-conscious laughter." Smedley insisted that Grahame transcribe the charming animals onto paper. And so Grahame composed *The Wind in the Willows*.

The setting for *The Wind in the Willows* was drawn from Grahame's memories of his childhood in Cookham Dene. Grahame was born in Scotland but moved to England after his mother succumbed to scarlet fever. His father, devastated by the loss, turned to alcohol and was no longer fit to take care of his children. Grahame lived in a cottage with his uncle, grandmother, and three siblings. Nearby lay the winding River Thames, with tall grass and willow trees swaying along its banks. River otters, toads, moles . . . Grahame saw all of these creatures splashing about in the water while he lived in Cookham Dene. Years later, he returned to the same area with Elspeth and Alastair, and the memories from childhood were still fresh in his mind. He noted, "The queer thing is, I can remember everything I felt then, the part of my brain I used from four till about seven can never have altered. Coming back here wakens every recollection." It was around that time that Grahame sat beside Alastair's bed and began to tell his unforgettable tale, conjuring the same setting and creatures that had captured his imagination as a child.

Publishers were not immediately charmed by *The Wind in the Willows*. The children's tale was not like Grahame's previous books, which were geared toward adult audiences and focused on people rather than river creatures. Even though Smedley had encouraged Grahame to transcribe his bedtime story into a manuscript, *Everybody's* declined to publish it. This was followed by a rejection from John Lane, the publisher of Grahame's other titles in the United Kingdom. It seemed that no one had faith that a story starring animals would sell.

The Wind in the Willows was finally accepted by the London-based company Methuen Publishing, albeit with great caution. They offered escalating royalties and no advance, so that if the book failed, there would be little loss for the company. Grahame wanted to place the book with Charles Scribner's Sons in the United States, but the firm felt the book was "altogether lacking in human interest." Luckily, Grahame had a fan that Scribner's could not ignore. President Theodore Roosevelt had responded enthusiastically to Grahame's work in the past, so, in a savvy move, the author sent him a copy of his latest manuscript. According to Grahame's agent, Curtis Brown, Roosevelt described the novel as "such a beautiful thing that Scribner *must* publish it." Not surprisingly, Scribner's had a change of heart and accepted *The Wind in the Willows*, and the book evolved into a bestselling classic for children on both sides of the Atlantic.

Winnie-the-Pooh

1926

A. A. MILNE

A YOUNG boy who preferred to be called by his nick-name, Billy Moon, lay wide awake in bed. Billy's father, A. A. Milne, was in the middle of narrating a brand-new bedtime story about a bear with a fondness for honey. Milne's tales were typically guaranteed to have a somnolent effect. On this night, however, Billy's eyelids did not begin to droop as soon as the story began. There was something special about the good-natured bear named Winnie-the-Pooh.

Milne had recently finished a popular book of poems for children called *When We Were Very Young*. The success of this collection established Milne as a new voice in children's literature, and he was in high demand for family-oriented articles and short stories. His latest assignment was a Christmas story for the *Evening News*. With the deadline looming, Milne struggled to come up with an idea. His wife, Daphne, suggested he consider one of his bedtime stories. None of those tales stood out to Milne, until he thought back to the bear. The story that appeared in the paper on December 24, 1925, became the first chapter in *Winnie-the-Pooh*, a book filled with the adventures of the tubby character and his friends.

Milne pulled Winnie-the-Pooh right out of Billy's nursery. Edward Bear, as he was originally named, and the young boy were always together. They often conversed, with Christopher Robin—which was Billy's real name—responding on his friend's behalf in a series of thunderous growls. One day it was decided that Edward Bear needed a new name. It must have seemed like a natural decision, since Milne's son went by a nickname. Without hesitating, Christopher selected "Winnie-the-Pooh."

Christopher had combined two words that he knew well to come up with an unusual name for his bear. He had once called a swan on a lake Pooh, and the word lingered in his mind. Milne recalled that when they walked away from the elegant bird, "We took the name with us, as we didn't think the swan would want it any more." Winnie, on the other hand, came from a black bear who resided at the London Zoo. Captain Harry Colebourn had brought the bear from Canada to England during World War I. She was named Winnie, or Winnipeg, after her owner's hometown. When Colebourn left to fight in France, he donated his unusual pet to the zoo.

Unlike many bears, Winnie was very friendly. She ate straight from outstretched hands and every now and then she gave visitors a ride on her back. Christopher was even able to hug the gentle bear! It is not surprising that he was inspired to name his darling toy after Winnie.

Milne did not have to look far to find friends for Winnie-the-Pooh. His son was part of the story right from the beginning, appearing as himself, the sweet and well-mannered Christopher Robin. The toys in Christopher's nursery were perfect friends for his bear. Eeyore sat there, in all of his gloom, right alongside adorable little Piglet and energetic Tigger. When Milne needed new animals, he and Daphne visited Harrods to survey the toys, after which Kanga and Roo were added to the mix.

Winnie-the-Pooh's world was based on one of Milne's favorite places. The Milne family often traveled to Ashdown Forest on weekends, and the verdant landscape was transposed directly onto the pages of the book. Milne even brought illustrator Ernest H. Shepard to the forest so that he could capture the backdrop accurately. Though some of the names of areas in Ashdown Forest were slightly altered—Five Hundred Acre Wood and Gills Lap were fictionalized as Hundred Acre Wood and Galleons Lap—according to Christopher, each place in the book is visually "identical" to its real-world counterpart.

Winnie-the-Pooh lives inside a tree trunk home that was modeled on an old walnut tree just north of Ashdown Forest on Cotchford Farm, which the Milnes bought in the summer of 1924. Christopher loved to crawl through a gap in the side of the hollow tree, bringing his favorite bear along for company. He later noted, "So if anyone wonders why in the stories so much time seems to be spent in trees or up trees, the answer is that this, in real life, was how it was." And it seems that so much in *Winnie-the-Pooh* was just how it was. Milne captured his little boy's universe, from the nursery to the garden and beyond.

Lord of the Flies

1954

WILLIAM GOLDING

WILLIAM Golding paused to turn the page while his children, eager to know what happened next, fought the urge to drift asleep. Storytelling was a bedtime ritual in their household. This night's tale may have been *The Coral Island* or *Treasure Island*. Golding could only recall that it was an island adventure. Though the name of the book was forgotten over time, the story itself is not important. It was the exotic setting that made an impression on Golding. Bright reefs and long stretches of sand were a distant reality from his tiny apartment in Salisbury, England, and as he read aloud, each sentence lulled him a little further away from his unsatisfactory life as a poor schoolteacher.

Golding shut the book, tucked the children into bed, and

went to sit by the fire with his wife, Ann. As he stared into the crackling flames, the aspiring writer was carried back to that distant island, where another fire might just as easily have burned. Suddenly an idea sparked and prompted Golding to turn to Ann and ask, "Wouldn't it be a good idea if I wrote a book about children on an island, children who behave in the way children really would behave?" Ann looked back at her husband, an eccentric man who wore a beard even though it was unfashionable at the time, and insisted that he start writing immediately.

When Golding picked up his pen to begin, he knew this would be the first story that belonged to him. In retrospect, previous manuscripts felt as though they had been "written by other people," but his life had been leading up to this very book. Golding later noted that *Lord of the Flies* came from three things:

1. Five years of war service
2. Finding out, afterwards, what the Nazis did
3. Ten years of teaching small boys

These experiences fused into a single idea by the warmth of the fire, but they had all consumed Golding's thoughts long before he began the new work.

In December 1940, Golding joined the British Royal Navy to fight in World War II. He was twenty-nine years old, with a wife and a baby boy at home. Golding began as an ordinary seaman, but by the time his service ended, he had commanded a rocket-launching ship. During this time, he witnessed first-hand the glory and horror of war. Golding's service inspired him to forge a new set of moral principles. But he also realized that he could—and had—fallen short of these ideals, which made him understand the Nazis and their weaknesses to an extent. It was "partly out of the sad self-knowledge" of his own sinister side that Golding wrote *Lord of the Flies*. Some of his characters revert to extreme brutality when they are stranded on a desert island.

Golding also knew that wickedness was not restricted to the battlefield. As a teacher at Bishop Wordsworth's School, an all-boys institution, he studied the students with a scientific eye. He was particularly intrigued by the actions the boys would take once standard rules were abandoned. Golding pushed the pupils just to see how far they might go. He recalled, "I gave them more liberty, and I gave them more liberty, and more, and more, and more—I drew further away. My eyes came out like organ stops as I watched what was happening." He often pitted two groups against one another to see how they would react. In one case, during a field trip to an ancient fort called Figsbury Rings, Golding choreographed a warlike game for the students to play. These social experiments provided glimpses of the dark turns that boys can take in unusual circumstances and were mirrored by the marooned children in *Lord of the Flies*.

Golding often found it difficult to concentrate on school-work, distracted by his dream of becoming a published writer. His fellow teachers ridiculed this seemingly unattainable goal, but Golding stubbornly held on to his vision. And perhaps he had the final laugh, since he composed much of *Lord of the Flies* during school hours. When he wanted to write during class, Golding assigned his students a quiet task, and while they toiled away, he dealt with a different set of boys on the page. Some students recalled listening to Golding read parts of his novel to the class. It is fitting that *Lord of the Flies* was recited aloud, transporting a group of students from their dreary classroom to a remote fictional island, much as Golding was swept away during the storytelling session that first inspired the book.

CATCH ME IF YOU CAN

A little figure rose before me—the figure of a man, or of a woman, who said, "My name is Brown. Catch me if you can."

—VIRGINIA WOOLF, "CHARACTER IN FICTION"

IMAGINE TWIRLING AROUND A BALLROOM WITH THE HAND-some and impeccably dressed Mr. Darcy. Or mastering the art of detection with Sherlock Holmes. Perhaps you'd prefer to attend an elite event with the vibrant socialite Mrs. Dalloway. Be home by midnight, though, so that you can sneak out and cause trouble with Huckleberry Finn. These escapades could only happen to us fictively, but for a handful of authors, they were just as real as the people who inspired them.

Often characters are a combination of real people, shards of personalities and physical traits forged together in the fires of an author's imagination. But sometimes a person is so singular and charismatic that he or she seems to cry out, just like

Woolf's Brown, "Catch me if you can!" The famous writers in the following section all heeded that call. Armed only with a pen and paper, they set off in pursuit of real people and chased them into the depths of the written page.

Pride and Prejudice

1813

JANE AUSTEN

J ANE Austen stepped out of the coach and stopped to admire Manydown Park. The manor looked particularly enchanting against a darkening sky. In the background, a greenhouse twinkled with candles lining the windows just for the occasion. Austen always looked forward to a ball. She loved to dance and pick up the latest tidbits of gossip from other guests. But this night was different. Inside, a charming Irishman waited to spin her across the floor and, with each turn, steal a little more of her heart.

Austen's dance partner was Thomas Langlois Lefroy. He was visiting Hampshire with his family over the Christmas holidays, before returning to London to study for the bar exam. Sparks flew between Austen and Lefroy and after dancing at three balls, they had fallen for each other. The budding relationship must have felt thrilling to the two twenty-year-olds. In a letter to her sister, Austen described her flirtation with Lefroy: "Imagine everything most profligate and shocking in the way of dancing and sitting down together." The young couple soon became the latest scandal in town, and many locals suspected that Lefroy would propose. It is a love story that seems pulled from one of Austen's own novels.

Sadly their relationship was doomed to fail. Lefroy did not come from an upper-class family, and as the eldest son, he was under great pressure to marry a wealthy woman and build a successful career as a lawyer. Despite her wit, humor, and warmth, Austen had very little to offer in terms of a dowry. Just as their relationship was taking off, Lefroy abruptly left town for London. According to his cousin George, Lefroy's aunt sent him away so "no more mischief might be done." Poor Austen never saw or heard from Lefroy again. Three years later, she found out that he was on his way back to Ireland to practice law. By that time their brief affair had dwindled to a memory, but it may have offered Austen lasting inspiration for her fiction.

Many Austen fans believe that Lefroy was the model for Fitzwilliam Darcy in *Pride and Prejudice*. Austen began writing the novel in October 1796, less than a year after her ill-fated affair. The heroine, Elizabeth Bennet, meets Darcy at a ball, just as Austen first encountered Lefroy. And like the real couple, they experience intense feelings for one another. Yet some scholars argue that there are several differences between Austen's fictional and real heartthrobs. Lefroy overlooked Austen's poor economic status when they first met, but he was still forced to abandon her. Darcy, on the other hand, is not nearly as open and engaging when he meets Bennet. He eventually overcomes his snobbery and falls for the woman he once felt was beneath him. Perhaps Austen decided to rewrite her ill-fated affair and offer a happy ending for Darcy and Bennet. It was virtually impossible to overcome social expectations in the real world, but anything could happen in fiction.

Austen faced a fair share of obstacles in both love and in writing. Her novels were composed in secret, a difficult task as she had no writing space of her own. Austen's immediate family knew about her pastime, but she carefully guarded it from anyone beyond this small circle, including servants and friends. Austen was forced to work in the drawing room, where visitors could stroll in unannounced at any time. A squeaky door acted as a convenient alarm. When the door swung open, Austen quickly hid the small slips of paper she had been working on.

In the privacy of her home, when there were no visitors, Austen entertained her family with her latest work. Her father liked *First Impressions* (the original title for *Pride and Prejudice*) so much that he sent the manuscript to publisher Thomas Cadell without mentioning the name of the author. The manuscript was promptly returned with an inscription: "Declined by Return of Post." It seems that Cadell and his colleagues did not even bother to peek at the pages. Several years later, *Pride and Prejudice* was finally published by Thomas Egerton of Whitehall.

Long after she danced with Lefroy at Manydown, Austen received a proclamation of love under the same roof. Harris

Bigg-Wither, heir to the estate, proposed and she accepted. Their engagement lasted for one short night and by the next day, Austen had called it off. In theory, it was an ideal match for Austen. She would be moving into a higher social standing. Yet she remained a romantic at heart and refused to spend her life with someone she cared for only as a friend.

After Lefroy died, his nephew revealed that he had "said in so many words that he was in love with [Austen], although he qualified his confession by saying it was a boyish love." Austen may have clung to that same thrilling spark, bringing it eternally to life in the relationship between Darcy and Bennet.

"The Raven"

1845

EDGAR ALLAN POE

GRIP the raven paced the length of the coach house, wobbling from side to side with each step. When the clock struck noon, Grip faltered, but he was determined to continue the interminable march. He regained his composure, took a few strides, and then stopped to call out his favorite refrain, "Halloa, old girl." The familiar greeting turned out to be a final farewell . . . Grip stumbled, fell over, and died. Charles Dickens captured the sad and comical scene in a letter to a friend.

The day before Grip's death, Dickens recorded in his diary that Mr. Herring had paid a visit to administer a dose of castor oil to the sick bird. Grip perked up long enough to bite Topping, the coach man, but the effect was short term. The talking raven had been a treasured member of the Dickens family, even though he enjoyed nipping the children's ankles and often exclaimed, "I am a devil!"

Dickens adored Grip and never grew tired of recounting his amusing antics. Once at a party, an acquaintance jokingly exclaimed that the writer was "raven mad." The comment morphed into "raving mad" as it was passed from one guest to another, and by the next day, many people throughout London were convinced that Dickens had been placed in a mental asylum. Fortunately, the only mania that Dickens suffered was for his pet bird, though his affection did border on abnormal. When Grip died, he was immortalized not only in fond memory, but also in physical form when Dickens had his body stuffed.

A few months before Grip's decline, Dickens had already begun to preserve him on the written page. He was working on a new novel called *Barnaby Rudge*, a murder mystery set amid riots in England, and he needed a companion for his slow-witted protagonist. In his diary, Dickens wrote: "Barnaby being an idiot, my notion is to have him always in the company of a pet raven who is immeasurably more knowing than himself. Accordingly have been studying my bird, and I think I could make a very queer character of him." Grip was clearly the model for Barnaby's loquacious companion. Dickens did not try to mask the connection between the two birds, as he named the feathered character after his departed pet.

While Dickens was writing *Barnaby Rudge*, his wife gave birth to a boy whom they planned to call Edgar. He was ultimately christened Walter Landor, but Dickens may have stuck with the original name had he known that another Edgar would bestow enduring fame on his talking raven.

Across the ocean, Edgar Allan Poe selected *Barnaby Rudge* for book reviews in the Philadelphia *Saturday Evening Post* in May 1841 and *Graham's Magazine* in February 1842. Though he had not yet reached widespread fame, Poe was in the process of building his literary career. He was an editor at *Graham's Magazine*, had sold a few poetry collections to small presses, and had placed short stories in national publications. *Barnaby Rudge* received high praise from Poe, though he criticized its weakness in plot. Poe read the story in serial installments and too easily predicted an important twist in the end. He also noted that Grip was an underdeveloped character whose "croaking might have been prophetically heard in the course of the drama." Poe felt that there was great potential in a talking bird.

In 1844, when Poe was in the process of composing a new poem and needed a "non-reasoning creature capable of speech," he first thought of a parrot. However, he soon realized that a brightly colored bird clashed with the tone of his dark and ominous piece. Poe must have then thought back to *Barnaby Rudge* and the bird named Grip. A raven was far better suited to the task of disturbing the bereft man in his poem. Poe never claimed that Dickens's bird was his muse. The connection is based on popular speculation, but there are definite similarities between the two ravens.

Every time the raven gently taps at the chamber door in

Poe's poem, he seems to invoke Grip. In a similar scene in *Barnaby Rudge*, Grip taps on the window and a widow exclaims, "'Tis some one knocking softly at the shutter." Whether this allusion was deliberate or not, it shows that *Barnaby Rudge* probably led Poe to his choice of bird.

Since the publication of "The Raven," many of Poe's fans have expressed their belief that Grip was a source of inspiration for the poem. After Dickens's death, his stuffed raven was sold at auction to Poe enthusiast Colonel Richard Gimbel, who brought him over to the United States. Grip is currently perched in the Rare Book Department on the third floor of the Parkway Central Library in Philadelphia.

The Adventures of
Tom Sawyer

1876

MARK TWAIN

Mark Twain waited for the signal. It was late at night, dark enough for young boys to scuttle through town unnoticed. He heard the whistle from behind the house and sprang to action. Twain silently climbed out the window, scrambled onto the roof of the shed, and landed on the ground to face Tom Blankenship and a group of boys, all eager to stir up mischief and embark on daring quests while everyone else slept.

Tom Blankenship was a scruffy boy who lived in a dilapidated house near Twain in Hannibal, Missouri. With eight siblings and an alcoholic father, Blankenship was free from scrutiny. No one cared if he ventured outside unchaperoned in the middle of the night. "He was the only really independent person—boy or man—in the community," recalled Twain, "and by consequence he was tranquilly and continuously happy and envied by all of us." While most boys, like Twain, suffered through painfully boring tasks, such as memorizing Bible verses, Blankenship fished and soaked in the sunshine, free to enjoy life according to his own whims. The Blankenships were not viewed as respectable members of the community, and Twain was instructed to stay away from them, but that only made him more determined to spend time with Tom.

As an adult, Twain turned back to his childhood to write *The Adventures of Tom Sawyer*, and he plucked one of his most memorable characters, the rebellious Huckleberry Finn, straight from the dusty streets of his hometown. Even Twain's family could not mistake the carefree character for anyone other than the real boy. "Why, that's Tom Blankenship!" exclaimed his sister Pamela Moffett, after she listened to passages about Huck.

To write the novel, Twain simply mined his memory. His family had moved to Hannibal, Missouri, when he was four years old and he immediately discovered that the bustling port town was full of possibility. In every direction lay new terrain—bluffs, a cave, an island, a creek, vast woods and fields. And the great Mississippi River coursed right alongside Hannibal. Twain almost drowned in the river six times, narrowly escaping death again and again, but nothing daunted the young boy. Rather than developing a fear of water, he decided that he was practically invincible. Twain spent his childhood exploring the wilderness, seeking out thrills and grand exploits.

In the introduction to *The Adventures of Tom Sawyer*, Twain wrote, "Most of the adventures recorded in this book really occurred; one or two were experiences of my own, the rest those of boys who were schoolmates of mine." He deposited many people he knew right onto the page, most obviously Blankenship as Huck. But Tom Sawyer was a combination of three boys, two of whom were most likely Twain's friends John Briggs and Will Bowen, and the third the author himself.

Twain was a mischievous child and he replicated many of his antics in the book. His daughter Susy wrote, "Clara and I are sure that papa played the trick on Grandma, about the whipping, that is related in *The Adventures of Tom Sawyer*." Twain confessed that he did use this ruse to avoid punishment. He was just about to be whipped, but interrupted his mother to warn her of some unknown danger in the other direction. The moment she turned around, he dashed away! Twain's brother Henry was his exact opposite. He followed the rules and was always truthful, even if that meant telling on Twain, who inevitably had done something wrong. Twain brought him into the book as Sid, but noted, "Henry was a very much finer and better boy than Sid ever was."

Twain drew upon real life for his novel, but he also harnessed his boyhood imagination, which had made the world seem so magical at the time. When Twain was young, folklore was not simply meant for entertainment; it held secrets and could even lead to lost treasure. According to Hannibal lore, two French trappers hid a chest of gold just north of the town, and they never dug it up. Blankenship enlisted Twain and their friend Briggs to help locate these riches, and they trekked out into the wilderness, shovels in hand. Despite their best efforts, the treasure remained underground—if it existed at all. Twain eventually managed to unearth a fabled box of gold, though only in fiction, in *The Adventures of Tom Sawyer*.

Twain began writing *The Adventures of Tom Sawyer* in the winter of 1872, when he was thirty-seven. He was a successful writer at the time. He had composed articles and short stories for publications nationwide, and his first book, *The Innocents Abroad*, a humorous travel memoir, had become a big bestseller when it was released in 1869. After he started his novel in 1872, Twain put the manuscript aside until the summer of 1874. During those hot months, he and his family stayed at Quarry Farm in Elmira, New York. The farm belonged to Twain's sister-in-law, Susan Crane, and she had a writing studio built just for him. It was an octagonal room with a little chimney on the side. Twain sat at a desk surrounded by windows that looked out over valleys and hills. He wrote from morning until late afternoon, dashing off almost fifty pages a day. No one knocked on the studio door while he was at work. If he was urgently needed, a horn would blow, calling him back to the house.

Twain often wrote pieces only to stop midway, dropping the work until inspiration struck again, and that summer, despite his furious progress, he abruptly discontinued working on the book. He turned his attention to the script for a play based on his only novel at the time, *The Gilded Age*, which had been published in 1873. Twain did not return to *The Adventures of Tom Sawyer* until the following summer, when he finally finished the tale that captured his childhood antics and made its way into print in December 1876.

Sherlock Holmes

1887–1927

ARTHUR CONAN DOYLE

DOCTOR Joseph Bell stood in front of a lecture room full of medical students, his eyes twinkling mischievously above a pointed nose. The assignment of the day tested the students' abilities to use their senses. They would have to taste and smell a particularly nasty liquid to determine its identity. Everyone was required to try the foul concoction, which smelled awful. Bell was a good sport, though, and said, "As I don't ask anything of my students which I wouldn't be willing to do myself, I will taste it before passing it around." He dipped his finger into the beaker and licked it, proving the amber fluid was harmless despite a severely bitter taste. The students then suffered through the test one by one, and before any of them could guess what it was, Bell announced that they had failed. The class had been so focused on tasting and smelling that they forgot to look. Bell had deceived them by licking a clean finger rather than the one he dipped into the beaker at the beginning of the experiment. No one noticed this small but important detail, which was exactly what the professor wanted to demonstrate with his sleight of hand. Bell stressed that a doctor must take note of even the most seemingly insignificant clues in order to reach a correct diagnosis.

Bell was a professor at the University of Edinburgh and served as a doctor at the Royal Infirmary. He was highly regarded in the medical field and was known for his uncanny ability to pinpoint even the most obscure illnesses. Patients could walk into Bell's medical office and within moments he knew all about their lives, much to their surprise.

In one instance, Bell took one look at a patient dressed in civilian clothes and announced that he was a recently discharged, noncommissioned officer from a Scottish Highlands regiment. To top off this display of brilliant deduction, Bell also noted that the man had served in Barbados. On the surface, these observations seem like lucky guesses or some form of trickery, but they were all based on logic. Bell described his thought process: "The man was a respectful man but did not remove his hat. They do not in the army, but he would have learned civilian ways had he been long discharged. He has an air of authority and he is obviously Scottish. As to Barbados, his complaint is elephantiasis, which is West Indian and not British, and the Scottish regiments are at present in that particular land." A faded tattoo, a slightly peculiar stride, a scuff on a pant leg . . . each idiosyncratic detail clued Bell in to a secret about someone's life. And it was that type of deductive reasoning that led him to solve difficult medical problems that stumped so many of his peers.

If you met Bell today you might think he admired Sherlock Holmes. You would probably say that Bell bore a striking resemblance to the handsome detective, with his angular features, tallness, and slender frame. Bell even liked to recline in a chair with his fingers pressed together when considering possible solutions to a problem, just like Holmes. But the truth is that Bell was the inspiration for the iconic sleuth. As Arthur Conan Doyle once said, "Sherlock Holmes is the literary embodiment, if I may express it, of my memory of a professor of medicine at Edinburgh University, who would sit in the patients' waiting-room . . . and diagnose people as they came in, before they had even opened their mouths."

From the moment Conan Doyle walked into Bell's classroom, he was captivated by the eccentric professor. He must have been thrilled when he was selected to be an outpatient clerk assisting Bell, who was in his early forties at the time. It would have given him the opportunity to observe Bell's impressive skills in both the hospital and the classroom, probably with greater enthusiasm than for his typical curriculum. Yet despite his fascination with Bell, Conan Doyle did not write about him until almost a decade after they first met.

Shortly after graduating, Conan Doyle started his own medical practice in Portsmouth, England. Fortunately for the literary world, his career as a doctor was not immediately successful; business was often slow, which meant that he was able to work on fiction during the day. In 1886, after years of writing short stories with some success, Conan Doyle finally brought his old professor to life on the page. He had decided to write a mystery and needed a protagonist. Bell had all the characteristics of a winning detective—an exceptional, almost superhuman ability to rustle up clues, an eccentric personality, and quirky habits.

From early March through April, the young doctor fervently wrote his first Sherlock Holmes story, a novella called *A Study in Scarlet*. Holmes first appeared in print in the 1887 *Beeton's Christmas Annual*, which featured *A Study in Scarlet*. Conan Doyle went on to write many accounts of Sherlock Holmes and his friend Doctor Watson, and they were published regularly in the *Strand Magazine* beginning in 1891. But as the readership for these stories increased, Conan Doyle grew less interested in Holmes and felt that the popular series kept him from focusing on "better things." Eventually Conan Doyle decided to get rid of Holmes by sending him to a dramatic death in "The Final Problem." There was immediate uproar when this story was published in 1893. Holmes fans were devastated; some even wore black armbands to mourn the fictional sleuth. Conan Doyle did not share his readers' grief, merely writing "Killed Holmes" in his diary after he finished the story.

Finally Conan Doyle was able to move on to what he considered more esteemed writing, ranging from serious nonfiction to historical and adventure fiction. But, true to form,

Holmes outmaneuvered the man who was perhaps his greatest adversary: his creator. In 1901, immense demand prompted Conan Doyle to pick up his pen and write about Sherlock Holmes again, offering new stories about the sleuth until 1927. The brilliant detective had defied death, returning to puff away on his trademark pipe and solve another series of complex cases.

Peter and Wendy

1911

J. M. BARRIE

FIVE-YEAR-OLD George Llewelyn Davies raced into Kensington Gardens with his younger brother Jack. Down the path they spotted a strange man. He was very short, around five feet tall, with neatly combed hair and a mustache, and he was accompanied by a large Saint Bernard. They made a comical pair, the hefty dog and his diminutive owner. The boys looked back at their nurse, Mary Hodgson, who was pushing their brother Peter in a baby carriage, before bounding ahead. J. M. Barrie went out of his way to introduce himself and his pet, Porthos, to the young boys. There is no firsthand account of how this fateful meeting unfolded, so we can only guess whether the boys were racing or strolling down the path that day, but we do know that George and Jack soon discovered that Barrie could wiggle his ears! He also came up with the most amazing make-believe games to play. And so the children struck up a friendship, one that would last a lifetime, with a man who was not all that much bigger than them.

After that first encounter in the park, Barrie timed his walks so that he would bump into the Davies boys. Though he adored children, Barrie had none of his own, and the Davies bunch filled that gap. Meanwhile, George and Jack were captivated by their new friend. They often told their mother about the funny man in the park. Then, at a New Year's Eve party, Barrie spotted a pretty woman stuffing candy into her handbag. He amicably brought up her transgression, and she told him that the goodies were for her son Peter. Barrie soon realized that the partygoer was Sylvia Llewelyn Davies, and now that he had met the boys' mother, he began visiting them at home, too.

Barrie was a successful playwright and novelist, and he naturally loved to entertain the boys with stories. He wrote one of his favorite tales into *The Little White Bird*, a novel based on his friendship with George (named David in the book). In the story, all children can fly when they are very little, but they usually lose this ability as they grow up. A little boy named Peter Pan manages to fly away from home while he is still young. He escapes to Kensington Gardens and becomes stuck in limbo, not quite a child or a bird. He lives on a nearby island and is never able to move back home.

The notion of mortality had haunted Barrie since his own childhood. When he was six, his older brother David was killed in an ice-skating accident. Barrie's mother never recovered from the loss. In a way, his brother remained immortal, an eternally perfect child. Even though Barrie sometimes wore David's old clothes, he could never fill his brother's absence. But he may have found a way to express the loss on the page. Peter Pan was trapped in childhood, much like Barrie's own brother. The story in *The Little White Bird* was only the beginning of the Peter Pan saga. There were no pirates or lost boys in this version of the story. It would later evolve over the course of a summer.

In 1901, the Barries spent the summer months in their country home, Black Lake. The Davies family was at Tilford, only a five-minute walk away. One of Barrie's favorite books was *The Coral Island*, a swashbuckling tale of shipwrecks, pirates, and violent battles. With a flick of his imagination, Barrie transformed the lakeside into an exotic island, and the Davies boys were delighted to play along (except for Michael, the latest addition to the family, who was too young to participate). George, Jack, and Peter wielded makeshift weapons to fight off foes, including the dreadful pirate dog (Porthos) and Captain Swarthy (Barrie). Sometimes Sylvia and her husband, Arthur, had to suspend the games to reprimand the children for almost—and every now and then actually—injuring one another. Barrie did not worry about danger the way parents did. He was much more concerned with having fun and hated to think that one day the games would end. In an effort to immortalize their exploits, Barrie compiled a book, called *The Boy Castaways*, filled with photographs of the boys striking poses and gallivanting around the lake.

Barrie later took their adventure to the stage in a play called *Peter Pan, or The Boy Who Wouldn't Grow Up.* Their summertime exploits were blended into the Kensington Gardens fairy tale. And though the protagonist was named Peter, he was a combination of all the Davies children. In the script's dedication, Barrie wrote to the boys: "I suppose I always knew that I made Peter by rubbing the five of you violently together, as savages with two sticks produce a flame." (The fifth boy was Nicholas, born a couple of years after their memorable summer.) Barrie transformed the popular production into a book called *Peter and Wendy,* which was published in 1911. He had been compelled to write the play because, one after another, the boys were growing too old for make-believe. The stories of Peter Pan and the pirates on Black Lake had begun to lose their magic, much to Barrie's dismay. But the play could be repeated again and again and, just like Peter Pan, never grow old and die.

The Great Gatsby

1925

F. SCOTT FITZGERALD

ONE "not-forgotten summer night" in the early 1920s, F. Scott Fitzgerald listened to a story told by Robert Crozier Kerr Jr., a fellow golf club member. When he was fourteen years old Kerr had spotted a yacht preparing to moor in Sheepshead Bay, Brooklyn. Eager to get a closer look at the new arrival, Kerr rowed across the water. As he approached the grand vessel, he noticed that it was dangerously positioned. The boat would break into pieces if it was not moved before the tide ran out. Kerr, barefoot and shabbily dressed, tried to warn the captain, who shooed him away. But the owner, Edward Robinson Gilman, heeded his advice and was so impressed with the bold teen that he offered him a job on the spot, and then he took him to buy a fancy new wardrobe. Gilman was a wealthy and eccentric businessman, who was in an illicit relationship with Nellie Bly, the reporter who famously traveled around the world in under eighty days (see *Around the World in Eighty Days*, pages 7–10). Kerr lived on the yacht as a personal assistant until his boss died, three and a half years later. This unusual work experience helped propel Kerr to success, and he eventually settled in the prosperous town of Great Neck, Long Island, which was where he found himself talking to a promising young author.

Fitzgerald later wrote to his friend about an upcoming novel: "I have my hero occupy the same position you did and obtain it in the same way. I am calling him Robert B. Kerr instead of Robert C. Kerr to conceal his identity (this is a joke—I wanted to give you a scare. His name is Gatsby)." Jay Gatsby followed in Kerr's footsteps: he landed a job after saving a yachtsman named Dan Cody from hazards in the ocean. Fitzgerald even mentioned that Cody had a fling with a newspaper reporter named Ella Kaye, just like Gilman and Bly.

Fitzgerald replicated Kerr's fairy-tale beginning with Gatsby, but he knew little about his character beyond the yacht, and it showed. After reading a draft of *The Great Gatsby*, editor Maxwell Perkins voiced his concern that Gatsby was too mysterious and "the reader's eyes can never quite focus upon him." Fitzgerald needed to establish more background for his character and so he drew upon a notorious scandal at the time.

When he sent revised pages back to Perkins, Fitzgerald noted, "After careful searching of the files (of a man's mind here) for the Fuller Magee case + after having Zelda draw pictures until her fingers ache I know Gatsby better than I know my own child." Not only was Edward M. Fuller notoriously famous at the time, he was also a neighbor of the Fitzgerald family. Fuller appeared in elite circles in Great Neck and Manhattan after starting his own brokerage firm, but his prosperity did not last long. He gambled illegally with clients' funds and came up short, forcing the company into bankruptcy. The Fuller-McGee case was top news throughout New York. During the course of four trials, it became clear that corruption stretched well beyond Fuller and his vice president, William F. McGee, to politicians, well-known businessmen, and Arnold Rothstein, a notorious gambler. Rothstein appears as secondary character Meyer Wolfshiem in *The Great Gatsby*. Just like his real-world counterpart, Wolfshiem is reported to have fixed the 1919 World Series.

Fitzgerald blended Fuller's dark business background with Kerr's fairy-tale beginning to create Gatsby's path to riches. And despite these two obvious inspirations, it is impossible to pinpoint a precise model for his character. Fitzgerald once acknowledged, "I never at any one time saw him clear myself— for he started as one man I knew and then changed into myself."

Gatsby was an elusive persona, but the lights of West Egg always shone bright and clear in Fitzgerald's imagination. The affluent town was based on Great Neck, where the Fitzgeralds moved in October 1922. Fitzgerald's wife, Zelda, saw little difference between New York City and her new home, which she described as "nothing so much as Times Square during the theatre hour." High society rubbed shoulders in Great Neck just as they did in the city, only the scenery had changed from towering buildings and bustling streets to glittery mansions on the coast. The Fitzgeralds' house was modest compared to their neighbors' impressive homes, but that did not stop them from soaking in the local scene, visiting golf clubs, attending parties, and staying up late to converse with millionaires. Fitzgerald was fascinated by the vast amount of wealth that surrounded him, and it was a perfect setting for a novel about a man's rise and fall from riches.

Though Fitzgerald had originally called his novel *The Great Gatsby*, he never felt that the title was quite right. Perhaps he never liked the title for his novel because Gatsby was always a puzzle, even to him. West Egg, however, remained vivid in his mind, and it was in a few of the suggestions he sent to Perkins. Between drafts, Fitzgerald suggested a series of titles to Perkins, including *Among Ash-Heaps and Millionaires*, *Trimalchio in West Egg*, *On the Road to West Egg*, *Gold-Hatted Gatsby*, and *The High-Bouncing Lover*. But Perkins always ushered him back to *The Great Gatsby*. Not long before the book was published, Fitzgerald sent a frantic telegram to Perkins: CRAZY ABOUT THE TITLE "UNDER THE RED WHITE AND BLUE" STOP WHAT WOULD DELAY BE. It was too late to make the change and when the book was published, Fitzgerald lamented that it might not sell because "the title is only fair, rather bad than good."

The Great Gatsby, Fitzgerald's third novel, performed as dismally as he had feared. Despite favorable responses from literary greats, including T. S. Eliot and Edith Wharton, the book did not garner enthusiastic praise from reviewers. Fitzgerald remained convinced that the title had worked against the novel. He also felt that the book did not cater to female audiences—a large portion of the book-buying market—because it had "no important woman in it." It was not until after Fitzgerald's death in 1940 that *The Great Gatsby* finally crystallized into a classic novel.

Mrs. Dalloway

1925

VIRGINIA WOOLF

BLUE-EYED, blond-haired, and full of poise, Katharine "Kitty" Maxse was a picture-perfect socialite. She followed rules of etiquette that were cherished by the elite. At parties, Kitty swept from person to person, conversing artfully and enthusiastically. Kitty's mother was close friends with Julia Stephen, a beautiful and melancholy middle-class woman. Julia respected the expectations of society, just like Kitty. And she played an important role in Kitty's life, as matchmaker between her and Leopold Maxse. Kitty was devoted to the older woman. When Julia passed away, from rheumatic fever, Kitty felt compelled to help her teenage daughters, Virginia and Vanessa. So she did what she knew best and trained the girls to become accepted members of upper-class society.

Kitty preferred to spend time with Vanessa, who was out-going and gregarious, unlike her shy, awkward sister. Virginia may have been hurt by the slight, but she never really liked their mentor anyway. Kitty was far too fashionable for her taste. Much later, when Kitty was fifty-five years old, she fell over the banister in her home and was fatally injured. On her deathbed, Kitty lamented, "I shall never forgive myself for such carelessness." But forty-year-old Virginia was not con-vinced and strongly suspected it was suicide. Perhaps Kitty was not flawless, as she had appeared to be. The enigmatic socialite had already danced her way into Virginia's pages as Clarissa Dalloway in her debut novel, *The Voyage Out*. Kitty was the ideal model for Mrs. Dalloway, a polished woman whose life revolves around social expectations. Still, Virginia felt compelled to explore the character in greater depth in another work of fiction.

Virginia brought Mrs. Dalloway back in a short story called "Mrs. Dalloway on Bond Street." She intended to use the piece in a collection of interconnected stories, tentatively called *At Home* or *The Party*. But soon after Virginia heard about Kitty's supposed accident, she decided to expand the story into a full-length book. Strangely, Kitty's death also seemed to save Mrs. Dalloway's life. Virginia noted, "Mrs. Dalloway was originally to kill herself, or perhaps merely to die at the end of the party." Yet within a week after hearing about Kitty, Vir-ginia shifted away from focusing on one woman's ominous plight. Death would still loom at the end of the book, but Mrs. Dalloway would live.

Virginia now envisioned what she described in her diary as "a study of insanity & suicide: the world seen by the sane & the insane side by side." It seems likely that Kitty's death was a catalyst for this change, since her suspicious passing is mentioned in the same diary entry. Still, it is a mystery why Virginia did not want Mrs. Dalloway to share the same fate as her real-life counterpart. Virginia introduced Septimus Smith to function as Mrs. Dalloway's insane double. Septimus, a disturbed World War I veteran, had earlier appeared in an unpublished story, "The Prime Minister." He provided a striking contrast to the courteous hostess. At first glance, the two characters are completely unalike, but surprising connections surface throughout *Mrs. Dalloway*.

Virginia found inspiration in her own life for several characters in *Mrs. Dalloway*. When she was around fifteen, Virginia was enamored with Madge Symonds Vaughan, a fellow writer bursting with passion and enthusiasm. Vita Sackville-West, one of Virginia's lovers, wrote in her diary: "V[irginia] told me the history of her early loves—Madge Symonds who is Sally Seton in *Mrs. Dalloway*." In the novel, Mrs. Dalloway recalls a euphoric kiss with Sally Seton, and her feelings echo Virginia's affection for Madge. Virginia was disappointed to see Madge's spark dull after years in a traditional marriage, and she painted a similar portrait of Sally, who fades over time.

Septimus's wife, Lucrezia Warren Smith, was based on the Russian ballet dancer Lydia Lopokova. Virginia knew Lydia through her friend John Maynard Keynes, a fellow member of their unofficial club, the Bloomsbury Group. Even though she was married to John, Lydia was treated like an outsider by the exclusive set of intellectuals. Through Lydia, Virginia grew to understand what it was like for an immigrant to navigate life in a new country, and she projected these experiences onto the Italian Lucrezia. Virginia became so involved with her character that she once slipped and embarrassingly called the ballet dancer Rezia.

Though she captured the world of a socialite in *Mrs. Dalloway*, Virginia personally rejected that way of life. When she and Vanessa began to spend time with a scruffy bunch of intellectuals in Bloomsbury, Kitty was appalled. After meeting these new friends, she exclaimed, "Oh darling, how awful they do look!" Virginia, on the other hand, was thrilled to be around people who did not scold her for looking bored after a party. She felt comfortable in their midst, and even married one of them, Leonard Woolf. Though this circle of friends never called themselves the Bloomsbury Group, they were eventually referred to by that name, inspired by the area of London where their informal gatherings took place.

Many Bloomsbury regulars became authors of Hogarth Press, a small independent publishing company started by Virginia and Leonard. According to Virginia, their goal was simply to publish "all our friends' stories." Virginia acted as the typesetter, painstakingly arranging all of the letters and punctuation marks in blocks. The first publication of Hogarth Press was *Two Stories*, which included "The Mark on the Wall," by Virginia, and "Three Jews," by Leonard. Eventually Hogarth grew to incorporate writers beyond their circle of friends. By that time, Virginia and Leonard had purchased a bigger press and worked with other printers on large-scale jobs.

The success of the company opened up new opportunities for Virginia. Her work had previously been published by her half brother Gerald Duckworth, but she decided to move to Hogarth so she would no longer have to worry about the demands of a commercial publisher. In 1923, Virginia and Leonard moved to Tavistock Square and set up their business in the basement. Virginia finished writing *Mrs. Dalloway* in a storeroom beside the printing press, where she sat in a wicker chair surrounded by piles of books. The floor was damp and Virginia no doubt heard the bustle of work in the background, but tucked away in that enclosed space, she was free. In the margins of her new novel, she wrote: "A delicious idea comes to me that I will write anything I want to write."

The Old Man and the Sea

1952

ERNEST HEMINGWAY

SANTIAGO Puig was fishing off the coast of Cuba with his son when the line pulled taut. They tried to reel in the fish but were no match for the force under the water. It was a huge marlin, far too formidable for a man in a rickety little boat. Ernest Hemingway spotted the midsea battle from across the water. He sailed alongside their boat in *Pilar*, his forty-foot, black-and-green cruiser. With Hemingway's help, Puig landed the catch. The exhausted fisherman then asked Hemingway for a glass of water. Hemingway offered one of his preferred beverages—beer—as an alternative. As they drank and talked about fishing, the two men became friends.

The Old Man and the Sea is the story of a battle between an old fisherman and a marlin. It is what might have happened if Puig was out fishing on his own, without his son or Hemingway. When the book was published, Cuban men lined up to claim that they were Hemingway's true protagonist, much to the author's chagrin. Hemingway forced one of those imposters into a local restaurant and demanded a public explanation for his trickery. The fraudster, who was not even a fisherman, simply admitted that he had lied "because they gave me five dollars." Only Hemingway knew his true source. "If the old man is anybody," he said, "it's Chago's father [Puig] . . . I fished with him many times." Hemingway probably suggested that producers contact Chago about his father's boat for the movie adaptation of the book, which was released in 1958. The little vessel made the long trip from Cuba to California for its Hollywood debut. And yet the origin of Hemingway's "old man" has become literary folklore. Most self-proclaimed models are fakes, but at the very least, some of them offer insight into the author and his drive to write about the sea.

Gregorio Fuentes was a lean man who worked on Hemingway's boat, *Pilar*, for almost thirty years. During this time he survived three hurricanes, cooked delicious meals (his specialty was pompano), caught countless fish, and probably served even more drinks. With Fuentes at his side, Hemingway transformed his boat into an undercover patrol vessel during World War II. Packing explosives, bazookas, and other weaponry, Hemingway and a small crew sailed around the coast on the lookout for submarines, though they never actually confronted one. Fuentes's long-standing relationship with Hemingway gave him credibility among the author's fans. He convinced droves of tourists that he was the real old man, charging for photos and stories about his role in the book, until he died, at 104 years old, in 2002. It is unlikely that Fuentes was all he claimed to be, particularly since Hemingway never credited him. Still, it seems that Fuentes did witness the first encounter between Hemingway and Puig. In a *CBS News Sunday Morning* interview in 1999, he recalled, "When we went to sea, we found the old man and the sea. We found him adrift on a little boat with a big fish tied there. And when he went to write, he wanted to give it a name. I named it *The Old Man and the Sea*." Perhaps Fuentes did come up with the title for the book. At this point, Hemingway was no longer alive to confirm—or deny—any of Fuentes's stories.

Carlos Gutierrez was captain of the *Pilar* before Fuentes. Though he did not chase fame like his successor, Gutierrez is a more likely candidate for Hemingway's old man. In April 1936, *Esquire* published an article by Hemingway about fishing in the Gulf Stream. Hemingway included an event that he had heard from Gutierrez: "An old man fishing in a skiff out of Cabanas hooked a great marlin. . . ." According to Gutierrez, the fish pulled the boat right out to sea, where the old man struggled to reel him in, fending off hungry sharks that chomped at the great prize. Hemingway decided to transform the true account into a short story. He wrote to his editor, Maxwell Perkins, about the piece. "I'm going out with old Carlos [Gutierrez] in his skiff so as to get it all right," he noted. "Everything he does and everything he thinks in all that long fight with the boat out of sight of all the other boats all alone in the sea. It's a great story if I can get it right." Even if the old man was not based on Gutierrez, the captain's storytelling and expertise certainly lent themselves to Hemingway's novella.

It is impossible to know who, if anyone, Hemingway had in mind when he wrote the epic tale of a lone fisherman out in the open sea. *The Old Man and the Sea* was an instant hit upon its release in 1952. It was first published in *Life* magazine and then in book form, and it was embraced by critics and readers alike. Hemingway received a Pulitzer Prize for the novel in 1953. Naturally fans were intrigued by the background of this powerful story. The race to claim ownership of the old man was unlike the reaction to Hemingway's other reality-based fiction, like *The Sun Also Rises*, in which the thinly veiled characters enraged the real people they were based on. And then there's Hemingway himself, who may not be the old man, but who was a passionate fisherman. When interviewed about *The Old Man and the Sea* for the *Argosy* magazine in 1958, Hemingway stated, "I wrote that story from thirty years of fishing around here [in Cuba], and before that, too." He was a master with the fishing reel almost from the day he could walk. Hemingway's knack for the sport was recorded in a scrapbook, in which his mother proudly noted that her son, who was two years and eleven months old, went fishing with his father and "caught the biggest fish of the crowd." At that young age, Hemingway had already begun to develop an appreciation for landing a difficult catch.

Doctor Zhivago

1957

BORIS PASTERNAK

IN October 1946, the renowned poet Boris Pasternak walked into the headquarters of the Moscow-based literary journal *Novy Mir*. There he was introduced to junior editor Olga Ivinskaya, who was an ardent fan of his work. Ivinskaya was thrilled to be meeting one of her literary heroes. Pasternak was a handsome man, with a well-defined jaw. The thirty-four-year-old, twice-widowed editor was beautiful, too. Sparks flew immediately, and Ivinskaya could not mistake her own allure. It was not long before Pasternak began to court his loyal reader. During that initial meeting, he told Ivinskaya that he was writing a novel, though neither of them would have realized what an important role she would play in the book.

Within six months Ivinskaya and the married Pasternak

were involved in a serious affair. News of their illicit relation-ship spread throughout Ivinskaya's office, making it difficult for her to remain at work. So Pasternak offered to help free Ivinskaya from the magazine by training her to become a translator. This was not the first obstacle they would face. Ivin-skaya pleaded with the poet to leave his wife, Zinaida, so they could enjoy a legitimate life together, but he refused. Zinaida knew all about their romance. Even though she had no power to prevent Pasternak from seeing Ivinskaya, Zinaida refused to let him abandon his family—and she let Ivinskaya know her feelings during a heated conversation. Despite the romantic tumult, Pasternak's affair continued and he remained married to his wife.

Meanwhile, he was writing *Doctor Zhivago*, the book he had told Olga about when they first met. It was the epic saga of Yuri Zhivago, a poet and doctor. Zhivago was involved in the medical field and looked nothing like Pasternak, and yet the protagonist shared some similarities with the writer. Both men were poets, were born the same year, and had a wife and a mistress. Pasternak's affair became a central inspiration for the book. Zhivago's mistress, Lara Antipova, was based on Ivinskaya. And while Pasternak spent his days romancing the young editor, Zhivago was falling in love with the beautiful Lara.

In 1949, rumors of Pasternak's work in progress reached Russian authorities. Apparently the book was anti-Soviet and he had to be stopped before he reached the end. Pasternak was a well-known literary figure and arresting him would have caught the attention of people worldwide. So the government arrested Ivinskaya instead. She was questioned about Pasternak, their relationship, and the nature of his work. During this time, she discovered that she was pregnant with Pasternak's baby, but the child was lost in miscarriage due to the stress of her imprisonment. Then she received a formal punishment: five years of hard labor for being in close contact with suspected spies. Pasternak was devastated by Ivinskaya's fate and the death of his unborn child. He wrote to the government asking to switch places with her, but he could not bring himself to do what they really wanted and give up his novel.

Ivinskaya was released by the time Pasternak finished *Doctor Zhivago*. The author had no luck placing his novel with a Russian publishing house, but international editors were eager to consider the book. Sergio d'Angelo from the Italian company Feltrinelli paid Pasternak a visit at his own house. Pasternak gave him the manuscript, and soon it was published for the first time abroad, in Italian rather than the author's native language.

The book quickly became an international bestseller, picked up by publishers across the globe. In 1958, Pasternak was awarded the Nobel Prize for *Doctor Zhivago*, much to the Soviet government's chagrin. At first the author expressed immense joy in a telegram to the Nobel Committee. But only days later, they received another message from Pasternak: a respectful decline. Pasternak had received a volley of bad press, orchestrated by the government, for his lack of patriotism. He and Ivinskaya also lost most of their translation work due to this negative political standing. It seems that the award was far less important to Pasternak than his love for Ivinskaya, proven in a telegram he sent to the Russian government: HAVE RENOUNCED NOBEL PRIZE. LET OLGA IVINSKAYA WORK AGAIN.

THESE MEAN STREETS

Down these mean streets a man must go.
—RAYMOND CHANDLER, "THE SIMPLE ART OF MURDER"

SUNLIGHT CUTS THROUGH METAL BARS AND DROPS DOWN TO the dusty prison floor. The room is bare except for an uncomfortable bed and a grimy sink. It does not resemble a writer's workspace, yet the path to literary glory is not always glamorous. Miguel de Cervantes and Fyodor Dostoevsky were both inspired to create great novels while locked up. They probably left with very little when they were set free, but Cervantes carried the seeds of *Don Quixote* from his prison in Spain, and Dostoevsky was armed with the idea for *Crime and Punishment* when he was released from his jail cell.

In the following pages, you will encounter authors who broke the law or delved into crimes that others committed. Their muses were nothing like the goddesses from Greek mythology. They were drug-induced visions, fistfights, and murder scenes. These writers ventured into dark places—sometimes willingly, and other times not—where many of us might never want to go. And it is on these mean streets that they were spurred to write.

Don Quixote

1605

Miguel de Cervantes

M IGUEL de Cervantes sat in jail surrounded by fellow criminals, and as a stench curled through the room, he embarked on an imaginary adventure across the Spanish countryside. Beyond the prison bars, an eccentric hero sought unconventional quests with his loyal sidekick. And when Cervantes finally emerged from confinement after thirteen months, he set to work on his tale of Don Quixote.

Cervantes left us with few clues about his life. We can only guess how his cell smelled or how many people he shared it with. Only through public, political, and criminal records are we able to track his movements, from the jailhouse to the battlefield and in between. There is no way to be certain that he invented his inimitable protagonist in a cramped cell. But the author deposited a small hint about the origin of his story in the "Prologue" of *Don Quixote*, noting that it was "engendered in a prison." Many scholars agree that Cervantes was most likely referring to his incarceration in Seville. He had been working as a government commissary, but was never very good at his job, more than once neglecting to maintain proper records. Commissaries were often corrupt and a number of Cervantes's colleagues were hanged for exploiting their power. Cervantes's life was never at stake, but in 1597, after failing to produce an official record of a tax reduction that he had granted, he was thrown into the biggest jail in Spain. Seville's prison housed about two thousand people, from petty criminals to dangerous murderers. Amid the fights, executions, and torture, it is possible that Cervantes drew upon his vivid imagination as an escape.

Though Cervantes never mastered his job as a commissary, he was able to use his experiences on the job in *Don Quixote*. He traveled through southern Spain collecting goods and money on behalf on the government, but he also met colorful characters and soaked up the local dialogue. Cervantes's occupation would not have made him very popular with the locals (at one point, he was excommunicated from the Church). And yet, as he traveled from one roadside inn to the next, he must have felt a certain warmth and humor in the people he encountered, and they likely inspired the rustic characters in his tale.

For the backdrop to his hero's quest, Cervantes may have turned to his time in an unhappy marriage. Catalina de Salazar was twenty-two years younger than Cervantes, and the new-lyweds found little bliss in their union. They lived in a small village in southern Madrid in an area called La Mancha. The wind blew strong across the plateau of La Mancha and farms scattered the land. Cervantes later separated from his wife, but he must have held on to the memory of that arid landscape, as Don Quixote's hometown lies within La Mancha. Perhaps Cervantes thought back to one of the peaceful windmills near his old home when he envisioned his courageous character valiantly attempting to conquer the stationary foe.

Cervantes did not always pursue a career as a writer. He served as a soldier in the Spanish army, fighting in several battles. He was wounded twice at sea and left with a permanently paralyzed hand. At one point, Cervantes was captured by Turkish pirates. He spent five years in captivity before returning to Spain. Soon after his arrival, Cervantes tried to make a living as a writer, composing a novel and several plays, but none allowed him to focus solely on the craft. He married Catalina and then became involved in grain and oil trade before securing a job as a commissary.

In 1590, Cervantes begged the Spanish royalty to send him to America, reminding them of his loyal service to the crown. They declined, noting, "Let him look on this side of the water for some favor that may be granted him." Cervantes was offered few favors as he struggled through financial difficulty in the following years. Seven years later, he was thrown into the jail in Seville, where he remained for thirteen months. But perhaps he would not have struck creative gold if he traveled to America, and then Don Quixote and his horse would never have galloped across the literary stage. In 1605, the first part of *Don Quixote* was published by Francisco de Robles. This tale of an indefatigable hero eclipsed everything else that Cervantes had written and brought him instant literary fame.

The Count of Monte Cristo

1844–1846

ALEXANDRE DUMAS

FRANÇOIS Picaud was euphoric when he met three friends at their favorite Parisian café in 1807. He had big news to share. Marguerite de Vigoroux had agreed to marry him. Mathieu Loupian, owner of the café, overheard the elated fiancé and seethed with envy. Vigoroux was an ideal candidate for a wife, wealthy *and* beautiful. Picaud was destined for an ideal life, unlike Loupian's struggling existence running the café and raising two children alone after the loss of his wife. Loupian decided to reverse his fate by snatching away Picaud's good fortune. He convinced two of Picaud's three friends to play an awful trick on him. They would tell the authorities that Picaud was spying for England. Picaud had no way to defend himself. It was his word against three others, and so he was secretly imprisoned, leaving the bride-to-be with no knowledge of his whereabouts. Two years later, Loupian married Vigoroux and, with his newfound wealth, opened a high-end café.

Picaud spent seven years in prison, all the while dreaming of revenge. And a few months before his release, he received a gift that would help wreak havoc on Loupian's stolen life. Picaud's cell mate, who had become his good friend, died and left him a vast fortune. When the wrongfully accused man returned to Paris, he was a multimillionaire. Picaud had changed physically during his years in captivity, and none of his old friends recognized him upon his return. The thirty-six-year-old waltzed into Paris under the assumed name Joseph Lucher and executed an intricate plan to punish the men who had betrayed him. One by one, each man was murdered, and Loupian and his family were brought to ruin. Vigoroux had waited loyally for Picaud before giving up hope and marrying Loupian, but even she could not escape a doomed fate. Just after Loupian's café burned to the ground, Vigoroux died of exhaustion and an apparent stroke. Picaud then murdered the mastermind behind his demise, but only after revealing that he was responsible for Loupian's misfortune.

While Loupian's blood was still warm, Picaud was attacked by none other than Antoine Allut, the only one who had declined to take part in the wicked plot years before. When Allut realized that Picaud had returned from captivity a wealthy man, he hatched his own greedy plan. Allut kidnapped Picaud and planned to starve him until he revealed the location of his fortune. Picaud was stubborn and after days without food or water, he still refused to say a word. Allut became enraged and stabbed Picaud to death, then fled to London. In 1828, just before dying, Allut confessed the entire tale of murder and deceit to a Catholic priest.

This sordid affair could easily have been pulled from the pages of a suspense novel. Instead, it was tucked away among a series of stories in a true crime book by criminologist Jacques Peuchet. Alexandre Dumas, a prolific and bestselling French writer of both fiction and nonfiction, had read Peuchet's work and mentally flagged the account of François Picaud. In 1843, forty-one-year-old Dumas agreed to write a travel book about Paris for Béthune and Plon, but the publishers changed their minds and asked for a novel with the same setting. To fulfill their request, Dumas decided to re-create the real-life story of a man bent on exacting justice against those who wrongfully had him imprisoned.

Peuchet's story served as a basic framework for the plot of *The Count of Monte Cristo*, though Dumas changed the circumstances of the crime. The fictionalized version includes political intrigue and more twists in the plot. Dumas also fashioned his characters to suit the epic proportions of the story. Dumas' hero, Edmond Dantès, is a sailor, unlike the cobbler Picaud. And when he returns from captivity, Dantès travels ostentatiously, flaunting his wealth and using the impressive title of Count of Monte Cristo, rather than Picaud's simple pseudonym. The hero's name was a nod to Prince Napoleon, who had sailed past the island of Monte Cristo with Dumas in 1842. Dumas told his companion that he would include the enchanting location in an upcoming work of fiction, and he dutifully fulfilled his promise.

In the mid-1830s, serialized novels became a popular staple in daily newspapers in France. Dumas wrote *The Count of Monte Cristo* as a serial, and it appeared in installments in *Les Journal des Debats* from 1844 to 1846. French readers eagerly consumed Dumas' compelling tale. The story was soon translated into multiple languages and became a worldwide sensation as a full novel, flying out of bookstores across the globe.

Crime and Punishment

1866

FYODOR DOSTOEVSKY

FYODOR Dostoevsky felt the weight of his leg irons. The heavy shackles never came off during his captivity in Omsk, Siberia. He spent four years in prison, forbidden to read and write, forced to conduct manual labor. During this time, he began to think about a character who, like him, had begun to unravel. It was a story that Dostoevsky felt he had to live through before he could write it. He later recalled, "I conceived it in prison as I lay back on my bunk in a heavy-hearted moment of sadness when I felt I was losing grip of myself." Prison life drew Dostoevsky to consider criminals and their motives, and though he had not committed murder, as his protagonist would, he did understand what it meant to suffer punishment for one's actions.

In early 1847 Dostoevsky began to attend weekly meetings

at Mikhail Petrashevsky's home in St. Petersburg. During these gatherings, a wide variety of topics were discussed, including literature, philosophy, and politics. Almost a year later, Dostoevsky woke up at 4:00 a.m. to find a man in his room. He was under arrest for his association with the so-called Petrashevsky Circle. Czar Nicholas I was disturbed by the political unrest in Europe. If France could become a republic, then what about Russia? Determined to maintain political order—and his role as ruler—the czar kept a close watch on potentially revolutionary groups, like Petrashevsky's associates.

After four months of intensive questioning, the Petrashevsky intellectuals were all sentenced to death by firing squad. On a cold December morning, the men were brought to a secret location. Twenty-eight-year-old Dostoevsky stood in a line with the other prisoners. They were ordered into groups of three, and sixteen gunmen stood twelve yards away. Hoods were placed over the heads of the first three men (Dosteovsky was in the next group), and then they heard the orders: "Load. . . . Aim. . . ." But there was no final shot. A new order was read aloud. The czar would spare their lives, offering periods of imprisonment rather than death. Nicholas I had orchestrated the execution charade so that all of the men understood the gravity of their actions before he lightened their sentences. Dostoevsky was soon carted off to Omsk. He arrived at the jail in January 1850 and remained there for four years. During his captivity, in that heavy-hearted moment on his bunk, the dark prison walls were illuminated by the first spark of his novel *Crime and Punishment*.

Dostoevsky knew since his time in Omsk that he wanted to write about a criminal confession, but it was not until 1860 that he stumbled across an ideal model for the protagonist in his book. At the time, Dostoevsky was a contributor for his brother Mikhail's hefty five-hundred-page monthly journal, *Vremya*, which focused on the place of common people within society. Dostoevsky scoured through court trials in France for news that he might include in the journal, and he came across an unusual story.

Pierre-François Lacenaire was a criminal unlike any other. He was witty, well-read, egotistical . . . and a murderer. Lacenaire's spiral into crime began when he won a duel to the death. Rather than feeling guilty about his transgression, Lacenaire experienced a newfound sense of self-worth. After his release from prison, Lacenaire turned his attention to poetry, but he was not satisfied with a literary life. He committed a series of burglaries, which culminated in murder. Lacenaire was imprisoned again, but he did not spend his time behind bars lamenting the crime. Instead he developed new ideas about literature, politics, and religion.

Dostoevsky was fascinated by this criminal intellectual, and the man became the inspiration for the fallen protagonist Rodion Romanovich Raskolnikov in *Crime and Punishment*. Both the fictional and the real man justified murder as a means to wealth, and each was punished for his violent act. But Lacenaire did not suffer the extreme poverty of his fictional counterpart. Dostoevsky was far more familiar with money woes than the incarcerated Frenchman.

Dostoevsky was constantly under the threat of being thrown into prison for his debt. In 1865 he traveled to Wiesbaden, Germany, to get away from financial pressures and focus on writing. And yet he was not able to escape his own weakness for gambling and was soon broke. He often pinpointed this moment of loss as the origin of *Crime and Punishment*, when his ideas came together in the framework of a story. Hungry and almost completely broke, Dostoevsky toiled away on the book, often deferring to creative demands over monetary needs. At one point, he had finished a large portion of the manuscript and decided to start over again, despite his lack of funds. "I burned it all," he noted. "I got interested in a new form, a new plan." His instincts must have been right, because the pages flew after he returned to page one.

Three months later, in January 1866, the first part of *Crime and Punishment* was printed in the literary journal *Ruskii Vestnik*. Dostoevsky had written several novels, but this one stood out from his previous works. One critic noted that it "promises to be one of the most important works of the author." *Crime and Punishment* appeared in twelve monthly installments and drew five hundred new subscribers to the journal. The novel was published in book form the following year, but the journal publication had already established its worth on the Russian literary scene.

Naked Lunch

1959

WILLIAM S. BURROUGHS

ILLIAM S. Burroughs added one more line to his letter and then signed off "Love, Bill." The message would make its way through the dusty streets of Tangier to the hills of San Francisco, until it landed in the hands of Allen Ginsberg. Burroughs wrote hundreds of letters from northern Africa to his friend and unrequited love. The forty-year-old writer had mixed feelings about living far away from the United States in a city nestled between the Atlantic Ocean and the Mediterranean Sea. Tangier was controlled by eight different countries in Europe. As a crossroads between language, currency, and politics, it was also a center for shady business. Drugs coursed through the streets and over countertops, and prostitutes lined the corners.

In January 1954, Burroughs was on the hunt for a place where he could survive on the two hundred dollars he received from his parents every month. Burroughs came from a wealthy family and his parents sent him the same allowance from the time he graduated from Harvard University until the early 1960s, when he could finally support himself. Tangier offered cheap living and an escape from the rest of the world, but Burroughs was often lonely and dove into heavy drugs to numb the pain. He began taking a variety of substances, including Eukodol, a German morphine that induced a feeling of euphoria. All the while, Burroughs wrote to Ginsberg, who described the letters as "Bill's faithful record of his heroic battle with depression and junk." Eventually Burroughs traveled to an institution in England, unable to wean himself off the junk alone.

After recovering, Burroughs stayed briefly in Venice before moving back to Tangier, where he worked furiously on *Naked Lunch*, a fictionalized version of his experiences on drugs. Burroughs recalled, "I wrote and I wrote and I wrote. I'd usually take majoun every other day and on the off days I would have a big bunch of joints lined up on my desk and smoke them as I typed." Burroughs said that he had to quit using heavy drugs before he could focus on the novel, and yet much of the book was gleaned from his correspondence to Ginsberg while still on junk. In March 1957, Ginsberg arrived in Tangier to help Burroughs complete the book. He carried with him folders filled with letters from Burroughs, all assembled in chronological order.

Ginsberg was not the only person to help Burroughs pull together his sprawling novel. Another writer was already clacking away on typewriter keys, transcribing the pages that sat in Burroughs's room at Hotel Muniriya. It was their mutual friend Jack Kerouac (see pages 183–186). The three men met in New York about a decade before convening in Tangier. Burroughs owed his title to Kerouac, who came up with it before he began work on the novel. Ginsberg had been looking through one of Burroughs's previous manuscripts and misread the phrase "naked lust" as "naked lunch." Kerouac caught the slip and insisted that Burroughs use it for a book.

Kerouac did not take to Burroughs's run-down, exotic city, staying only four weeks and leaving the day after Ginsberg arrived. Ginsberg remained for several months and worked about six hours every day on the manuscript. He and Burroughs scoured the letters for worthwhile observations, which they lifted into the book. Ginsberg later observed, "The letters merge with the novel, the life merges with art." Poet and playwright Alan Ansen joined the pair. He had extensive experience as a research assistant and was able to add an element of control to the unwieldy mass of writing. When Ginsberg and Ansen departed in June, they left behind a two-hundred-page manuscript, but the book was still not finished. Burroughs continued to toil away on it. He traveled to Scandinavia, which became a backdrop in the book, in addition to Tangier, Mexico, and the United States. He returned to Tangier and then traveled to Paris, all the while revising *Naked Lunch*. Burroughs may have revised for much longer if an excerpt from the book in progress had not been published by the *Chicago Review*.

In the fall of 1958, a Chicago gossip columnist deplored the work by William S. Burroughs in the *Chicago Review*. The next issue, which would have featured another excerpt from *Naked Lunch*, never made it to the press—it had been prohibited by Chicago University faculty because of Burroughs's graphic work. A handful of editors were outraged about the censorship and quit the magazine to start their own venture, *Big Table*. The rebellious magazine published Burroughs's excerpt and hundreds of copies were held at a post office after being deemed unfit to send due to explicit content.

Almost immediately, Burroughs had a book deal. Maurice Girodias from the Parisian publisher Olympia Press offered to buy *Naked Lunch*. He wanted the manuscript within a couple of weeks, planning to publish it while the literary scandal was still fresh. So, in one great flurry, the book was finished. *Naked Lunch* was published by Grove Press in the United States in 1962, though not without difficulty. Burroughs had received little recognition for his debut novel, *Junkie*, which was also based on his drug experiences, but the controversy surrounding *Naked Lunch* pushed him into the literary spotlight. A man was arrested in Boston for carrying profane material—he had placed *Naked Lunch* in his bookstore. The book was evaluated by a court in Boston, only to be judged unacceptable, even though it was passionately defended by Ginsberg and Norman Mailer. The discussion escalated to a Supreme Court trial, in which *Naked Lunch* was finally ruled as having literary merit.

Burroughs was no stranger to notoriety. In 1951, he was living in Mexico City with his wife, Joan, and their two children.

Drunk at a party, Burroughs decided to play a spontaneous game. He recalled saying to Joan, "I guess it's about time for our William Tell act." Joan was sitting about six feet away and she complied, placing a highball glass on her head. Burroughs leveled his .380 automatic, an old and defective gun that he had planned to sell at the gathering. He pulled the trigger and shot his wife in the head. Joan was pronounced dead upon arrival at a nearby Red Cross hospital. Burroughs was shocked. He could not understand why he chose to fire the gun and attributed it to a dark side that had usurped him. Burroughs later admitted that the horrendous act propelled him to become a writer. He observed, "The death of Joan brought me in contact with the invader, the Ugly Spirit, and maneuvered me into a lifelong struggle, in which I have had no choice except to write my way out."

To Kill a Mockingbird

1960

HARPER LEE

O N Christmas Day, 1956, thirty-year-old Harper Lee received a note from her friends Michael and Joy Brown: "You have one year off from your job to write whatever you please. Merry Christmas." Lee had been struggling for some time to get by as an unpublished writer in New York City, far away from her sleepy hometown of Monroeville, Alabama. She managed to finish five stories while working menial jobs, but there was never enough time to write. The Browns' gift changed all that. Lee was free to quit her job and channel all of her energy onto the page. The tall, shy brunette sat down to work, and within one month she had fifty pages of a novel. She marched over to the office of literary agent Maurice Crain and handed him the beginning of her book, at that time called *Go Set a Watchman*. Crain had read Lee's short stories the previous year and encouraged her to write a full-length work. By February, after Crain had received several installments, an entire manuscript sat on his desk. Crain was willing to send the book out to publishers, but he suggested Lee simplify the title, changing it to *Atticus* after one of the main characters. He mailed the manuscript to the publishing house J. B. Lippincott, and its editorial board expressed interest in the book, though not in its current form. Lee was invited to meet with the editors at their office to discuss the structural problems of her plot. She listened attentively to the criticism and submitted a revised manuscript a few months later. In October, she accepted an offer from the company. She had landed a book deal within a year from the day she began her novel.

Before publication, Lee's book underwent countless rounds of revisions and another title change, but Atticus kept his name to the very end. He was named after Titus Pomponius Atticus, close friend to the Roman philosopher and politician Marcus Tullius Cicero. Lee modeled the character on her father, lawyer Amasa Coleman Lee. In 1919, twenty-nine-year-old A. C. Lee defended two black men in court. They were tried for the murder of a white shopkeeper. Both men were found guilty and hung, and parts of their scalps were sent to the victim's father. It was a horrific expression of criminal justice.

Lee selected a different trial for her book when she sat down to write nearly forty years later, but one that was also fraught with racial prejudice. She dug deep into the history of her hometown and pulled up a decades-old criminal case. In 1933, Naomi Lowery had accused Walter Lett of raping her on the outskirts of Monroeville. Lowery was white and Lett was black, which basically meant that he was cast as guilty before the trial began. Lett was sentenced to death. Many locals questioned his guilt and his punishment was eventually changed from execution to life imprisonment, but by that time, he had suffered a mental breakdown that he would never recover from. In *To Kill a Mockingbird*, Atticus Finch represents a black man in a similarly controversial case. The defendant, Tom Robinson, is accused of raping a white woman. The evidence against Robinson is flimsy, but he lives in Alabama during the 1930s, a place and time rife with racism, which means there is a good chance that justice will not be served.

Lee prefers not to link specific people to characters in the book. And yet much of the story is clearly influenced by her childhood. Her six-year-old protagonist, Scout, is a bold tomboy, much like Lee was when she was young. The mysterious and reclusive Boo Radley is based on a real man, too. Son Boulware was just a teen when he was caught robbing a drugstore, among other minor delinquencies. The judge planned to send him to a state industrial school, but his father intervened. He promised the judge that if Son returned home he would not cause any more trouble. Son was rarely seen outside the house again. Truman Capote (see pages 145–148) was Lee's best friend in Monroeville and he later recalled fetching presents that Son left in trees, just as Boo does in the novel. In fact, Capote wrote Son into his novel *Other Rooms, Other Voices*, but removed him in later drafts. Of Boo Radley's story, Capote insisted, "Everything [Lee] wrote about it is absolutely true."

Capote also declared that he was Dill, Scout's imaginative friend in *To Kill a Mockingbird*. The eccentric author was just like his fictional counterpart, both inclined to come up with elaborate stories. Lee and Capote were inseparable when they were young, and one day Lee's father gave them a gift that foreshadowed their literary careers—an Underwood typewriter. The pair spent hours hunched over the machine. As children, they wrote all about the local people in Monroeville, and years later Lee returned to the same setting for her novel. Though this time around, the writing did not flow as easily. During one of her many revisions, Lee became so exasperated that she threw her manuscript out her apartment window, the pages fluttering down into the New York snow. Lee's editor, Theresa Von Hohoff, convinced her to race outside and pick everything up. Hohoff had faith in Lee's ability and, perhaps even more importantly, her drive. Hohoff recalled, "She wanted with all her being to write—not merely to 'be a writer.'"

When *To Kill a Mockingbird* was published in 1960, Lee probably hoped for modest success. There is no way she could have predicted that her book would become a huge bestseller. It hit the *New York Times* bestseller list and remained a fixture there for eighty-eight weeks. A year after its publication, *To Kill a Mockingbird* won the Pulitzer Prize and was a finalist for the National Book Award. And then in 1962, a movie version of the book starring Gregory Peck was released. Almost overnight, Lee was transformed from a struggling writer into a public personality. She received a torrent of interview requests and fan letters (at one point, sixty-two messages were delivered for her in one day). A shy and private person, Lee found it difficult to remain in the spotlight, so she retreated back into her own life. She no longer grants interviews and only rarely makes public appearances. Though fans eagerly await Lee's next book, it has never arrived, and we can only guess why. Perhaps it was too difficult to write in the shadow of her phenomenal success. Lee made a rare appearance at an awards ceremony at the Alabama Academy of Honor in 2007, and she captured her departure from the public eye in a pithy, sentence-long speech: "It is better to be silent than to be a fool."

In Cold Blood

1966

TRUMAN CAPOTE

O N November 16, 1959, Truman Capote flipped through the *New York Times*, skimming the articles until he noticed a headline on page 39: "Wealthy Farmer, 3 of Family Slain." Tucked away in the newspaper was a horrific story. In a small town in Kansas, four people from a picture-perfect family had been brutally murdered by someone the local sheriff concluded must be "a psychopathic killer," and the culprit was still on the loose. Capote sensed that there was much more to the story than the basic facts presented in the article. So he pitched his own investigation of the crime to William Shawn at the *New Yorker*. It did not matter to Capote that the police had yet to catch the perpetrator. He would focus on the extreme act of violence and its impact on a seemingly serene town.

Within a few weeks, Capote received a green light on the piece, packed his bags, and boarded a train to Holcomb, Kansas. The young writer was rarely intimidated by a new challenge, but he was not sure what to expect in the sprawling countryside that loomed ahead. Capote did know that he was much more at home among the eclectic crowds of New York than amid conservative Midwesterners, so he invited a research partner to travel with him. Harper Lee had been friends with Capote since childhood, and she promptly accepted the offer. She recalled, "Crime intrigued him, and I'm intrigued with crime—and, boy, I wanted to go. It was deep calling to deep." The trip was also a perfect distraction from her soon-to-be-published debut novel, *To Kill a Mockingbird* (see pages 140–144).

Capote stood out from the moment he stepped off the train. He was an eccentric writer with a high-pitched voice, an outgoing personality, and a flamboyant wardrobe—not the type of person you would expect to find in the country. Still, he hoped to win over the locals with warmth and charisma. To his dismay, it seemed impossible to break through to the townspeople, who were still reeling in shock from the murders. Luckily for Capote, as a product of Monroeville, Alabama, Lee had perfected the art of small-town charm. Lee was no stranger to saving Capote in a rural setting. When they were young children in Monroeville, Lee had stood up to the bullies who harassed the unconventional Capote. In Holcomb, now an adult, she traded those raised fists for a warm smile. She befriended the women almost instantly, paving the way for them to give Capote a chance. Finally one family took pity on the peculiar outsider and invited him to Christmas dinner at their house. Not long after the dishes were washed, dried, and put away, news had spread like wildfire: the New York reporter was actually funny and entertaining. More invitations soon rolled in and Capote was finally able to accumulate intimate details about the victims and the town.

If you peeked through the window into a living room when Capote was visiting, you would probably assume that he had stopped by for a friendly chat. He was determined to cultivate trusting relationships with the people of Holcomb. Neither Capote nor Lee used a tape recorder or took notes during an interview. They jotted down everything they could remember after their meetings and then compared notes each night. Through their combined efforts, Capote began to assemble a compelling story about Holcomb before and after the murders, but nothing could prepare him for the next development in the investigation.

On December 30, 1959, two suspects were apprehended in Las Vegas and supervising investigator Alvin Dewey traveled all the way to Nevada to pick them up. When Dewey returned, a large group of people were waiting outside the county courthouse. Capote stood in the crowd, curious to see what type of men might commit such a gruesome crime. A peculiar pair stepped out of the police car. Richard "Dick" Hickock was tall with light hair and a disfigured face, and Perry Smith was short with dark hair and a noticeable limp. And they had already confessed to the murders. It was not long before Capote lined up a series of meetings with Hickock and Smith.

A masterful conversationalist, he managed to lure both men beyond the bounds of a standard interview. Over time, they opened up to Capote, offering facts about their pasts, their motivation for murder, and even the night of the crime. As he forged an unusual friendship with the two criminals, Capote pieced together portraits of troubled, charismatic, and violent men. And he realized that his story would no longer fit in just one article; it would have to be a book. Capote described *In Cold Blood* as the first nonfiction novel, "a narrative form that employed all the techniques of fictional art but was nevertheless immaculately factual."

It took six years to complete the manuscript. Capote spent much of that time impatiently waiting to find out the fate of the murderers so that he could write the last chapter of the book. The men were eventually executed and Capote was finally able to finish the book.

In Cold Blood was published in serial installments in the *New Yorker* in 1965 and sales for the magazine immediately skyrocketed. This success only hinted at the fanfare that would erupt when the book was published the following year. Capote became a hot news item, stealing the spotlight on television, on radio, and in major publications nationwide.

The Outsiders

1967

S. E. HINTON

A TEENAGE boy with slicked-back hair strolled home from school in Tulsa, Oklahoma. He was a Greaser, part of a group of students who smoked cigarettes, wore black leather jackets, and were notorious for making trouble. The young rebel had nowhere to run when a car full of Socs pulled up alongside him. The Socs were a rival gang from the more affluent part of town. Tensions ran high between the two groups, often culminating in fierce words and physical fights. On this afternoon, the Socs had the advantage and decided to beat up the defenseless teen.

Susan Eloise Hinton was furious when she heard about her injured friend. Hinton had been writing stories for years, so it was not surprising that she carried her rage directly to the typewriter. She recalled, "I just went home and started pounding out a story about this boy who was beaten up while he was walking home from the movies—the beginning of *The Outsiders*." Hinton wanted to write about what life was really like as a teen in the 1960s. Other young adult books featured glossy, clean-cut teens that did not resemble any of the kids she knew. Unlike the authors of those books, Hinton was actually the same age as her characters and so she wrote with an authority they lacked. She was fifteen years old and a sophomore in high school when she began the book.

A self-proclaimed loner, Hinton was not aligned with any particular group at school. Even though most of her pals were Greasers from the poor side of town, she was friends with some of the Socs, too. At a young age, Hinton realized that every teen, no matter what social status, struggled in his or her own way. This insight helped her write about both groups with understanding and compassion. Many of Hinton's friends became the inspiration for characters in the book. In a letter to her literary agent, Hinton wrote: "You might like to know that quite a few people from the book are from real life. The true-life counterpart of Two-Bit Mathews, for instance, drove me to school yesterday. He and his friends are my real inspiration. I mentioned that to them one time, and they got a nice laugh out of it."

Hinton had been writing since she was a little kid, first composing stories on her father's Underwood typewriter. It was a clunky old machine and difficult to type on, but that did not bother Hinton as she tapped out tales about cowboys and horses. Finally, in ninth grade, Hinton invested in a new type-writer. Hinton's pet cocker spaniel had given birth to a litter of puppies and she had sold them for a nice profit. She earned enough money to buy a modern machine (though it was not electric), which she used to write her debut novel.

When Hinton finished *The Outsiders*, she had extra incentive to find a publisher. Her mother half jokingly agreed to buy her a car if she sold the book. Hinton's younger sister Beverly desperately wanted her to get the car and so she personally mailed the manuscript to a literary agent. Ever since, Beverly has taken credit for her role in the success of the book, but Hinton reminds her, "Yeah, and you put the first dent in the car." The literary agent was Marilyn Marlow of Curtis Brown in New York. Marlow called Hinton and said, "I think you've caught a certain spirit here, and I'm going to see what I can do with it." Hinton received a D in creative writing her junior year, but neglecting her schoolwork paid off. On her high school graduation day, she received her first book contract. Marlow had sold the book to the second publishing house she sent it to.

After *The Outsiders* was published, Hinton suffered from severe writer's block. Her debut novel was a blockbuster bestseller and a tough act to follow. Hinton's boyfriend helped motivate her to sit down at the typewriter again with an ultimatum: they could only go out if she wrote two pages that day. Eager to spend time with her future husband, Hinton finally had all the inspiration she needed to get back to work. Her second novel, published in 1971, was called *That Was Then,*

This Is Now, an apt title given her struggle to move beyond the success of *The Outsiders*. None of Hinton's books came close to the phenomenal success of *The Outsiders*, but Hinton has remained upbeat about her literary career. When asked during a radio interview how it felt to be known only for her debut novel, she replied, "From what I hear, it beats being not known at all."

Slaughterhouse-Five

1969

KURT VONNEGUT

ON February 13, 1945, Kurt Vonnegut heard the air-raid sirens blare. He and his fellow prisoners of war trudged down two flights of stairs into the depths below the slaughterhouse. The top floor had been converted for the soldiers and outfitted with bunks and straw mattresses, but carcasses were hung in the meat locker below. They could hear sounds of the Allies bombing Dresden, Germany, and yet there was no way to tell what the damage would be. The attack was devastating. "When we came up the city was gone," recalled Vonnegut during a 1977 interview for the *Paris Review*. Over 130,000 people were killed within a matter of hours, and a vast number were civilians. Vonnegut and the other POWs were ordered to help dispose of the bodies. Memories of the bombing haunted Vonnegut long after he was freed in May 1945.

Vonnegut had enlisted in the army in 1943 and went on to fight in the infantry during World War II. In December 1944, the twenty-two-year-old private was captured by the Germans in Belgium during the Battle of the Bulge. Vonnegut witnessed a lot of bloodshed during this surprise attack from the Germans, but nothing could prepare him for the immense death toll in Dresden. He was sent there as a POW and put to work with a group of privates. They spent their nights in a slaughterhouse the Germans called *Schlachthof Fünf*, or Slaughterhouse Five, which later inspired Vonnegut's title. During the day, they worked in a factory that produced malt syrup for pregnant women. Dresden produced all sorts of products, such as clarinets and cigarettes, but not weapons. The city had little to do with the war effort and was not prepared for a large-scale attack. It was shocking when Allied forces wiped out the entire metropolis.

Vonnegut considered writing about the war when he returned to the United States, but felt as if he had missed the major action and had little to offer. The Dresden bombing was only mentioned briefly in American newspapers. Vonnegut's knowledge of the event was limited to the portions of the city he was ordered to work in. He had no idea how many people had lost their lives. Then, in 1963, David Irving's *Destruction of Dresden* revealed the full extent of the massacre. Vonnegut realized, "By God, I saw something after all!" So he finally decided to write about World War II. The only problem was that so much time had passed it was difficult to remember everything that took place in Dresden. He reached out to men who had served alongside him, but most preferred to forget their horrific experiences. Veteran Bernard V. O'Hare was one of the few people who supported Vonnegut's endeavor. During a meeting with O'Hare, Vonnegut had an important epiphany about the book. O'Hare's wife, Mary, interrupted to scold both men for contemplating a glamorous portrait of the war. She reminded them that World War II was fought by children—boys in their teens or early twenties—not by flawless men. The observation made an impression on Vonnegut. He observed, "She freed me to write about what infants we were: 17, 18, 19, 20, 21." He was no longer bound to writing about heroes. With Mary's caution in mind, Vonnegut added "The Children's Crusade" to his title.

Slaughterhouse-Five is not a typical war novel. Rather than following a chronological sequence or sticking to the front lines, the book jumps back and forth through time and blends science fiction with scenes based on Vonnegut's experiences during World War II. Vonnegut later observed, "The science-fiction passages in *Slaughterhouse-Five* are just like clowns in Shakespeare." These otherworldly sections offer a thought-provoking comparison to the battlefield.

Vonnegut had already written several novels, but this was his first big book. When it was published in 1969, *Slaughterhouse-Five* jumped to number one on the *New York Times* bestseller list. But the book's unconventional approach, particularly its controversial religious and sexual scenes, prompted a strong negative response from some readers. *Slaughterhouse-Five* has become one of the most censored and banned books in the United States. Many concerned parents have lobbied to exclude the book from school curricula. And yet it was children, soldiers who had only recently graduated from high school, who Vonnegut was writing about in the first place.

THE GREAT CHASE

You can't wait for inspiration. You have to go after it with a club.

—JACK LONDON

ANTOINE DE SAINT-EXUPÉRY FLEW BENEATH A STARRY SKY. Jack Kerouac pressed on the gas, hurtling from one side of the United States to the other. Jack London trudged through snowy mountains. And Herman Melville spotted a whale spout on a voyage through the Bahamas. Rather than waiting for ink and a pen to carry them away on fictional adventures, these authors packed their bags and embarked on their own grand expeditions.

Whether they were looking for thrills or simply bound for a relaxing holiday, each writer in the following section discovered that some of the best ideas are found away from home. Some were struck by the beauty of a new setting or the compelling history of a place. Others came close to death as they ventured into dangerous territory. Their experiences were more valuable than anything you would find in your standard gift shop: they were literary gold, the foundation for novels that no one would soon forget.

Jane Eyre

1847

CHARLOTTE BRONTË

SHOCKING news swept through the classrooms at Roe Head School. A governess in the nearby city of Leeds had discovered that her husband had a secret wife from a previous marriage. The poor woman had recently given birth to a baby, and she was devastated. When confronted, her husband explained that his first wife was mentally disturbed. The situation was unbearable for him, but divorce was out of the question. So he had resolved to find a new bride and never let the two women know about one another. A deceitful husband, a nonexistent marriage, an illegitimate baby . . . the governess's life fell apart. The scandal must have resonated with nineteen-year-old Charlotte Brontë, who was a teacher at Roe Head. Years later she wrote a novel based on the true story of the unfortunate brides and groom.

A trip away from home offered Brontë the inspiration she needed to plan the book. In July 1845, Brontë visited her old friend Ellen Nunney in Hathersage, England. Nunney was staying at the home of her brother Henry, helping to prepare the house for the arrival of his new bride. Henry had first proposed to Brontë, who declined his businesslike offer, but six years later he'd found another suitable woman to marry. Brontë stayed with Nunney for three weeks and they spent much of that time moving from one place to the next.

One of their stops was North Lees Hall, an impressive manor about a mile north of Hathersage. In the past, a mistress of the hall was deemed crazy and confined to a padded room, where she died in a fire. When Brontë visited North Lees and learned of its terrible history, she must have been reminded of the mentally disturbed wife from Leeds. She melded both tales together in the pages of *Jane Eyre*, in which a young governess falls in love with a man who hides a terrible secret. The mysterious man lives in Thornfield Hall, a replica of North Lees. In fact, Brontë re-created many of the places from her trip in her novel. The fictional town of Morton, which lies near Thornfield, is clearly based on Hathersage. Brontë did not try to disguise the model for her setting: she named the town after a local inn owner in Hathersage and her protagonist's surname was inspired by the Eyre family, who had lived in the area for generations.

A year after returning from Hathersage, Brontë put pen to paper and wrote *Jane Eyre*. She worked by her father's bedside in a quiet, dark room, watching over him while he recovered from eye surgery. The tale unfolded on square pages that Brontë pulled close to her shortsighted eyes. Brontë grew increasingly involved in the story, writing furiously until she came down with a fever and had to take a break. Her zeal was contagious. In August 1847, Brontë sent the manuscript to Smith, Elder, and Company. George Smith read the book in almost one sitting, canceling his appointments for the day and staying up late, just so he could reach the end. By October that year, he had released *Jane Eyre*, Brontë's first published novel. The book was an immediate hit, but no one would have recognized the author if they passed her on the street, not even her own publisher.

Jane Eyre was originally attributed to a writer named Currer Bell. Brontë insisted that she and her sisters, Emily and Anne, also writers, use pseudonyms for their published work. After all, women at the time were subjected to harsh criticism based solely on their sex. Brontë explained, "We had a vague impression that authoresses are liable to be looked on with prejudice; we had noticed how critics sometimes used for their chastisement the weapon of personality, and for their reward, a flattery, which is not true praise." The sisters decided to name themselves Currer, Ellis, and Acton Bell. They plucked the surname from Arthur Bell Nicholls, a man who worked for their father, Reverend Patrick Brontë. Though she had no idea at the time, Brontë would marry Nicholls later in life.

The sisters giggled over reviews of poetry and prose by the Bell brothers. Brontë observed, "How I laugh in my sleeve when I read the solemn assertions that *Jane Eyre* was written in partnership, and that it 'bears the marks of more than one mind and one sex.'" Little did those reviewers know that the book was in fact written by a woman and just one brilliant mind.

Moby-Dick

1851

HERMAN MELVILLE

N 1838, a sea captain spotted a spray of water on the horizon just off the coast of Chile. A call followed: "There she blows!" Boats were lowered from the ship. Men raced toward the spout, bold and courageous . . . until they noticed a streak of white. It was Mocha Dick, the notorious albino sperm whale whose name was whispered in awe on ships around the world. Hundreds of sailors had tried to conquer the "ferocious fiend of the deep," and he wore the scars of each battle with irons wedged into his pale back. Some of the most skilled whalers had died in pursuit of the great whale.

So it was not surprising that the harpooner's knees shook when he looked up at Mocha Dick, with his gaping jaw and barnacle-studded head. The sailor drew his arm back, took aim, and missed, and the whale swam away. The next day, the ship crossed paths with Mocha Dick again, and this time a harpoon landed in his side, a rare hit in one of his weakest points. The whale thrashed in pain, hurtled toward the little boat, and then plunged into the ocean. Just as the men were about to cut the line that was attached to the harpoon, for fear of being pulled into the deep, Mocha Dick rose to the surface, weak and wounded. The fierce creature fought until his last breath, and then at last the sailors celebrated their victory.

J. R. Reynolds wrote about the true story of Mocha Dick's final days for *Knickerbocker Magazine* in 1839. Just over a decade later, Herman Melville sat down to write a novel that would combine great whaling adventures with his own experiences on the open sea. Melville must have heard about the legendary whale first spotted near Mocha Island on the Chilean coast. He changed the name only slightly for the novel, *Moby-Dick*, in which an obsessive captain seeks a seemingly invincible white whale. But there was another midsea adventure that resonated with Melville.

In 1820, Captain George Pollard directed his ship toward a group of whales near the Galápagos Islands. The sailors were in the middle of their hunt when one of the whales broke from the pack and tore right into the ship. The boat began to sink and orders were given to abandon ship when the whale attacked again. The survivors were stuck in three boats in the middle of the ocean with few supplies. In desperation, some of the men resorted to cannibalism. A harrowing account of this tale from sailor Owen Chase "had a surprising effect" on

Melville. It was virtually unheard of for whales to turn on ships, and this story was the stuff of nightmares for sailors. Yet for Melville, the writer, it was inspiration for an epic ocean saga that pitted man against whale.

Moby-Dick was not simply pieced together through second-hand accounts. Melville was a whaler for a brief stint. In January 1841, with few other prospects, he joined the crew of the whale ship *Acushnet* bound for the South Seas. Whales were in high demand at the time, and their value could be seen in everyday life, from the lighting of an oil lamp to the tightening of a whalebone corset. Twenty-one-year-old Melville took well to life on the high seas, where he experienced every part of the whaling process. The hunt began with the harpooning, but that was only the beginning of the struggle, as the whale was then stabbed to death. Depending on its size, preparing a whale could take several days. Barrels of oil were sent from the *Acushnet* back to the United States, proof of the crew's successful encounters across the water. And all the while, Melville soaked in the ocean life, listening to stories from fellow sailors and gazing up at the albatrosses circling above. Midway through the voyage, Melville abandoned his ship with a fellow sailor on an island in the South Pacific. After a month on the island, he jumped on board another whale ship.

Melville never encountered a vicious whale bent on destroying a ship, but for a little while, he lived just as his characters did in *Moby-Dick*, chasing fortune and adventure on the open seas. Ten years after setting out to sea as a whaler, Melville wrote that he was composing "a strange sort of book." He was back on the ocean, only this time, his captain was a fiery man who lost his leg to Moby-Dick and was bent on revenge.

Melville had written a couple of memoirs and three novels before he penned his whale story. He dedicated the book to a friend, the writer Nathaniel Hawthorne, citing "admiration for his genius." But in this novel, Melville had expressed his own literary genius. His story was not merely the tale of a man and a whale. It was filled with insight, literary allusion, and experimental narrative technique. And yet when the book was published in 1851, readers did not rush to pick up a copy. Only a portion of the three thousand copies that were first printed ever sold. It was not until the early twentieth century, decades after Melville's death in 1891, that his novel received widespread acclaim. In the 1920s, *Moby-Dick* was adopted by literary critics, who marveled not only at the story, but at Melville's modern style, which differentiated him from his contemporaries. In 1921, D. H. Lawrence observed that Melville was "a futurist long before futurism." Melville's white whale continues to ripple through literary waters today.

Heart of Darkness

1902

JOSEPH CONRAD

As a young boy, Joseph Conrad dreamed of exploring uncharted territory. Blank spaces on maps were filled with possibility. He pointed at unknown regions of Africa and swore that one day he would travel there. Decades later, Conrad fulfilled his promise. In August 1890, the thirty-two-year-old voyaged up the Congo River to Stanley Falls, which he described in his memoir, *A Personal Record*, as the "blankest of blank spaces on the earth's figured surface."

Conrad traveled along the winding river in a wood-burning steamship called *Roi des Belges*. He had originally intended to report as a captain for a Belgian trading company in Africa, but when he arrived, he discovered that his ship was in disrepair. While he waited to take charge of another boat, Conrad joined the crew of *Roi des Belges* for a preview of navigating African waterways. The rattling vessel passed few villages or boats en route to their isolated destination. In the mornings, a white mist enveloped them, blocking out the murky water and lush vegetation on the banks. When they arrived at Stanley Falls, they picked up Georges-Antoine Klein, who worked for the same company that had hired Conrad. Around the same time, the captain of *Roi des Belges* became ill and Conrad took charge. On the way back, tragedy struck when Klein died from dysentery. The expedition turned out to be Conrad's only stint as a captain in Africa.

Conrad had signed a contract to work in the Congo for three years, but the professional venture was ruined by a curmudgeonly manager. Camille Delcommune and Conrad disliked one another immediately. In a letter to his friend Marguerite Poradowska, Conrad complained, "The director is a common ivory-dealer with sordid instincts who imagines himself a merchant while in fact he is only a kind of African shopkeeper. His name is Delcommune. He hates the English, and I am of course regarded as one." (Conrad was Polish by birth, but in 1886 he became a British citizen.) Conrad had large dark eyes and animated facial expressions that gave away every emotion, and his animosity toward his Belgian employer must have been equally clear. Unfortunately, this meant that Conrad would lose the opportunity to take charge of his own ship in Africa. After his venture on the *Roi des Belges*, Conrad was assigned to menial tasks, such as handling ivory and overseeing a forestry project. In October he became severely sick with dysentery, and by January 1891 he was back in London.

Conrad was disenchanted by his work in Africa, but the long-awaited expedition had sparked his imagination. Almost a decade later, he would climb aboard another steamship, though this time he sailed from page to page and had full control of the vessel, charting its fictional course with his pen.

Conrad sailed across the globe on many adventures before he left the high seas when he was thirty-six to concentrate on writing full time. He sold several short stories and a few novels to various outlets before establishing a relationship with *Blackwood's Magazine*. The publication adopted Conrad as an emerging talent and gave him the freedom to write with little editorial input. *Blackwood's* printed several pieces by Conrad, including a serialization of his Congo novel, *Heart of Darkness*, that ran from February through April 1899. *Heart of Darkness* was published in book form in *Youth: A Narrative, and Two Other Stories* in 1902.

To write the novella, Conrad returned to the banks of the Congo. In an "Author's Note" for *Youth*, Conrad noted that when he wrote *Heart of Darkness*, he "pushed a little (and only very little) beyond the actual facts." He described the same landscape that he recorded in his diary during his months in Africa. And he brought real people into the tale, including characters based on the awful manager and the sickly Klein (whose German surname, meaning "small," was fictionalized as Kurtz, based on *kurz*, or "short").

Yet the novella was not simply a retelling of Conrad's trip up the river. His gentle nudge beyond the facts transformed a basically uneventful journey into a harrowing adventure.

Conrad received little critical attention for *Heart of Darkness*. In fact, he did not become a bestselling author until the publication of his novel *Chance* in 1914. But over the years, readers have flocked to the depths of the Congo, with *Heart of Darkness* growing into one of Conrad's most popular works.

The Call of the Wild

1903

JACK LONDON

IN August 1897, Jack London stopped to survey the Chilkoot Pass. The mountains loomed high above, offering a treacherous route through Alaska to British Columbia. London and his companion, Captain Shepard, had already traveled one hundred miles through the wilderness just to reach the pass. Beyond the snowy peaks lay a vast amount of gold, there for the taking for anyone who could reach the Klondike River alive.

Twenty-one-year-old London had survived severe poverty in San Francisco and was eager to catapult into prosperity, but he was also there for the adventure. Shepard was London's brother-in-law and supported their journey financially, mortgaging his house so that they had enough money for supplies.

But he was also decades older than London, and upon reaching the Chilkoot Pass, Shepard, like many other travelers who reached that point, decided to return home. London forged ahead. When he reached the other side of the pass, he built two boats, crossed a lake, and barely survived foaming white rapids. London was forced to pause for the winter, holed up in an abandoned cabin with a few other men. As soon as the snow melted, he sailed up the Yukon River to Dawson City. There London joined the vast number of miners who had already set up camp.

The streets of Dawson were not paved with gold. It was a run-down place where around five thousand men struggled to survive. Many people lost what little money they had at local casinos. And most of the riches had already been claimed. London found no yellow nuggets to bring back home, but he did acquire a prize that outweighed any substance that could be unearthed from the ground. He absorbed his surroundings—the rugged outdoors, the ambitious men, and their loyal pets.

London placed his tent beside Marshall and Louis Bond's cabin. After the long journey, London was just as scruffy as the rest of the miners in town. Marshall recalled, "His face was marked by a thick stubbly beard. A cap was pulled down low on the forehead. . . . He looked as tough and as uninviting to us as we doubtless looked to him." The Bonds had two pet dogs and one of them was named Jack. He was a Saint Bernard–Scotch collie mix and an honorable, good-natured animal. London soon became friends with his canine neighbor, and he never spoke down to him as other men might. "It always seemed to me," observed Marshall, "that [London] gave more to the dog than we did, for he gave understanding. He had an appreciative and instant eye for fine traits and he honored them in a dog as he would in a man." Though London only spent about six weeks in Dawson City, he never forgot the dog named Jack.

London returned to San Francisco empty-handed but filled with determination to become a writer. He slept for only three hours a night and wrote at least a thousand words a day. As a form of training, London copied out stories by his literary hero, Rudyard Kipling, striving to learn what it takes to create great fiction. Despite his hard work, London found little success, and at one point, he began to consider suicide. He was broke, barely published, and was forced to search for menial jobs. But then he received a message in the mail. The *Black Cat* magazine wanted to publish one of his teen adventure stories. "Literally, and literarily, I was saved by the *Black Cat* story," noted London. The story inspired London to hurtle forward, and he soon had articles published on the east and west coasts that were based on his experiences during the Gold Rush. He had finally crossed the literary Chilkoot Pass after trudging up a near-impossible summit.

London did not slow down from his writing regimen, even when he had begun to reach a level of success. Several of his short story collections and a couple of novels were published, and then he received an offer from George Brett at Macmillan. Brett offered to sign up London for six books, for $150 each, over the course of two years. Two of the books were already finished: a memoir that captured a few months he spent in the East End of London and an epistolary novel that he had cowritten with Anna Strunsky. It was up to London to decide what to write for the third book on the contract.

Most of London's work at the time focused on his life in Canada, but this deal would allow him to venture into new territory. "I want to get away from the Klondike," he noted. And yet, for some reason, when London sat down to write he was drawn magnetically north. He trekked back to Dawson City, picked up Jack the dog, and brought him to life on the page. The story is told through the perspective of Buck, an intelligent mutt just like Jack, who is thrust into the Alaskan wilderness after being kidnapped and sold in California. *The Call of the Wild* captured many of London's own impressions of the treacherous and beautiful outdoors that he encountered during the Klondike Gold Rush. He became completely engrossed in the canine story, and within three weeks it was finished.

The Magic Mountain

1924

THOMAS MANN

THE Waldsanatorium was perched in the Swiss Alps. At the grand altitude of over five thousand feet, this medical resort offered patients brisk mountain air and breathtaking scenery. In March 1912, Katia Mann, struggling with sickness in her lungs, was prescribed extended rest in a beneficial climate. So she traveled from Munich, Germany, to Davos, Switzerland, and checked into the upscale sanatorium. During her six-month stay, Katia wrote regularly to her husband, Thomas. In her correspondence, she described an often ludicrous world within the walls of the institution. Thomas visited Katia for four weeks in mid-May and he, too, was captivated by the strange place.

If the doctors had their way, Thomas would have joined his wife and stayed for six months. He developed a nasty cough and was, to his mind hastily, diagnosed with a serious infection. The thirty-seven-year-old writer rejected the medical advice, shrugging it off as an attempt to bring in more money, and traveled back to Munich. Still, he did not leave the sanatorium behind. In July the following year, Thomas picked up his pen and brought the medicinal atmosphere to life within the framework of a novel.

This was not the first time Thomas had been inspired by a journey away from home. He traveled to Venice with Katia in the summer of 1911, and their vacation provided more than simple relaxation. A fellow traveler at the same hotel became the catalyst for a work of fiction. Katia recalled, "In the dining-room, on the very first day, we saw the Polish family, which looked exactly the way my husband described them: the girls were dressed rather stiffly and severely, and the very charming, beautiful boy of about thirteen was wearing a sailor suit with an open collar and very pretty lacings. He caught my husband's attention immediately." Shortly after returning home, Thomas began work on the tragic story of a man who becomes consumed by his obsession with a boy, modeled on the child from the hotel.

In late 1912, *Death in Venice* was published in two installments in the German literary magazine *Die Neue Rundschau*, and a full book was released in October 1913. The novel received high acclaim in literary circles, but Thomas did not pause for very long to celebrate. In July 1913, he decided to write a comedic novella about death, a story that would deliberately contrast with his dark Venetian tale. And the Waldsanatorium provided the perfect backdrop for a satirical exploration of mortality.

At first the new work progressed at the steady clip of about a page a day. Thomas adhered to a strict writing regimen, which involved three hours of writing every morning. But in 1914, World War I broke out and distracted Thomas from the novella. He turned his attention to political works, and his creative writing slowed. World War I continued until 1918, and over time Thomas began to reenvision his story within the current political climate. It would now take place in the years leading up to the war. As years passed, it became clear that the story had grown beyond the scope of a novella. In the midst of composition, Thomas researched the medical aspects of his tale to ensure accuracy. He had his hand x-rayed and attended a couple of hospital operations, in order to bring firsthand experience to the text. By the time he had finished the novel, it had grown into a thousand-page tome. It was published in two volumes in 1924, and though some critics complained about the length, others agreed that it was a monumental work.

The Little Prince

1943

ANTOINE DE SAINT-EXUPÉRY

Antoine de Saint-Exupéry was dozing in an airplane when the pilot, René Riguelle, suddenly shouted: "Damn! There goes the connecting rod." The two men were accompanying a mail plane over the Sahara (airplanes often fell apart en route across Africa, so they traveled in pairs to ensure that packages arrived at their destinations). Riguelle had pulled out of the desert to fly above the ocean, where it was cooler. Even though he was falling in and out of sleep, Saint-Exupéry was conscious enough to think it was a bad idea to fly over the water, as they would inevitably drown if they crashed. Before Saint-Exupéry managed to voice his opinion, the connecting rod broke. Soon they were on a steady trajectory down, but Riguelle managed to steer toward land.

They crashed into the desert and with each dune it hit, the plane lost a piece—the wheels, a wing—and then it stopped, wedged into the sand.

When Riguelle discovered that neither he nor Saint-Exupéry was seriously hurt, he exclaimed, "Now that's what I call piloting a ship!" It was not long before they were discovered by their colleagues, but there was only room for one more on board that plane, and Saint-Exupéry was left to wait alone. The young pilot was not scared of solitude. He soaked in the majesty of the rolling sands and later wrote of that afternoon, "The love of the Sahara, like love itself, is born of a face perceived and never really seen. Ever after this first sight of your new love, an indefinable bond is established between you and the veneer of gold on the sand in the late sun." Saint-Exupéry never lost his deep affection for the desert and he was not fazed by the crash—it would be the first of many.

Years later, Saint-Exupéry returned to the same crash site, though this time it was in the pages of his book *The Little Prince*. Saint-Exupéry fled to the United States after the 1940 armistice between France and Germany. In June 1942, he was living in New York. He was already a bestselling writer, renowned for his near brushes with death and other adventures in the air.

Elizabeth Reynal, the wife of his U.S. publisher, suggested that he fill his free time with a new project. Why not write a children's story about the little prince that he had been doodling on manuscripts, letters, and scraps of paper? It is not clear when the little prince popped into Saint-Exupéry's imagination, but he had been drawing the royal character for several years. Inspired by Reynal's suggestion, Saint-Exupéry visited a drugstore on Eighth Avenue to buy a children's set of watercolor paints, and he got to work. Throughout June, Saint-Exupéry wrote and painted late into the night. He then found that Manhattan was too hot in July, so he asked his wife, Consuelo, to find a summer home where he could work on the book more comfortably. Consuelo secured a mansion on Long Island that was much more extravagant than her husband had wanted, but it served as a welcome escape from the city, and it was there that he finished the manuscript.

A pilot crashes into the Sahara Desert in *The Little Prince* and his predicament is almost identical to Saint-Exupéry's. Left alone to ponder the surrounding landscape, he experiences something quite magical. In the book, though, the enchantment lies in a visit from a little prince from outer space. Many of Saint-Exupéry's experiences in flight, whether hurtling to the ground or coasting through the sky, come to life in the book. He once wrote, "I know nothing, nothing in the world, equal to the wonder of nightfall in the air." After marveling at the beauty of a vast night sky while zipping through the sky, it is not surprising that Saint-Exupéry decided his little prince would live in an asteroid among the stars.

Saint-Exupéry fell in love with the desert his first time alone in the Sahara, but his most famous plane crash brought him so close to death that it changed him forever. It also inspired a secondary character in *The Little Prince*. In December 1935, Saint-Exupéry attempted to beat the record for fastest flight from Paris to Saigon. A fortune-teller warned the pilot that his trip was doomed and the prediction proved correct. Saint-Exupéry and his navigator, André Prévot, crashed into the Libyan Desert. Round black pebbles on the desert floor acted like ball bearings, causing the plane to coast into the sand, which helped soften the crash, probably saving the pilots' lives.

After three days in the desert with very little food and water, Saint-Exupéry experienced a series of vivid hallucinations, including a vision of Consuelo's eyes beneath the brim of a hat. Desperate for sustenance, Saint-Exupéry set traps outside holes that belonged to desert animals, including fennecs (small foxes). He followed a set of fennec footprints until they led to a hole, where he imagined an animal was crouching below. He leaned down and said, "Fox, my little fox, I'm done for; but somehow that doesn't prevent me in taking an interest in your mood." After four days, Saint-Exupéry and Prévot were finally rescued. In Saint-Exupéry's picture book, a desert fox convinces the Little Prince that the rose on his planet is special and unique. The wise character was most likely inspired by the imaginary fennec that Saint-Exupéry spoke to when he was delirious in the desert.

A year after *The Little Prince* was published, just after his forty-fourth birthday, Saint-Exupéry was flying over Nazi-occupied France when he crashed for the last time. His death was shrouded in mystery and it was decades before the remnants of his plane were discovered off the coast of Marseilles. Shortly thereafter, German pilot Horst Rippert confessed that he had shot down Saint-Exupéry during World War II. They were sworn enemies at the time, fighting on different sides of the war, but Rippert still had tears in his eyes when he spoke about discovering that he'd killed Saint-Exupéry, the great pilot and writer whom he had revered.

On the Road

1957

JACK KEROUAC

IN July 1947, twenty-five-year-old Jack Kerouac stood on the side of the road in Yonkers, New York, and stuck his thumb out to oncoming traffic. A car slowed and stopped to pick up the young writer, his blue eyes sparkling with excitement. It was the beginning of his first big road trip west, a direction that seemed full of adventure and possibility. He planned to stop in Denver before advancing to his final destination, San Francisco. Unfortunately, once Kerouac reached Route 6, which led west, the only ride he could get pulled him north to upstate New York. Though money was limited, he had to resort to paying for bus tickets to reach Chicago. But after he got off the bus, he was soon back on the side of the road, depending on strangers to facilitate his cross-country quest.

In Denver Kerouac reunited with his good friend Neal Cassady, a charismatic wanderer he met in New York the previous October. Cassady's energy was intoxicating; he had a magnetic pull on Kerouac, who was eager to experience life as fully as possible. Kerouac soon discovered that Cassady was entangled in a complicated love triangle. Every now and then Cassady visited his sometimes lover, Allen Ginsberg, while his wife, LuAnne, waited for him in a hotel room nearby. He was also chasing after Carolyn Robinson, a graduate student at the University of Denver. And while Cassady raced from one sexual encounter to the next, he paused to spend time with his newly arrived pal. Kerouac soaked in his surroundings, dabbling in drugs, visiting pool halls, and dropping into jazz joints. After a short stay, Kerouac broke away from the group to take a bus to San Francisco. Cassady and Ginsberg took off in a different direction, south to visit William S. Burroughs (see pages 135–139) in Texas.

From San Francisco, Kerouac traveled to Oakland and then Los Angeles before making the long trek back to the East Coast in November the same year. The next time Kerouac went west, it was January 1949. He traveled in a Hudson Hornet, with Cassady at the wheel, zipping along highways at tremendous speed. During his adventures from one end of the country to the next, and south to Mexico in 1950, Kerouac carefully filed away his experiences. He kept a journal, jotting down observations with the intention of pulling them into a novel.

Kerouac had many false starts trying to capture his road trips on the page. Then, in December 1950, he received a long letter from Cassady. It was a recap of Cassady's sexual exploits, including a relationship with a woman named Joan. But the content was less important than the style. The Joan Anderson letter, as it was later called, was bursting with spontaneity, jumping from one thought to the next, all based on Cassady's whims. Upon reading the stack of pages, Kerouac suddenly knew how to approach his novel. In a 1967 interview for the *Paris Review*, he recalled, "I got the idea for the spontaneous style of *On the Road* from seeing how good old Neal Cassady wrote his letters to me, all first person, fast, mad, confessional, completely serious, all detailed, with real names in his case however (being letters). . . . [The Joan Anderson letter] was the greatest piece of writing I ever saw." The next time he sat down to work on the book, Kerouac barely stood up again until it was finished.

In April 1951, on a steady diet of soup and coffee, Kerouac wrote most of the manuscript of *On the Road*. He taped together sheets of tracing paper into one long scroll to avoid having to reload his typewriter every time he finished a page. After twenty days of nonstop writing, Kerouac's wife, Joan, kicked him out of their house. He moved in temporarily with his friend Lucien Carr, bringing with him the typewriter and precious manuscript. Kerouac did not let marital discord slow him down. He soon finished the book, which was 120 feet long.

During this remarkably productive time, Kerouac called upon his journals and notes, but the novel is filled with spontaneous impressions that came to him in the furious act of writing. Only one part of the manuscript needed to be rewritten, due to outside circumstances rather than Kerouac's doubts about the text. Carr's cocker spaniel chewed up a few feet of the scroll. Kerouac reworked that section of the book, which was then ready to be shopped around to publishers.

Kerouac first presented his scroll to Robert Giroux, who had edited his debut novel, *The Town and the City*, in 1949. Giroux did not eagerly snatch up the unconventional manuscript, as Kerouac had hoped he would. In fact, Kerouac had to retype the book on normal sheets of paper before submitting it to Harcourt, Brace for consideration. Giroux's subsequent rejection was the first of many. Kerouac's sprawling novel did not appeal to editors' commercial sensibilities.

Finally, more than five years after he finished *On the Road*, Kerouac received word that Malcolm Cowley at Viking was interested in the book. There was only one concern. Kerouac used the real names of the people he had encountered during his travels, which could cause legal issues upon publication. But this proved to be a small matter—Kerouac changed the names of his characters—and Cowley bought the book.

On the Road was released in September 1957. A *New York Times* review praised the novel as the "most important utterance yet made by the generation Kerouac himself named years ago as 'beat,' and whose principal avatar he is. . . . *On the Road* is a major novel." Other critics chimed in with more praise, flooring the accelerator to Kerouac's overnight transition from virtually unknown writer to voice of a generation.

ON THE JOB

How vain it is to sit down to write when you have not stood up to live.

—HENRY DAVID THOREAU, JOURNAL, 1851

IF SOMEONE TELLS YOU NOT TO QUIT YOUR DAY JOB, DON'T feel dismayed. You may want to heed the advice. A biweekly paycheck could translate into much more than just that, if you know where to look for literary inspiration. Dashiell Hammett found his muse between car chases and knife fights, working as a private eye. John Steinbeck stumbled upon an idea while working as a ranch hand on idyllic fields in California. And Ken Kesey discovered inspiration as a professional tester of psychedelic drugs. These may not be your average desk jobs, but they were what each author relied upon to survive. Some of these writers penned their novels while on the clock, and others waited until well after they had moved on. And even if the work was grueling, it was well worth it. Without their jobs, these authors might never have become literary legends.

Anne of Green Gables

1908

L. M. MONTGOMERY

Lucy Maud Montgomery scanned the worn pages of her notebook. Ever since she was a child she had recorded story ideas and now hoped to discover a long-forgotten gem to use as the basis for a serial in a Sunday school paper. As the thirty-year-old Montgomery glanced at each line, none of the ideas seemed quite right, until she stopped at an entry she had written years before: "Elderly couple apply to orphan asylum for a boy. By mistake a girl is sent to them." The concept tugged at her imagination, and she decided it suited her project perfectly.

The brief line captured an event from when Montgomery was seventeen years old. Her cousin Pierce Macneill and a fellow farmer had arranged to adopt two boys, but to their surprise, a three-year-old girl and her five-year-old brother dis-embarked from the train at the local station. Despite the mix-up, Macneill took in the young girl and gave her a new name, Ellen. She grew up on a farm in Cavendish, Canada, not far from Montgomery's home. Montgomery replicated this beginning for her eleven-year-old protagonist Anne, who is adopted by an aging brother and sister who originally wanted a boy to help on their farm. However, the author vehe-mently rejected any claim that her cousin Ellen was anything like the red-haired orphan in her novel.

Montgomery fiercely guarded her role as sole creator of Anne. In her journal, she wrote that the fictional girl "flashed into my fancy already christened, even to the all important 'e'." From the moment Anne strode into her imagination, it was clear that she was unlike anyone the Canadian writer had dreamed up before. A few years earlier, Montgomery had writ-ten *A Golden Carol*, a novel that featured a sweet-natured young woman. The book was rejected over and over again until Montgomery finally gave up and burned the manuscript. She later realized that her main character had been flat, and she was determined to create someone entirely different in Anne. Her new protagonist was imaginative, courageous, and fun loving, and Montgomery soon realized that she was too special for a fleeting serial. So in the spring of 1905, Montgom-ery sat by the window in her little gable room overlooking new blossoms and fresh green grass and attempted to write another novel.

In her writing room, Montgomery hung a portrait of a

model that she had plucked from a magazine. The teenage girl looked out of the photograph and into the distance with her head tilted to one side, highlighting an angular nose and small, delicate lips. Two large chrysanthemums were attached to a ribbon that rested on her forehead, giving her the appearance of a fairy from another land. The Canadian writer often looked over at the picture and wondered whether the model realized she had played an important part in the creation of Anne. Montgomery had come across the photograph in a copy of *Metropolitan Magazine*. The young woman was the red-haired beauty Evelyn Nesbit, a famous model at the turn of the century, and she became the physical embodiment of Anne of Green Gables.

When Montgomery reached the end of her story in January 1906, almost a year after thumbing through her old journal, she pulled out her secondhand typewriter to transcribe the handwritten manuscript. The rickety machine resisted capitalization and would not stamp *w* onto the page, but Montgomery clicked away until she had a neat stack of pages to submit for publication. She sent the book out to different publishing houses, but after five rejections, she packed the manuscript into an old hatbox and stored it out of sight.

Montgomery must have felt utterly dejected after the failure of her previous novel, and yet she was not compelled to burn *Anne of Green Gables*. Instead, she resolved at some point to cut the story down into the serial that she had originally planned. Less than a year later, Montgomery pulled the hatbox out of storage. She sat down and read the manuscript from the beginning to the end and found herself drawn into Anne's world all over again. She decided that if her book could appeal to her after all that time, then perhaps it was worth sending it out to publishers again. The manuscript was wrapped up and sent to the Boston-based L. C. Page and Company, and Montgomery soon had another entry to add to her journal, commemorating the fact that her book had been accepted for publication.

The Phantom of the Opera

1911

GASTON LEROUX

IN 1889, Gaston Leroux graduated with a degree in law and was set on a course to become a prominent Parisian lawyer. But he soon realized that he had made a terrible mistake. He hated practicing law and quit his first job almost immediately. Leroux had no alternative prospects at the time, but his father died and left him a fortune of almost one million francs, freeing him from the responsibility of earning a living. Leroux was not prepared to handle such a large sum. He cast away funds on drinking and gambling, rather than letting his inheritance sit in the bank. Within six months, the money had evaporated. Leroux was forced to find a new job, though this time he selected a completely different line of work as a reporter.

Journalism suited Leroux perfectly. He sprang into action

with each new report, tirelessly striving to uncover the truth. And his law degree could be used to his advantage in this field. He covered court cases for the daily newspaper *L'Echo de Paris*, and in one instance, his coverage helped prove the innocence of an accused man. From the courtroom, Leroux then moved beyond French borders to write international stories, traveling as far as Russia to witness scenes from the 1905 revolution. Leroux also penned stories about local theater, and a tour of Paris's opera house, Palais Garnier, was the catalyst for his novel *The Phantom of the Opera*.

In 1858, Napoleon III had a near-fatal encounter with a group of assassins. They threw bombs under his carriage on a narrow street outside a local opera house, which was the ruler's destination. Napoleon survived, surprisingly without any wounds, and went on to attend the performance that evening. Determined to outmaneuver any future attacks, Napoleon had a new opera house built. It was perched in a wide open space so that no one could hide in the shadows and attack him en route to the opera again. In a national competition, Charles Garnier won the honor of designing the grand new building, which opened its doors in 1875.

Palais Garnier was an impressive structure, seventeen stories high, with a magnificent multicolored marble staircase. Leroux sensed that the opera house would be an ideal setting for a novel. Beyond its grandeur, the building contained hidden nooks both above and below the ground, perfect for Leroux's grotesque character to move stealthily from one point to the next. During construction, a marsh had been discovered below the theater.

Leroux transformed the watery pool into a fictional subterranean river for his phantom to sail through. A tragic event in 1896 also made its way into Leroux's story. A huge chandelier hung in the Palais Garnier, and during a performance, one of the counterweights fell, killing an audience member. In Leroux's tale, the actual chandelier plunges into the audience.

Leroux quit his job as a journalist in the early 1900s and shifted to fiction. He wrote several novels, including two popular mysteries, before penning the story of a ghost who haunts the Parisian opera house. *The Phantom of the Opera* was published in serial form in the French newspaper *Le Gaulois* during 1909 and 1910. Pierre Lafitte and Company brought it out as a bound book in 1910, and an English version was published by the Bobbs-Merrill Company in the United States the following year. The *American Review of Reviews* praised the book, noting, "It offers all the gasps and thrills a devotee of 'ghost stories' could possibly ask for . . . belongs to the genus 'Best Seller.'" But positive reviews were not enough to boost the book to bestseller status.

Despite Leroux's previous success as an author, his novel received little attention. It was not until 1925, when the story hit the big screen as a silent movie starring Lon Chaney, that the opera ghost captivated viewers nationwide. And he continued to haunt audiences through a variety of media for decades to come. In 1986, Andrew Lloyd Webber's musical *The Phantom of the Opera* was performed for the first time in London. Two years later, it opened in New York and became the longest-running show in Broadway history.

Red Harvest

1929

DASHIELL HAMMETT

TWENTY-ONE-YEAR-OLD Dashiell Hammett was thumbing through the newspaper when he stumbled across an advertisement. A watchful eye peered over the motto "We Never Sleep." Just as the logo promised, Pinkerton operatives were alert and observant. They were renowned for protecting presidents, uncovering spies, and breaking up violent union strikes. Detective work seemed perfectly suited to Hammett, who admired qualities like strength and stealth, and he applied for a job in Pinkerton's Baltimore office.

Though his case reports were supposedly lost in a fire, Hammett clearly had to flex his muscles in the field. As Hammett's daughter Jo recalled, "[I got] to feel the dent in his head from being hit by a brick when he bungled a tailing job, and he let me see the knife tip embedded in the palm of his hand." But detective work consisted of more than violent encounters; Hammett acquired an entirely new skill on the job.

A tough, stocky detective proved to be the ideal mentor for Hammett. After years of experience, James Wright had developed into a gritty operative whom few people would double-cross. He taught Hammett everything he needed to know, from perfecting surveillance skills to developing an ethical code. Hammett treasured this education, and he never forgot Wright. Years later, Hammett's old adviser served as a model for a fictional hard-boiled detective.

Hammett began writing literary fiction in his late twenties. Then he read a selection of detective stories that were riddled with errors a true operative would never dare record on paper. Hammett knew that he could pull off a superior pulp story. Not only was he a talented writer, he also had real-life experience working for Pinkerton. So Hammett turned back to the dark streets where he used to track down crooks, and he invoked James Wright as a character simply known as the Continental op.

Hammett was a methodical writer. He began each story with a series of notes, which he used to handwrite a first draft. He then typed the finished piece on his Underwood. Despite the slow process, Hammett sold twelve mystery stories to magazines within a year. And in 1923, he introduced the Continental op to the public in a story called "Arson Plus." The short, heavyset man was tough, but not reckless like many of his contemporaries. He took his job as an operative seriously, chasing down clues and crooks until he had achieved his end of the arrangement. The nameless detective struck a chord with mystery readers and was featured in several short stories before Hammett decided to use him in a book-length work.

For his debut novel, Hammett ventured back to Anaconda, Montana, where he had been sent on jobs for the Pinkerton Detective Agency. The state was full of mining towns and, at the time, they were prone to violent union strikes. Operatives were called in to maintain order, a difficult task given that corruption ran rampant throughout the mining community. Hammett invoked this seedy world in a book he called *Poisonville*. In the story, the Continental op travels to Personville, nicknamed Poisonville by those who live there. Crime courses through the town, and the op confronts crooks at every turn.

Poisonville was published in four installments in the *Black Mask* before Hammett sent it to Alfred A. Knopf for consideration. Knopf's wife, Blanche, accepted the book for the Borzoi Mysteries imprint but only after Hammett made a few key changes. She asked him to tone down the violence, which he did with a few exceptions, and that he change the title. Hammett sent his revised manuscript along with a list of possible titles and Blanche selected the last one, *Red Harvest*.

Gone with the Wind

1936

Margaret Mitchell

ARGARET Mitchell lay on the bed in her tiny apartment in Atlanta, Georgia, and wondered if she
would ever walk without crutches again. She had
been an active journalist, chasing interviews and feature items
across town, until a broken ankle slowed her down. The injury
led to painful arthritis, forcing Mitchell to quit her job and
remain virtually housebound for three years. Her only escape
from domestic confinement was through books.

She was eager to read anything at all, highbrow and low-
brow, from literary fiction and history to mystery and romance.
Her devoted husband, John, carted armfuls of books to and
from the library, until one day he arrived home without anything to read. He handed a stack of blank paper to Mitchell

and said, "Write a book. I can't find anything at the Carnegie that you haven't read, except books on the exact sciences." It was a tempting suggestion. Reading distracted Mitchell from her captivity in the apartment for short bursts of time, but her own novel would carry her away indefinitely. Soon the sound of turning pages was replaced by the clicking of keys on the Remington typewriter that John bought for Mitchell. She wrote about the Old South, a subject that had been part of her life right out of the cradle.

Born in Atlanta, Mitchell grew up on stories about the South. She recalled visiting her relatives on Sunday afternoons and sitting on "the bony knees of veterans and the fat slippery laps of great aunts." The older generation spoke about surviving war and hardship, and their stories captured her imagination. Mitchell's favorite pastime was listening to someone talk about a topic they knew well, no matter what it was.

Years later, she worked as a journalist for the *Atlanta Journal Sunday Magazine* and naturally loved the job. The best assignments were interviews with "the Oldest Inhabitants" of Atlanta. She peppered these elderly people with questions and soaked up their stories just as she had done with her family. Mitchell noted, "I had no intention, at that time, of ever writing a book. I just wanted to know those things." But those interviews came in handy when she began her novel. The oral history that Mitchell absorbed as a child and a journalist became the foundation for an epic portrait of the Old South.

It took Mitchell several years to finish *Gone with the Wind*, though she would have made faster headway if she were not so popular. Even after she recovered from her injury, Mitchell found it difficult to write. Mitchell observed, "I labored under considerable difficulties in my writing. For one thing I have a large number of friends and kin to whom I am devoted and for five years there wasn't a day that some one of them wasn't in hospital with babies, gall stones, automobile accidents etc. . . ." Her apartment was always bustling, the phone rang constantly, and people swooped in for impromptu visits at all hours of the day and night.

To make matters worse, Mitchell had no space of her own to work in. She and John had little money and lived in a very small apartment that they nicknamed "the Dump." Mitchell often worked out in the open, but she was reserved about her work in progress. When a friend dropped by, Mitchell would pick up a towel, drop it over the typewriter, and turn her attention to the guest. Despite these social obstacles, Mitchell's novel crept along. She wrote and rewrote and then stacked the pages in her closet. She probably would have continued revising for years and years, but an out-of-towner spurred her to give the book a chance at publication.

In 1935, editor Harold Latham traveled to Atlanta in search of bright new writers for the Macmillan Publishing Company. Mitchell had returned to work for the *Atlanta Journal* at the time and, as a prominent figure in the local writing scene, she was asked to line up aspiring authors to meet with Latham. But when the editor found out that Mitchell had a hidden manuscript and asked to see it, she refused, feeling that it was not ready just yet. One of the young artists Mitchell had introduced to Latham was surprised to hear that she was working on a novel. She exclaimed, "Really, I wouldn't take you for the type who would write a successful book. You know you don't take life seriously enough to be a novelist." The opinionated writer went on to say that at least her novel had been viewed and rejected by a number of publishers, and then she suggested that Mitchell stop writing altogether.

Her dander up, Mitchell decided to hand her unfinished manuscript over to Latham so that at least she could jokingly say that her book had been rejected, too. Latham had to buy an extra suitcase to carry the lengthy manuscript, but his purchase was worth the effort. Soon after returning to New York, Latham made an offer for *Gone with the Wind*, and Mitchell never received her prize rejection after all. The book was an instant blockbuster, with over a million copies sold within six months after its release in June 1936. Mitchell was surprised and overwhelmed by her success. In January 1937, she lamented to Sidney Howard, the playwright and screenwriter who wrote the movie adaptation of her book, "Alas, where has my quiet peaceful life gone?"

Of Mice and Men

1937

JOHN STEINBECK

JOHN Steinbeck wiped the sweat from his brow and looked out across the vast expanse of fields. Work on a ranch could be exhausting, but Steinbeck preferred physical labor over being huddled up in a library. After abruptly dropping out of Stanford University, he had gotten a job as a bindle stiff, or migrant worker, at Spreckels ranches in California. There were no more papers or due dates out on the land, and the ex-student welcomed the change of pace.

Tall, tan, and blue-eyed, he even looked the part of a farmer. During one of these stints, a fellow worker was fired and a slow-witted farmhand became terribly upset about the loss of his friend. In a fit of rage, he plunged a pitchfork into the boss's stomach, killing him. Steinbeck witnessed the scene and recalled, "We couldn't stop him until it was too late." The murderer was sent to an insane asylum, which was probably the last that Steinbeck ever heard of him, but the event remained lodged in his mind.

Steinbeck traveled for months from ranch to ranch, but he never lost the urge to become a writer. He eventually traded the outdoors for a desk and a stack of paper and went back to school to study English and journalism. Steinbeck was a poor student, though, unable to concentrate during classes that did not grab his interest, and he never graduated. He left Stanford in the spring of 1925 and went through a string of odd jobs before settling down to focus solely on his writing in 1928. During this time, Steinbeck never completely let go of life on the farm. He invoked the California landscape and the hardworking bindle stiffs in his fiction.

Steinbeck returned to the brutal yet innocent murder at the ranch to write *Of Mice and Men* in 1935, though he changed the details of the crime and the identity of the victim. The story follows mentally disturbed Lennie and his friend George, two migratory farmhands who are doomed to a tragic fate. Steinbeck acknowledged that Lennie is based on the murderer from Spreckels. It is possible that George is a fictionalized version of the man who was fired. Or perhaps he is based on another worker Steinbeck met while roaming the fields. And then again, he may have materialized solely in the author's imagination.

Steinbeck was midway through *Of Mice and Men* when he moved into a new house that he and his wife had built near

Los Gatos, California. It was on two acres of land near a canyon, and Steinbeck settled happily into the rural locale, far removed from any distractions. A highly disciplined writer, Steinbeck rose early every morning and worked until he reached a personal quota of words, sometimes going beyond the allocated amount, particularly if he was drawing closer to the end of a story.

An incident with Steinbeck's dog set him back two months in *Of Mice and Men*. The setter pup tore apart almost half the manuscript in the middle of the night. The text on the damaged pages was barely recognizable and Steinbeck was forced to rewrite a large portion of the book. The frustrated writer understood that his dog had no idea what he had done and did not punish him any more harshly than he would have for a minor disobedient act.

Steinbeck preferred to write directly onto the page rather than use a typewriter. He would then read his draft on a tape recorder. He explained the methodology: "I've tried reading aloud but then my eyes are involved. I read on tape and listen back for corrections, because you can hear the most terrible things you've done if you hear it clear back on tape." It would have been particularly important to listen to the dialogue in *Of Mice and Men* because Steinbeck hoped that his book would translate directly onto the stage. Convinced that the novel was a dying art form, he decided to write a story that would double as a play, with actors reading dialogue from the finished book.

Of Mice and Men hit bookstores in February 1937. Steinbeck already had four novels published, but this book was by far his most successful. It was a Book-of-the-Month Club selection and sold almost a thousand copies a day during the month of its release. The same year the book was published, *Of Mice and Men* opened on Broadway. Steinbeck considered his novel-play a failure because parts of it had to be rewritten for the production. He decided not to attend the opening of the play and defended the choice, noting, "I don't go to the theatre much and I don't know a darn thing about actors." Still, the play was a huge success, running for 207 performances. And even if he was not there to see the curtain rise and fall, Steinbeck did ask his publisher, Pascal Covici, to report back with a detailed description of the first showing.

Casino Royale

1953

IAN FLEMING

N May 1941, Ian Fleming was en route to New York on an assignment with John Henry Godfrey, director of British Naval Intelligence. Though the trip was strictly business, a layover in Lisbon afforded them some recreation time. They stayed at the swank Palácio Hotel, where Fleming decided to try his luck at the hotel casino. He strode into the room with high hopes, but was none the richer at the end of the night. On the surface, Fleming lost at the gambling tables, though he was not one to let reality interfere with his ever-active imagination. As he walked out of the room, Fleming said to Godfrey, "What if those men had been German secret service agents, and suppose we had cleaned them out of money; now that would have been exciting." With that simple observation, Fleming dealt himself a winning hand.

Years later, when he sat down to write *Casino Royale*, he placed James Bond at a gambling table in France, immortalizing the exciting scene that had unfolded in his mind in Portugal. When describing the events that take place in the novel, Fleming explained, "I extracted them from my wartime memories, dolled them up, attached a hero, a villain, and a heroine, and there was the book."

Fleming was hired to assist Godfrey in May 1939. He threw himself wholeheartedly into the role, working long hours and with dedication that he had never experienced before. Though Fleming spent most of his time in the office, unlike his mission-bound protagonist, he still played an important part in intelligence during World War II. One of Fleming's tasks was to come up with creative ways to acquire critical information from the enemy. Fleming soon became known for suggesting missions that seemed better suited to fiction than reality. And yet Godfrey was not disappointed in his new hire. He felt that Fleming excelled in the job, despite, or perhaps because of, his outlandish ideas. Fleming also assembled the 30 AU, a small, elite assault unit, whose motto was "Attain by Surprise." The men of 30 AU could crack a code just as easily as they could beat an opponent in hand-to-hand combat. They were an army of real James Bonds.

Fleming may not have looked further than his own mirror for a model for his protagonist. Both Bond and his creator were tall, black-haired, blue-eyed, and handsome. During his career in the navy, Fleming rose from lieutenant to acting commander, a rank that he bestowed on Bond.

Though the phrase "Bond, James Bond" now holds a certain mystique, it was a deliberately dull choice. Fleming felt that an extravagant name would hinder a true spy. When he was in the process of writing *Casino Royale*, Fleming looked up at his bookshelf, scouring the spines for an appropriate choice. He stopped at *Field Guide to Birds of the West Indies*, written by the ornithologist James Bond. It was short, simple, and just about as generic as possible—it was perfect.

Bond's 007 code name has more exciting roots. During World War I, a secret telegram from Germany was seized by the British navy. The message proposed an alliance between Mexico and Germany against the United States. When U.S. officials found out about what became known as the Zimmermann Telegram, they were furious and soon declared war. The code used in the telegram was referred to as 0075. By the time Fleming joined the navy in World War II, the numbers were part of intelligence language. Fleming recalled, "When I was in the Admiralty during the war, all the top-secret signals had the double-0 prefix . . . and I decided to borrow it for Bond to make his job more interesting and provide him with a licence to kill."

In early 1952, Fleming was on his annual two-month vacation with his fiancée, Ann, when he wrote *Casino Royale*, the very first James Bond novel. He often spent his time off at Goldeneye, a beach house in Jamaica he had named after one of his assignments during World War II. Fleming often said that the book was a distraction from his impending marriage, much to Ann's chagrin. Still, it seems that he had been waiting for this opportunity for some time, because the moment he sat down to work, he wrote with lightning speed, adding two thousand words every day. He worked for about three hours every morning and then corrected the text at night.

Perhaps Fleming was able to write so quickly because he did not focus on small details in his first draft. Fleming later wrote to his friend Ivar Bryce, "Never mind about the brilliant phrase or the golden word, once the typescript is there you can fiddle, correct and embellish as much as you please. So don't be depressed if the first draft seems a bit raw, all first drafts do." Within a month, Fleming finished *Casino Royale*, even if it was a bit raw, and a week later he walked down the aisle in a small, intimate ceremony with his bride.

The same year, British publisher Jonathan Cape reluctantly accepted Fleming's debut novel, which he felt needed a lot of work. Cape also published travel memoirs by Fleming's adventurous older brother, Peter. In reference to *Casino Royale*, Cape noted, "[Fleming's] got to do much better if he's going to get anywhere near Peter's standard." But the publisher soon realized that this gambling espionage thriller was a literary gold mine. After the novel was published in April 1953, it quickly went back to print, and a few months later Cape proudly stated, "A copy of *Casino Royale* by Ian Fleming has been sold every six and a half minutes that the bookshops were open."

One Flew Over the Cuckoo's Nest

1962

KEN KESEY

EN Kesey worked the night shift at the veterans hospital in Menlo Park, California. He kept watch over the psychiatric ward, and there was little to do during those hours beyond making routine rounds and cleaning the floors. It was dull work, but Kesey secretly transformed the job into a psychedelic source of inspiration. He consumed hallucinogens while on the clock and watched as the sterile halls came to life.

All Kesey had to do was pull on a mask of sobriety whenever the night nurse swung by to check on the patients. Otherwise, he was free to explore his workspace under the influence of mind-altering drugs. The hallucinogens helped Kesey realize that the patients under his care might not be crazy after all. Kesey, who was in his midtwenties, was also a graduate student in creative writing at Stanford University, and it was not long before he began to compose *One Flew Over the Cuckoo's Nest*, a novel based on his experiences in the psychiatric ward.

During one of Kesey's shifts, eight peyote plants led the young writer to an epiphany. He recalled, "I was flying on peyote, really strung out there, when this Indian came to me." Kesey pulled out some paper and wrote a new opening for his novel from the perspective of Chief Bromden, the Indian from the drug-induced mirage. Kesey then decided to write the entire book from Bromden's viewpoint. In an interview for the *Paris Review* that took place in 1992 and 1993, Kesey said that he found it very difficult to write while under the influence of drugs. He noted, "It's like diving down to look at coral reefs. You can't write about what you've seen until you're back up in the boat." The peyote trip was a rare exception, offering a burst of inspiration that redefined the narrative framework of his debut novel.

Before he applied for the job in the psychiatric ward, Kesey was already a regular visitor to the Menlo Park Veterans Hospital. In 1958, Kesey had traveled from Oregon to Palo Alto to attend Stanford University. He and his wife, Faye, moved into a little cottage on Perry Lane, where they were surrounded by writers, scholars, and intellectuals. Vik Lovell, a psychology student, was one of Kesey's neighbors and became a close friend. In 1960, Lovell suggested that Kesey sign up for MK-Ultra, a series of paid government-sponsored experiments at the veterans hospital. During each session, volunteers would consume a wide variety of drugs and describe their experiences to doctors.

Kesey needed the extra cash, but he was also curious about the effect hallucinogens would have on his mind. Soon he was marching over to the hospital every week to participate in MK-Ultra, popping pills in whitewashed rooms and waiting for the drugs to take hold. He received seventy-five dollars a day, but this part-time job gave him much more than a paycheck; it set him on a lifelong journey of dabbling in hallucinogens.

When the research ended, Kesey continued his own personal experiments. He secured a job on the night shift at the hospital and received a set of keys that unlocked many doors in the building, including the office of a former MK-Ultra doctor who had a stash of drugs tucked away in his desk. Kesey helped himself to a large quantity of the doctor's hallucinogens, which he used both at home and while on the night shift.

Kesey wrote his novel within ten months, and in June 1961 he handed the manuscript over to Malcolm Cowley, an editor who helped usher emerging writers onto the literary scene. Four years earlier, Cowley had convinced his publisher, Viking Press, to take on a groundbreaking novel by a promising author: *On the Road* by Jack Kerouac (see pages 183–186). With an eye for talent, Cowley scouted out new writers while teaching creative writing at Stanford. Kesey was one of his star students, wowing the class with portions of *One Flew Over the*

Cuckoo's Nest when the book was still a work in progress. Cowley was eagerly anticipating the full manuscript when it arrived, and Viking promptly bought the debut novel. *One Flew Over the Cuckoo's Nest*, published in February 1962, was a critical success and launched the twenty-six-year-old writer to literary fame.

The Bell Jar

1963

SYLVIA PLATH

T the end of April, an eagerly awaited telegram arrived for Sylvia Plath. It read: HAPPY TO ANNOUNCE YOU HAVE WON A MADEMOISELLE 1953 GUEST EDITORSHIP. Only a small group of young women were selected from a highly competitive pool of applicants. The prize was a monthlong apprenticeship at *Mademoiselle* magazine in New York City. The job suited Plath perfectly. She was determined to carve out a life as a successful writer, and where better to launch her career than in one of the biggest literary hubs in the world. Plath had already begun to experience success, with several poems published in national magazines, and a new role as editor-in-chief of the *Smith Review* at her college. This internship was another step toward solidifying her literary future. Plath did not have long to prepare for her trip. On May 31, she took a train from Wellesley, Massachusetts, right into the center of Manhattan.

Beneath the looming skyscrapers and bright lights, the city must have seemed full of possibility. And yet at each turn, Plath became more disappointed. On her first day at the magazine, Plath hoped to be placed in the fiction department. Instead she was assigned to work with Cyrilly Abels, a tough managing editor. With Abels watching over her shoulder, Plath worked furiously from week to week. She conducted routine tasks in the office, in addition to writing her own pieces, and there was a long list of events to attend, ranging from ballet performances to baseball games.

In the background, Julius and Ethel Rosenberg counted their final hours. Images of the couple were plastered on newspapers nationwide. They had been convicted of spying for Russia and were sentenced to death by electrocution. Plath was deeply troubled by their impending death. As the summer wore on, she became depressed and overwhelmed. Just before she left the city, Plath asked one of her fellow interns for a set of clothes to wear home. Apparently, she had thrown her entire wardrobe off the roof of the hotel. She was clearly breaking beneath the weight of her own disenchantment.

Plath hoped to recuperate upon her return home, but she sank even further into depression upon hearing terrible news. Frank O'Connor had not selected her for his summer course at Harvard University. Plath was devastated. She spiraled down over the next few weeks and was particularly disturbed by her sudden inability to write and sometimes even to read.

She began cutting herself. When her mother noticed the scars on her legs, Plath suggested that they commit suicide together. Plath was soon subjected to treatment for her depression, in the form of electroshock therapy. The harsh sessions did not cure Plath. At the end of August, she attempted to commit suicide by swallowing almost forty-eight sleeping pills. She barely survived the ordeal and was subsequently committed to a hospital and was not released until the following January.

Years later, when she was married to poet Ted Hughes and living in London, Plath decided to write about her troubled summer in New York. She cast the book as fiction, though it closely followed her own journey from the big city into the hospital ward. Plath decided to write under a pseudonym to add some distance between herself and the book.

The Bell Jar was published in England in 1963, but Plath did not live to see it come out in the United States. She wrote part of a sequel to her novel, about a young woman in London, just like her, with a handsome literary husband. But everything was ruined when she discovered that Hughes was having an affair. Plath burned the manuscript of the second book and fell into complete and utter despair. Just weeks after the publication of her debut novel, Plath committed suicide, placing her head in an oven and turning on the gas. The thirty-year-old writer had succumbed to the depression that she had battled since childhood. Sadly Plath was not alive to experience the literary recognition she had strived for during her brief life. *The Bell Jar* was published to wide acclaim in the United States in 1971, and in 1982 she was posthumously awarded the Pulitzer Prize for *The Collected Poems*.

SOURCES

When Lightning Strikes

Anna Karenina by Leo Tolstoy
Thorlby, Anthony. *Leo Tolstoy: Anna Karenina*. New York: Cambridge University Press, 1987.
Tolstoy, Alexandra. *Tolstoy: A Life of My Father*. Belmont, Russia: Norland, 1975.
Troyat, Henri. *Tolstoy*. New York: Grove Press, 1967.
Turner, C. J. G. *A Karenina Companion*. Ontario, Canada: Wilfrid Laurier University Press, 1993.
Wilson, A. N. *Tolstoy*. New York: W. W. Norton, 1988.

Around the World in Eighty Days by Jules Verne
Bly, Nellie. *Around the World in Seventy-Two Days*. New York: Pictorial Weeklies, 1890.
Lottman, Herbert. R. *Jules Verne: An Exploratory Biography*. New York: St. Martin's Press, 1997.

Sherard, Robert H. "Jules Verne at Home." *McClure's*. January 1894: 115–24.

Treasure Island by Robert Louis Stevenson
Harman, Claire. *Myself and the Other Fellow: A Life of Robert Louis Stevenson*. New York: HarperCollins, 2005.

Stevenson, Robert Louis. "My First Book." *Idler*. August 1894.

———. *Selected Letters of Robert Louis Stevenson*. Edited by Ernest Mehew. New Haven: Yale University Press, 1997.

The Sound and the Fury by William Faulkner
Blotner, Joseph. *Faulkner: A Biography*. New York: Random House, 1990.

Inge, M. Thomas, ed. *Conversations with William Faulkner*. Jackson: University Press of Mississippi, 1999.

Padgett, John B. William Faulkner on the Web: www.mcsr.olemiss.edu/~egjbp/faulkner/faulkner.html.

Parini, Jay. *One Matchless Time: A Life of William Faulkner*. New York: HarperCollins, 2004.

The Hobbit, or There and Back Again by J. R. R. Tolkien
Carpenter, Humphrey. *J. R. R. Tolkien: A Biography*. New York: Houghton Mifflin, 2000.

Norman, Philip. "The Prevalence of Hobbits." *New York Times*. January 15, 1967.

Tolkien, J. R. R. *The Letters of J. R. R. Tolkien*. Edited by Humphrey Carpenter. New York: Houghton Mifflin, 2000.

Animal Farm by George Orwell
Crick, Bernard. *George Orwell: A Life*. New York: Penguin, 1982.

Meyers, Jeffrey. *Orwell: Wintry Conscience of a Generation*. New York: W. W. Norton, 2000.

Orwell, George. *A Collection of Essays*. Orlando, FL: Houghton Mifflin Harcourt, 1953.

———. *The Collected Essays, Journalism and Letters of George Orwell*. Edited by Sonia Orwell and Ian Angus. New York: Harcourt, Brace, and World, 1968.

Taylor, D. J. *Orwell: The Life*. New York: Henry Holt, 2003.

Warburg, Fredric. *All Authors Are Equal: The Publishing Life of Fredric Warburg, 1936–1971*. London: Hutchinson, 1973.

The Lion, the Witch and the Wardrobe by C. S. Lewis

Duriez, Colin. *Tolkien and C. S. Lewis: The Gift of Friendship*. Mahwah, NJ: Paulist Press, 2003.

Gormley, Beatrice. *C. S. Lewis: The Man Behind Narnia*. Michigan: Eerdmans, 1998.

Green, Robert Lancelyn, and Walter Hopper. *C. S. Lewis: A Biography*. London: HarperCollins, 2002.

White, Michael. *C. S. Lewis: Creator of Narnia*. New York: Carroll and Graf, 2004.

Charlotte's Web by E. B. White

Elledge, Scott. *E. B. White: A Biography*. New York: W. W. Norton, 1985.

Ferguson, Andrew. "At E. B. White's Farm: Where Charlotte Wove." *Time*. June 12, 1999. www.time.com/time/magazine/article/0,9171,991473,00.html.

White, E. B. *Letters of E. B. White*, revised edition. Edited by Dorothy Lobrano Goth. New York: Harper Perennial, 2007.

Catch-22 by Joseph Heller

Nagel, James. "The Early Composition of *Catch-22*." *Bloom's Modern Critical Interpretations: Joseph Heller's* Catch-22. Edited by Harold Bloom. New York: Infobase, 2008.

Sorkin, Adam J., ed. *Conversations with Joseph Heller*. Jackson: University Press of Mississippi, 1993.

One Hundred Years of Solitude by Gabriel García Márquez

Bell-Villada, Gene H., ed. *Conversations with Gabriel García Márquez*. Jackson: University Press of Mississippi, 2006.

Martin, Gerald. *Gabriel García Márquez: A Life*. New York: Alfred A. Knopf, 2009.

In the Telling

Frankenstein by Mary Shelley

Goreau, Angeline. "Physician, Behave Thyself." *New York Times*. September 3, 1989.

Seymour, Miranda. *Mary Shelley*. New York: Grove Press, 2000.

Shelley, Mary. *Frankenstein*. New York: Penguin Classics, 2003.

Sunstein, Emily W. *Mary Shelley: Romance and Reality*. Boston: Little, Brown, 1989.

"Rip Van Winkle" by Washington Irving

Irving, Pierre M. *The Life and Letters of Washington Irving*, 2 vols. New York: G. P. Putnam and Company, 1869.

Jones, Brian Jay. *Washington Irving: An American Original*. New York: Arcade, 2008.

Roscoe, Thomas. *The German Romances*. Vol. 2. London: Henry Colburn, 1837.

Alice's Adventures in Wonderland by Lewis Carroll

Carroll, Lewis. *Alice's Adventures in Wonderland*. New York: Rand, McNally, 1902.

Cohen, Morton N. *Lewis Carroll: A Biography*. New York: Alfred A. Knopf, 1996.

Woolf, Jenny. *The Mystery of Lewis Carroll: Discovering the Whimsical, Thoughtful, and Sometimes Lonely Man Who Created "Alice in Wonderland."* New York: St. Martin's Press, 2010.

The Wonderful Wizard of Oz by L. Frank Baum

Baum, L. Frank. *The Annotated Wizard of Oz*, centennial edition. Edited by Michael Patrick Hearn. New York: W. W. Norton, 2000.

Rogers, Katharine M. *L. Frank Baum: Creator of Oz*. New York: St. Martin's Press, 2002.

Schwarz, Evan I. *Finding Oz: How L. Frank Baum Discovered the Great American Story*. New York: Houghton Mifflin Harcourt, 2009.

The Tale of Peter Rabbit by Beatrix Potter

Lear, Linda. *Beatrix Potter: A Life in Nature*. New York: St. Martin's Press, 2007.

Potter, Beatrix. *Beatrix Potter's Letters*. Edited by Judy Taylor. New York: Frederick Warne, 1989.

———. *Letters to Children from Beatrix Potter*. Edited by Judy Taylor. New York: Penguin, 1992.

The Wind in the Willows by Kenneth Grahame

Grahame, Kenneth. *The Annotated Wind in the Willows*. Edited by Annie Gauger. New York: W. W. Norton, 2009.

Green, Peter. *Beyond the Wild Wood: The World of Kenneth Grahame*. New York: Facts on File, 1983.

Winnie-the-Pooh by A. A. Milne

Thwaite, Ann. *A. A. Milne: The Man Behind Winnie-the-Pooh*. New York: Random House, 1990.

"Winnie." *Historica Minutes*. The Historica Foundation of Canada: www.histori.ca/minutes/minute.do?id=10193.

"Winnie-the-Pooh." *Ashdown Forest*. The Conservators of Ashdown Forest: www.ashdownforest.org/pooh/winnie_the_pooh.php.

Lord of the Flies by William Golding

Carey, John. *William Golding: The Man Who Wrote* Lord of the Flies. London: Faber and Faber, 2009.

Haffenden, John, ed. *Novelists in Interview*. London: Metheun, 1985.

Catch Me If You Can

Pride and Prejudice by Jane Austen

"Letters of Jane Austen: Brabourne Edition." The Republic of Pemberley: www.pemberley.com/janeinfo/brablet1.html.

Nokes, David. *Jane Austen: A Life*. New York: Farrar, Straus and Giroux, 1997.

Tomalin, Claire. *Jane Austen: A Life*. New York: Alfred A. Knopf, 1997.

"The Raven" by Edgar Allan Poe

Ackroyd, Peter. *Dickens: Private Life and Public Passions*. New York: HarperCollins, 1990.

Dickens, Charles. "A Dickens Diary." Edited by Walter Dexter. *The Dickensian: A Quarterly Magazine for Dickens Lovers* 37 (1941): 71–84.

Frank, Frederick S., and Anthony Magistrale. *The Poe Encyclopedia*. Westport, CT: Greenwood Press, 1997.

Keim, Albert, and Louis Lumet. *Charles Dickens*. New York: Frederick A. Stokes, 1914.

Poe, Edgar Allan. *Poe: Essays and Reviews*. Edited by G. R. Thompson. New York: Library of America, 1984.

———. *The Raven*. Commentary by John H. Ingram. London: George Redway, 1885.

Quinn, Arthur Hobson. *Edgar Allan Poe: A Critical Biography*. Baltimore: Johns Hopkins University Press, 1998.

Silverman, Kenneth. *Edgar A. Poe: Mournful and Never-Ending Remembrance*. New York: HarperCollins, 1992.

The Adventures of Tom Sawyer by Mark Twain

Kaplan, Fred. *The Singular Mark Twain*. New York: Doubleday, 2003.

Paine, Albert Bigelow. *The Boy's Life of Mark Twain*. New York: Harper and Brothers, 1915.

Powers, Ron. *Dangerous Water: A Biography of the Man Who Became Mark Twain*. Cambridge: Da Capo Press, 2001.

Twain, Mark. *Autobiography of Mark Twain*. Vol. 1. Edited by Harriet Elinor Smith. Berkeley: University of California Press, 2010.

Sherlock Holmes by Arthur Conan Doyle

Lennenberg, Jon, Daniel Stashower, and Charles Foley, eds. *Arthur Conan Doyle: A Life in Letters*. New York: Penguin Press, 2008.

Liewbow, Ely M. *Dr. Joe Bell: Model for Sherlock Holmes*. Madison: University of Wisconsin Press, 2007.

Lycett, Andrew. *The Man Who Created Sherlock Holmes: The Life and Times of Sir Arthur Conan Doyle*. New York: Free Press, 2007.

Wells, Carolyn. *The Technique of the Mystery Story*. Springfield, MA: The Home Correspondence School, 1913.

Peter and Wendy by J. M. Barrie

Birkin, Andrew. *J. M. Barrie and the Lost Boys: The Real Story Behind Peter Pan*. New Haven: Yale University Press, 2003.

Chaney, Lisa. *Hide-and-Seek with Angels: A Life of J. M. Barrie*. New York: St. Martin's Press, 2005.

Lane, Anthony. "Lost Boys: Why J. M. Barrie Created Peter Pan." *New Yorker*. November 22, 2004. www.newyorker.com/archive/2004/11/22/041122crat_atlarge.

The Great Gatsby by F. Scott Fitzgerald

Bruccoli, Matthew J., ed. *F. Scott Fitzgerald's* The Great Gatsby*: A Literary Reference*. New York: Carroll and Graf, 2002.

Mellow, James R. *Invented Lives: F. Scott and Zelda Fitzgerald*. Boston: Houghton Mifflin, 1984.

Mrs. Dalloway by Virginia Woolf

Briggs, Julia. *Virginia Woolf: An Inner Life*. Orlando, FL: Harcourt, 2005.

Gordan, Lyndall. *Virginia Woolf: A Writer's Life*. New York: W. W. Norton, 1984.

Lee, Hermione. *Virginia Woolf*. New York: Vintage Books, 1999.

Scott, Bonnie Kime. Introduction to *Mrs. Dalloway*, by Virginia Woolf. Orlando, FL: Harcourt, 2005.

Woolf, Virginia. *Moments of Being: A Collection of Autobiographical Writing*. Edited by Jeanne Schulkind. Orlando, FL: Harcourt, 1985.

The Old Man and the Sea by Ernest Hemingway

Bruccoli, Matthew J., ed. *Conversations with Ernest Hemingway*. Jackson: University Press of Mississippi, 1986.

Hotchner, A. E. *Papa Hemingway*. New York: Carroll and Graf, 1999.

Lynn, Kenneth S. *Hemingway*. Cambridge: Harvard University Press, 1995.

Osgood, Charles. "Inside La Finca Vigia: A Visit to Hemingway's Villa." *CBS News Sunday Morning*. May 12, 1999. www.cbsnews.com/stories/1999/05/12/sunday/main46804.shtml.

Reynolds, Michael. *Hemingway: The Final Years*. New York: W. W. Norton, 1999.

Scribner Jr., Charles. Introduction to *The Old Man and the Sea*, by Ernest Hemingway. New York: Simon and Schuster, 2002.

Doctor Zhivago by Boris Pasternak
Hingley, Ronald. *Pasternak: A Biography*. New York: Alfred A. Knopf, 1983.
Mossman, Elliott, ed. *The Correspondence of Boris Pasternak and Olga Freidenberg: 1910–1954*. New York: Harcourt Brace Jovanovich, 1982.

THESE MEAN STREETS

Don Quixote by Miguel de Cervantes
Canavaggio, Jean. *Cervantes*. Translated by J. R. Jones. New York: W. W. Norton, 1990.
Duran, Manuel. *Cervantes*. New York: Twayne, 1974.
Mancing, Howard. *Cervantes' Don Quixote: A Reference Guide*. Westport, CT: Greenwood Press, 2006.
Russell, P. E. *Cervantes*. New York: Oxford University Press, 1995.

The Count of Monte Cristo by Alexandre Dumas
Coward, David. Introduction to *The Count of Monte Cristo*, by Alexandre Dumas. New York: Oxford University Press, 2008.
Robb, Graham. *Parisians: An Adventure History of Paris*. New York: W. W. Norton, 2010.

Crime and Punishment by Fyodor Dostoevsky
Dostoevsky, Anna. *Dostoevsky: Reminiscences*. Translated and edited by Beatrice Stillman. New York: Liveright, 1975.
Grossman, Leonid. *Dostoevsky: A Biography*. Translated by Mary Mackler. New York: Bobbs-Merrill, 1975.

Naked Lunch by William S. Burroughs
Morgan, Ted. *Literary Outlaw: The Life and Times of William S. Burroughs*. New York: Henry Holt, 1988.

To Kill a Mockingbird by Harper Lee

Bloom, Harold, ed. *Bloom's Modern Critical Interpretations:* To Kill a Mockingbird. New York: Infobase, 2007.

Inge, Thomas M. *Truman Capote: Conversations.* Jackson: University Press of Mississippi, 1987.

Keillor, Garrison. "Good Scout." *New York Times.* June 11, 2006. www .nytimes.com/2006/06/11/books/review/11keillor.html.

Madden, Kerry. *Harper Lee (Up Close).* New York: Viking, 2009.

Shields, Charles J. *Mockingbird: A Portrait of Harper Lee.* New York: Henry Holt, 2006.

In Cold Blood by Truman Capote

Capote, Truman. *Too Brief a Treat: The Letters of Truman Capote.* Edited by Gerald Clarke. New York: Vintage Books, 2004.

Clarke, Gerald. *Capote: A Biography.* New York: Carroll and Graf, 1988.

Plimpton, George. *Truman Capote: In Which Various Friends, Enemies, Acquaintances, and Detractors Recall His Turbulent Career.* New York: Doubleday, 1997.

"Wealthy Farmer, 3 of Family Slain." *New York Times.* November 16, 1959. www.nytimes.com/books/97/12/28/home/capote-headline.html.

The Outsiders by S. E. Hinton

Hinton, S. E. *The Outsiders.* New York: Speak, 2005.

———. *Some of Tim's Stories.* New York: Speak, 2009.

Slaughterhouse-Five by Kurt Vonnegut

Allen, William Rodney, ed. *Conversations with Kurt Vonnegut.* Jackson: University Press of Mississippi, 1988.

Bloom, Harold, ed. *Kurt Vonnegut's* Slaughterhouse-Five. New York: Infobase, 2007.

Klinkowitz, Jerome. *The Vonnegut Effect.* Columbia: University of South Carolina Press, 2004.

Szpek Jr., Ervin E., and Frank J. Idzikowski. *Shadows of Slaughterhouse Five.* Edited by Heidi Szpek. Bloomington, IN: iUniverse, 2008.

The Great Chase

Jane Eyre by Charlotte Brontë

Barker, Juliet. *The Brontës*. New York: St. Martin's Press, 1994.

Gaskell, Elizabeth. *The Life of Charlotte Brontë*. Edited by Elizabeth Jay. New York: Penguin, 1997.

Gordon, Lyndall. *Charlotte Brontë: A Passionate Life*. New York: W. W. Norton, 1995.

Shorter, Clement King. *Charlotte Brontë and Her Circle*. London: Hodder and Stoughton, 1896.

Stead, J. J. "Hathersage and 'Jane Eyre.'" *Brontë Society Publications*. Vol. 1. Brontë Society. March 1898: 26–28.

Moby-Dick by Herman Melville

Delbanco, Andrew. *Melville: His World and Work*. New York: Alfred A. Knopf, 2005.

Parker, Hershel. *Herman Melville: A Biography*. Vol. 1. Baltimore: Johns Hopkins University Press, 1996.

Reynolds, J. N. "Mocha Dick, or The White Whale of the Pacific: A Leaf from a Manuscript Journal." *The Knickerbocker, or New-York Monthly Magazine*. Vol. 13. May 1839: 377–92.

Heart of Darkness by Joseph Conrad

Conrad, Joseph. *A Personal Record*. New York: Harper and Brothers, 1912.

Karl, Frederick R. *Joseph Conrad: The Three Lives*. New York: Farrar, Straus and Giroux, 1979.

Najder, Zdzisław. *Joseph Conrad: A Life*. Translated by Halina Najder. Rochester, NY: Camden House, 2007.

Simmons, Allan. *Joseph Conrad in Context*. New York: Cambridge University Press, 2009.

Stape, John. *The Several Lives of Joseph Conrad*. New York: Pantheon Books, 2007.

Tennant, Roger. *Joseph Conrad: A Biography*. New York: Atheneum, 1981.

The Call of the Wild by Jack London

Hedrick, Joan D. *Solitary Comrade: Jack London and His Work*. Chapel Hill: University of North Carolina Press, 1982.

Kershaw, Alex. *Jack London: A Life*. New York: St. Martin's Press, 1997.

London, Jack. *The Letters of Jack London*. Vol. 1. Edited by Earle Labor, Robert C. Leitz III, and I. Milo Shepard. Stanford, CA: Stanford University Press, 1988.

Walker, Franklin. *Jack London and the Klondike*. San Marino, CA: Henry E. Huntington Library and Art Gallery, 1994.

The Magic Mountain by Thomas Mann

Byatt, A. S. Introduction to *The Magic Mountain*, by Thomas Mann. Translated by John E. Woods. New York: Alfred A. Knopf, 1995.

Mann, Katia. *Unwritten Memories*. Edited by Elisabeth Plessen and Michael Mann. Translated by Hunter and Hildegarde Hannum. New York: Alfred A. Knopf, 1975.

Prater, Donald. *Thomas Mann: A Life*. New York: Oxford University Press, 1995.

The Little Prince by Antoine de Saint-Exupéry

Saint-Exupéry, Antoine de. *Wind, Sand and Stars*. New York: Harcourt, 1992.

Saint-Exupéry, Consuelo de. *The Tale of the Rose: The Love Story Behind The Little Prince*. New York: Random House, 2001.

Schiff, Stacy. *Saint-Exupéry: A Biography*. New York: Alfred A. Knopf, 1994.

Tagliabue, John. "Clues to the Mystery of a Writer Pilot Who Disappeared." *New York Times*. April 11, 2008. www.nytimes.com/2008/04/11/world/europe/11exupery.html.

On the Road by Jack Kerouac

Amburn, Ellis. *Subterranean Kerouac: The Hidden Life of Jack Kerouac*. New York: St. Martin's Press, 1999.

Gifford, Barry, and Lawrence Lee. *Jack's Book: An Oral Biography of Jack Kerouac*. New York: Thunder's Mouth Press, 1994.

Hayes, Kevin J., ed. *Conversations with Jack Kerouac*. Jackson: University Press of Mississippi, 2005.

Lawlor, William T. *Beat Culture: Lifestyles, Icons, and Impact*. Santa Barbara, CA: ABC-CLIO, 2005.

Maher Jr., Paul. *Jack Kerouac's American Journey: The Real-Life Odyssey of On the Road*. Cambridge: Thunder's Mouth Press, 2007.

ON THE JOB

Anne of Green Gables by L. M. Montgomery

Gammel, Irene. *Looking for Anne of Green Gables: The Story of L. M. Montgomery and Her Literary Classic*. New York: St. Martin's Press, 2008.

Montgomery, L. M. *The Alpine Path: The Story of My Career*. Toronto: Fitzhenry and Whiteside, 1975.

The Phantom of the Opera by Gaston Leroux

Ayers, Andrew. *The Architecture of Paris*. London: Axel Menges, 2004.

Opera National de Paris. "The Opera Palais Garnier." www.operadeparis.fr/cns11/live/onp/L_Opera/Palais_Garnier/PalaisGarnier.php?lang=en.

Shaw, Albert, ed. "Translations." *The American Review of Reviews* 43 (1911): 762.

Snelson, John. *Andrew Lloyd Webber*. New Haven: Yale University Press, 2004.

Sollars, Michael D. *The Facts on File Companion to the World Novel: 1900 to Present*. New York: Infobase, 2008.

Red Harvest by Dashiell Hammett

Hammett, Dashiell. *Selected Letters of Dashiell Hammett*. Edited by Richard Layman. Washington: Counterpoint, 2001.

Hammett, Jo. *Dashiell Hammett: A Daughter Remembers*. Edited by Richard Layman. New York: Carroll and Graf, 2001.

Layman, Richard. *Shadow Man: The Life of Dashiell Hammett*. New York: Harcourt Brace Jovanovich, 1981.

Gone with the Wind by Margaret Mitchell

Mitchell, Margaret. *Margaret Mitchell's* Gone with the Wind *Letters: 1936–1949*. Edited by Richard Harwell. New York: Collier Books, 1986.

Pyron, Darden Asbury. *Southern Daughter: The Life of Margaret Mitchell*. New York: Harper Perennial, 1992.

Taylor, Helen. *Scarlett's Women:* Gone with the Wind *and Its Female Fans*. Piscataway, NJ: Rutgers University Press, 1989.

Walker, Marianne. *Margaret Mitchell and John Marsh: The Love Story Behind* Gone with the Wind. Atlanta: Peachtree, 1993.

Of Mice and Men by John Steinbeck

Fensch, Thomas, ed. *Conversations with John Steinbeck*. Jackson: University Press of Mississippi, 1988.

Parini, Jay. *John Steinbeck: A Biography*. New York: Henry Holt, 1995.

Casino Royale by Ian Fleming

Lycett, Andrew. *Ian Fleming: The Man Behind James Bond*. Atlanta: Turner, 1995.

Macintyre, Ben. *For Your Eyes Only: Ian Fleming and James Bond*. New York: Bloomsbury, 2008.

One Flew Over the Cuckoo's Nest by Ken Kesey

Faggen, Robert. "Ken Kesey: The Art of Fiction No. 136." *Paris Review*. www.theparisreview.org/interviews/1830/the-art-of-fiction-no-136-ken-kesey.

"Ken Kesey: Digital Interview." Rossgita Communications. 2003. www.digitalinterviews.com/digitalinterviews/views/kesey.shtml.

Kesey, Ken. *One Flew Over the Cuckoo's Nest*. Edited by John Clark Pratt. New York: Penguin, 1996.

Lupack, Barbara Tepa. *Insanity as Redemption in Contemporary American Fiction*. Gainesville: University Press of Florida, 1995.

Silverman, Al. *The Time of Their Lives: The Golden Age of Great American Publishers, Their Editors and Authors*. New York: St. Martin's Press, 2008.

Silvers, Robert B., and Barbara Epstein, eds. *The Company They Kept: Writers on Unforgettable Friendships*. New York: New York Review of Books, 2006.

Stevens, Jay. *Storming Heaven: LSD and the American Dream*. New York: Grove Press, 1987.

Tanner, Stephen L. *Ken Kesey*. Boston: Twayne, 1983.

The Bell Jar by Sylvia Plath

Alexander, Paul. *Rough Magic: A Biography of Sylvia Plath*. New York: Viking Penguin, 1991.

Plath, Sylvia. *The Journals of Sylvia Plath*. Foreword by Ted Hughes. New York: Anchor Books, 1998.

ACKNOWLEDGMENTS

This book would not be possible without my dear friend Maria Gagliano. She is a brilliant and sharp-eyed editor, a true Renaissance woman, and I am grateful to have had the opportunity to work with her. My thanks to Beth Blachman, Nikki Van Noy, and my parents, Trish and Carl Johnson, who offered insightful comments when the book was in its preliminary stages. My brothers CJ, Colin, and Christian have remained enthusiastic champions throughout the process. I am also grateful to my mentor, the phenomenal Les Pockell, who showed me that with the right energy and zeal, anything can be accomplished. Most of all, I have to thank my husband, Ian McConnell, without whom I would be lost.

ABOUT THE AUTHOR

Celia Blue Johnson graduated from New York University with a master's in English and American Literature and went on to become an editor at Grand Central Publishing. She is the cofounder of Slice Literary, a Brooklyn-based nonprofit organization that has been featured in *Time Out New York*, the *New Yorker*, and the *New York Times*. Celia has also compiled two poetry anthologies, *100 Great Poems for Girls* and *100 Poems to Lift Your Spirits*. She grew up running around barefoot in Melbourne, Australia, but now wears shoes in Brooklyn, New York, where she lives with her husband and daughter. Visit her website at www.celiablue.com.

STAND
UP
FOR
AUTISM

A Boy, a Dog, and a
Prescription for Laughter

GEORGINA J. DERBYSHIRE

Jessica Kingsley Publishers
London and Philadelphia

First published in 2010
by Jessica Kingsley Publishers
116 Pentonville Road
London N1 9JB, UK
and
400 Market Street, Suite 400
Philadelphia, PA 19106, USA

www.jkp.com

Library of Congress Cataloging in Publication Data
A CIP catalog record for this book is available
from the Library of Congress

British Library Cataloguing in Publication Data
A CIP catalogue record for this book is available from the British Library

ISBN 978 1 84905 099 9

Printed and bound in Great Britain by
MPG Books Group

ACKNOWLEDGEMENTS

This will be a test in keeping things brief. I am so scared of missing out somebody vital that I am taking the advice of my dear friend, Claire, and doing my thank yous as follows:

To all those people who have supported me over the last decade, believed in me and encouraged me in writing this book, given me the opportunity to write in the past, proofread my waffle and hidden their boredom when I recount my stories; those who have gone beyond the call of duty when helping, supporting and encouraging Bobby; our families, teachers, friends and colleagues; and those who have helped me pull myself together when I thought I couldn't cope any more – I offer you my most sincere thanks. You know who you are and we love you all. For God-Mother Sarah – for taking this book under her wing and acting like a one-woman marketing phenomenon – you *go*, girl. You never did things by halves!

For those people who have been no help whatsoever, you know who you are and I offer you...nothing!

For my fellow unemployed Imaginatives (the Holloways) and the Imaginatives-in-Training (the Maddisons), I offer you all my love and *huge* amounts of never-ending gratitude (and a signed copy).

Bobby, you gorgeous little man – you're the best pal in the world.

CONTENTS

PREFACE

If you are anything like me, dear reader, you will have received a diagnosis for your child (or currently be undergoing the never-ending traumatic cycle of trying to get one) and are reading all sorts of material to educate yourself, grasping at any hints and tips to make life easier or gathering information to back up what you already know (and have probably known for a while).

As parents and carers, we absorb as much as we can, because knowledge is power. We then receive a diagnosis, stating what we knew all along, and then feel sad because it's there in black and white. We also subject ourselves to heartbreaking stories from families who are fighting for the rights of their children every hour of every day. It becomes easy to slip down into a dim, dark hole where the future looks bleak, and isolation (or a monastery) is the only option. I don't know about you, but there's no *way* I am ever going to look good in an outfit that belongs on a monk. Nor could I take a vow of silence, for that matter.

So what's the alternative? If we do not want to be mournful and lamenting, which I am sure we don't, then we need to be upbeat and constructive. Nobody ever changed the world by being negative, and the mainstream views of autism will never change unless we alter the way we, *ourselves*, view it. The way to start this journey is by smiling. If you feel you need permission to laugh – consider it granted. If you feel the need to *stand up for autism*, then, my friend, let us be upstanding together.

INTRODUCTION

Why Have I Written This Book?

'Mum, do I have autism or icebergers? If you catch icebergers, is it because you've eaten too much meat or is it something to do with the *Titanic*? Is that why I like the *Titanic*, Mum?'

It is very important to look at the lighter side of life – it keeps us sane and it reminds us that, for every dark cloud, there is a little ray of sunshine just bursting to get through.

Children, for example, can be very funny. Although the things they do and say can induce sudden bouts of parental flushed cheeks and a desire to crawl down the nearest hole, the offending comment or incident can become an anecdote that you will be able to regurgitate for many years to come. The more embarrassing the incident at the time, the more comedy factor it is likely to have in the future. Relayed in the right way, and with ample drama, you can keep a small group of people entertained for many a while.

A word of caution – remember whom you have told which particular story as, if you start to repeat yourself, there is only so much polite smiling and forced laughter that the listener can display. Your friends and family may clearly have had enough and are shuffling off to let out the dogs (that they don't actually have), while you stand like a lemon laughing your socks off and retelling a story that was, at one time, quite amusing. I have been that lemon on a few occasions, so now I have chosen to relay some stories to *you*.

Funny stories are also great to share with the child concerned – the star role – but this will inevitably result in him requiring you to retell the story an unlimited number of times. You will be required to repeat yourself with exactly the same emphasis at just the right places, and tell the story in exactly the same way as you told it the first time, second time and so on. That is partly why I know I have recorded the stories accurately. I have told them so many times that I have them word-perfect!

The child will laugh just as much at the third telling as he did the first. After that, it may start to wane, but he will just force out the amusement nonetheless. At the fifteenth telling of the story, *you* will be losing the will to live, while the child will be forcing amusement to such a degree that his laughter now sounds like a strangled toad with bronchitis.

I have retold various stories to my son (somewhere on the autistic spectrum, who knows where) who loves to hear what he has done in the past and some of the things he has said. He has laughed, he has looked at me as though I have grown two heads, and he has told me I should write all the stories down so that he can continue enjoying them for years to come. The egotistical side of him also wants everybody else on the planet to read the stories. He has, very importantly, given *me* permission to laugh too. This is another reason for writing this book – because my son has decided it would be a good idea. I know what's good for me, and that's following his orders. That isn't me lacking control or being a lazy parent – it's just that I know that my son often knows best. Occasionally, he has also told me that I need to go away and do something more interesting for a while.

My son likes to see people laugh – if he is 100 per cent sure that they are not laughing *at* him. He thinks it is quite strange when people laugh so much that they cannot talk, and his quizzical expression is a picture to see. I once laughed so much that I had tears running down my cheeks. Very slowly and cautiously, he walked up to me, stared at my eyes and asked me why they were leaking water. There were many possible replies I could have offered, including 'When I laugh, my eyes become incontinent just like the rest of me'. Obviously I did not say this; otherwise he would have repeated it during 'show and tell' time at school.

My son sometimes also responds to my comments by saying, 'You philistine!' I am still not sure whether he knows what it means, but he certainly likes saying it, along with a number of other obscure words, which one year he saved up ready for his trip to see Santa.

'Kiwi.'

'Ho, ho, ho. What would you like for Christmas, young man?'

'Kiwi.'

'Do you like kiwi?'

'Kiwi.'

'Okay…'

My own personal reason for writing this book began when I started to forget certain stories and thought it time to make a record of them. Some of the favourite ones have been told so many times that I have felt like a CD on repeat. I don't particularly mind, but it would be easier if I had a break between repeating sessions – even if I just got to visit the bathroom. Sadly, a full-on toilet break has not been forthcoming in the past, and I have been known to carry on repeating the same story while echoing in the bathroom and trying to rearrange my underwear. I often have visions of my neighbours with a glass tumbler to the wall: 'She's at it again…she's garbling and on repeat… I can hear running water… should we call someone? Maybe she's a philistine…'

A child on the autistic spectrum can be just like any other child – an unspoilt, unblemished version of our more mature, cynical and pessimistic selves. But children on the autistic spectrum are every bit as joyous, heart-warming and amusing as others – with a little added *spice*. Their honesty is likely to be more brutal and bordering on the offensive, and their actions can be shocking, disturbing, astounding, unsettling and hilarious in varying degrees. They can, in contradiction to what I have just said, be extremely pessimistic and grumpy and sound like cantankerous pensioners, bringing additional amusement to those within hearing distance. Personally, I say, 'Good for them!' because too many of us are incapable of saying what we really mean or doing what we want to. How many of us really have the courage of our own moral convictions and are able to express it? But, just like everyone else, *individuals* (a *very* important

word) on the autistic spectrum can be incredibly different
to each other and have their own personalities, strengths
and challenges.

*'Mum. Have you ever thought of expressing yourself more?
You could make a start by getting rid of those spots on your
chin and then wear nicer clothes. You might look pretty if you
wore a dress. I think I will dress you tomorrow.'*

I like to think of autism like this: there are two ways of
looking at a spectrum – one is a scientific mix of words
such as 'optics' and 'prism', and one is a rainbow. There
are also two ways of looking at a rainbow – one is the
never-ending search for the pot of gold which probably
doesn't exist, and the other is to enjoy the colours and
marvel at how nature can create such a beautiful display.
I choose to see autism as a rainbow. I love to live, smile
and laugh along with every shade and hue within it, and
at no point do I ever want to miss that vibrant concoction
of light and colour in the search for a crusty pot of old
metal. Keep the gold, because I am enjoying a magical
view.

I will never suggest that autism is all fun and games
but the important factor, and the message that I am
desperately trying to convey by writing this, is: it's okay
to laugh – *it is the laughter that reminds us of the absurdity of
life, not the absurdity of any individual.* The incidents that
cause the laughter make us realize that the *world* is an odd
place. People are odd and the rules of socializing are odd.
Whoever said that it was the monopoly of neurotypical
people to define 'imagination'? Come to think of it, *who*
decided which members of society are 'neurotypical'?!
If I had the chance to define that particular word, I
really don't think I would reach the same conclusion as
somebody else. Let's be honest: *neurotypical* doesn't exist,

and if it did, it would probably carry the warnings 'boring' and 'clone' alongside it. We are unique, our children are unique, and everyone with an autism label is unique. Just as vital is remembering that *none of us is perfect.*

I digress. Whereas my son tends to stick with one subject until he has exhausted the very life out of it, *I* tend to fly off on tangents with great frequency. We complement each other beautifully, even when I am not looking pretty in a dress.

We have also learned to tread on each other's eggshells, which is handy with there only being the two of us in the house. It would not do to be treading on the eggshells of other residents, as there would not be room for either them or the shells themselves. Visitors often don't know about the eggshells and so are not particularly welcome.

> *Carpet Cleaner: 'I will just go and have a look at the damage to the carpet.'*
>
> *'Don't you go and touch anything!'*
>
> *Carpet Cleaner: (laughs) 'Don't worry, I won't.'*
>
> *'Don't knock any Lego over!'*
>
> *Carpet Cleaner: 'I will be careful, don't worry.'*
>
> *'You had better! And I am worried!'*

Before we tiptoe beyond the eggshells, I have recently learned that they are, in fact, portable. Eggshells are taken to holiday homes too.

Children often tell things in a way that we, as adults, would like to tell it if only we had the ability or the nerve. Why would we call a spade a 'spade' when we can call it an 'all-purpose innovative compact ground-digging geological solution'? A child on the autistic spectrum would probably call it, well, a 'spade', but then go on to give technical specifications, a list of suppliers and the history of the man who invented it. Another may simply bang you on one of your two heads with the aforementioned offending article. Needless to say, the child would probably then repeat it all to ensure no one missed any of the detail or action. A question-and-answer session is likely to be provided after the event, and you *will* be expected to participate. I sincerely pity you if you have not been paying attention.

This is excellent news. Like it or not, there have to be people out there in society who can provide the technical specifications of a spade. There also has to be a lot of health and safety tests carried out. A perfect example of when an individual with autism is ahead of the *neurotypical* game.

Let us stay with the spade analogy for a minute, for no other reason than this could be leading somewhere. If that particular spade found itself being dropped on somebody's head from a great height, we would probably rush to the assistance of the injured individual and chastise the spade. We may shout obscenities at the spade, *blame* the spade or even become physically *aggressive* towards the spade. The child, however, would probably find the whole incident rather interesting, or perplexing. The spade can now be checked for damage to its external materials, the height from which the spade dropped can be calculated, and at some point the spade should be dropped again to see if the same thing happens. The spade could, in extreme circumstances, find itself in repeat mode. The child will look at the injured party, however, and wonder why on earth this person is verbally abusing a garden tool.

It all makes perfect sense when you think about it. There are many elements and factors that are combined to cause an accident. That child may not be being insensitive

– he may be just more interested in the specifics. The whole theory of cause and effect is, after all, incredibly important to the way the world works.

> *'Bobby, Granny and Granddad have been in a car accident today.'*
>
> *'Where?'*
>
> *'I will show you when we drive past the place it happened. A tree fell on the car, and they have been to hospital.'*
>
> *'How is the car?'*
>
> *'Well, it's got a lot of damage, but Granny and Granddad are going to be fine.'*
>
> *'Can we go and see the damage to the car?'*
>
> *'Not at the moment, no. Anyway, aren't you just pleased that Granny and Granddad are okay?'*
>
> *'Yes. Is the damage to the right or the left side of the car? Where is the tree?'*

Some children on the spectrum, understandably, will have no interest in spades, car accidents or anything related to them. They will stick with the original theory that the person has two heads and is, actually, a philistine with no dress sense. Incidentally, this could be a reason for lack of eye contact. As a parent, you are clearly mad, and therefore you do not *deserve* eye contact. If you are ignored, you may go away and stop embarrassing yourself and everyone around you. Yes, it is fair to say that the neurotypicals are quite odd. Especially, it seems, when they have spots and can't express themselves. Okay, it's time to leave the spade behind and move on.

I dedicate this book to my wonderful son, friend, personal advisor, skin-care expert, fashion advisor and constant source of inspiration, Bobby. Without him, I would not have become the person I am now (and I happen to like myself better now than I did before, although I can't comment for other people). I also dedicate this book to the millions of parents, teachers, families, friends and carers of children with autism all over the world – quite a few of you then! You are, by far, some of the most genuine and dedicated people I have ever met. In my humble opinion, you are more deserving of a good laugh than the rest of the population.

If my memory serves me right, the original question was 'Why have I written this book?' Answer: because people need to tell it as it is. We need to remind people that there is nothing politically incorrect, offensive or cruel about letting out a laugh every now and again. And *everybody* needs to know that that's okay.

'Bobby? Would you like to go ice-skating?'

'No. I will fall over.'

'I will hold you up.'

'You might fall over.'

'Then we will fall over together.'

'No. It's dangerous.'

'We could give it a go.'

'You can beat me, whip me, attack me, punch me, shout at me, be nasty to me, kill me, blackmail me and murder me, force me to go ice-skating, let me break my legs and die, and that will be just fine, won't it?! And then I won't be able to do anything or go to school, or play, and then I will be in a wheelchair and it will all be your fault!'

(Long silence)

'*Do you want to go ice-skating, then, Bobby?*'

'*No.*'

'*Okay.*'

'*It's a ridiculous idea. Philistine.*'

CHAPTER 1

THIS IS BOBBY

'When I feel frustrated, the people in my brain are messing up the computers and throwing them about. They are banging them and throwing them out of the windows. The control panel in my brain blows up and the people throw all the books off the shelves. When I am really frustrated and have silly behaviour, it's because the whole office has blown up. At night when I am asleep, the people in the office have a break and a snack.'

After a lengthy Introduction, you may feel as though you already know Bobby quite well. Here are a few more facts, figures and technical specifications about him that may help you bond a little more as we move through his first decade on Planet Earth (in body, if not always in mind). You will have noticed that I have included lots of direct comments, statements and responses from the boy himself. This is so you can hear things from the horse's mouth, so to speak. (I wouldn't dare mention the 'horse's mouth' in the presence of Bobby, however, as his face would not be able to hide the disdain at such a ridiculous concept.)

It would be a logistical nightmare (not to mention very time-consuming) to introduce *you* (and anybody else who does me the honour of reading my ramblings) to *him*, so this seems the most appropriate way to do it. This also serves to avoid any embarrassment that may be caused, should you have the misfortune of not immediately becoming one of his 'chosen few'. I will tell you more about that later.

Everything I have quoted and every incident I have mentioned is true. There may be a bit of artistic licence going on in relation to mentions of 'tumbleweed' and me dying every now and again, but I will not patronize you and think you actually believe those particular bits. I have not yet, to my knowledge, died.

Bobby was diagnosed at five years and two months old after a number of healthcare specialists and psychologists had been having an ongoing argument among themselves about what the 'problem' seemed to be. It went on for quite some time and was a very stressful period for all concerned, so, ultimately, we withdrew from the muddled discussions and I obtained an independent, professional opinion from a neurologist and then a psychologist. Eventually, a diagnosis of 'Autistic Spectrum Disorder' was forthcoming. The other professionals then stopped their arguing and apologized for taking so long. We proceeded to the next stage: someone gave me a leaflet, aptly named 'What to do next'.

I would like to stress that although Bobby has autism, he is, first and foremost, a *boy*. He is a son, a grandson, a great-grandson, a nephew and a *child*. Big brown eyes, button nose, a huge grin and a wicked sense of humour. He is his own person and that will always surface more than his autism. The majority of the time, his individual characteristics and the autism are blended together like a delicious smoothie. It's just that, sometimes, the smoothie may taste slightly bitter, get stuck in the throat or make one choke, if you get my meaning. We only talk about autism when it is appropriate or when there is a question to be answered, but we certainly don't shut it in a cupboard and pretend it isn't in our lives.

The neurologist had commented that Bobby had 'autism oozing out of every pore'. A wonderful analogy and a fine statement, I thought, although I could not actually see anything oozing out of any pores, and for this I was mighty glad. This was strange (not the oozing thing, something else), because while everybody else had been discussing things among themselves, a health visitor had stated she believed any autistic traits he had were very minor, if, indeed, they existed at all. (Okay, someone help me out here, because I don't get how there could be such a variation of opinion.)

Prior to the final diagnosis, and when I had first started the process, our doctor said I should not be concerned with his 'delightfully quirky traits'. This comment was in response to me telling the doctor that every time my son walked through the front door of our home, he removed his left sock. That is, Bobby removed his sock, not the doctor. I wouldn't want you to think that every time my son returned home, a doctor – in a surgery somewhere in the world – removed his left sock. Now that would just be weird, but delightfully quirky nonetheless.

Bobby is incredibly talkative. There was a short delay in his speech development and he soon caught up and went beyond what was expected of a child his age. Hurrah! But when I say he is 'incredibly talkative', I mean *incredibly* talkative. I suppose that's why I said it, really. I used to think he got that particular gene from me, but although I can bore anyone into submission while garbling about a number of subjects, Bobby can send you into a coma – which you would be pleased to be in just for a few hours' respite. Reality check: I acknowledge that I am lucky that he talks to me at all and would not want anyone to think that I am not grateful for this. At 5.15 a.m., midday, 10.30 p.m., midnight – I am grateful that the verbal skills are always more than willing and prepared to exhibit themselves.

Bobby can talk for hours without taking a break, without stopping to breathe and without any punctuation. He talks like he writes – one long sentence with no gaps. He once won a competition during assembly at school for being able to talk the longest about any one subject. He said he saw his head teacher slumping in his chair while the talk went on and on and on... He seemed particularly proud that half of the school was yawning and holding each other up.

It will seem surprising, then, that my chatty young boy had speech and language therapy shortly after diagnosis. The reasons for this were that, first, it ticked one of the boxes for what a child with autism should have (according to somebody, somewhere, who decided to write a list) and, second, he found it very difficult at the age of five (and still does) to talk to his peer group in an appropriate way. After all, as I have tried to explain to him, other children do not like being grammatically corrected or being talked at. To Bobby, this is a problem that they have to sort out for themselves, not the other way round. For him, it is the world that is odd and everybody else who needs help. He is quite right. To use one of my favourite analogies, nobody of sound mind would say to a person using a wheelchair, 'If you can't get up the steps, then you will have to get out and walk.' It's a good point.

There are no savant skills as such, other than his juggling of acronyms and his ability to remember where every last one of his toys was purchased and by whom (plus the time of day, the weather and who was wearing a dress).

There are rare occasions when my pensive son will not talk to me at all. The trip home from school can sometimes be made in complete silence, and then, foolishly, it is me who breaks the silence by asking him what is wrong. Yes, I know, a silly thing to do. One descriptive and very animated answer that I noted was:

> *'Well, my brain has been a bit busy today. The control panel blew up and the people using the computers had thrown books all over the place, smashed their computers and the whole office blew up.'*

It was traits like the above that originally pointed towards Asperger Syndrome. The obsessions, such as the lining up of toys and the serious fascination with trains to the exclusion of everything else, suggested the same. The Exclusion of Everything Else (EEE) deserves an acronym of its own really, it is used so often! Having spent some difficult sessions with a child mental health specialist, however, it was agreed that Bobby could slide from one end of the autistic spectrum to the other like an eel on an ice-skating rink. The same is still true today, and things can change from one minute to the next. For a boy who likes to plan things in advance, he certainly doesn't follow suit with his behaviour.

The Triad of Impairments (social interaction, communication and imagination) is sometimes a little difficult to apply to Bobby, but I have also heard other parents say that their children don't quite fit into the whole three-way thing. Perhaps nomadic-quad would be more appropriate, or triadic-octad. Whichever one suits you or *your* child; Bobby, for one, does not do the 'three' thing (other than many bouts of EEE).

Social interaction: Bobby *can* socially interact – he just prefers not to. That is unless he has the full attention of the social beings and he is not interrupted, argued with or suddenly startled by someone's ridiculous comment, humour or sarcasm. He would prefer for no one to be in his personal space (which is an approximate radius of three miles) and for people not to smell of anything too strong. He is unlikely to offer you full-on eye contact unless you have really upset him – in which case you will get the 'piercing eyes drilling right through to your skull' glare. And let me tell you – it hurts your brain and is more tortuous than a double choc-chip cookie hanging on a string under your nose when you are on a diet and tied to a chair. With a gag on.

Social communication: Bobby *can* socially communicate – if he is in the right mood, the weather is right, he is wearing the correct clothes and it is a monologue. Others *may* be able to speak, but only if they have incredibly fascinating information or are engaging in questions-and-answers so that Bobby can educate them.

Imagination (or Theory of Mind, or Flexibility of Thought, or Thoughts of Flexibility, or even Theories of Flexible Minds and Thoughts – or anything else that comes into this category): I can safely say that Bobby *has* imagination. What he cannot do is imagine things that are quite *possible*. He can imagine floating around in the Milky Way to help him relax, and he can imagine that he is a dog or a baby or an atomic bomb (sorry – did I say '*imagine*'?), but he struggles with the concept of imagining

a successful career when he is older. He cannot imagine a
time when he will ever be independent, content, at peace
with himself, or, more importantly, a time when he is too
grown-up to play. (I tell him that that's okay, though,
because boys grow into men, and men never really stop
playing. In fact, boys grow into men but the men are
still really boys.) Which reminds me of something rather
profound and slightly disturbing that was said in the
bathtub one night with no prior warning:

*'Mum. You know, you could try and take me away from the
autism, but you can't ever take the autism out of the boy.'*

I have no idea where it came from, but whatever the
source, the answer would be the same: 'Sweetheart – I
have no desire to change you in any way whatsoever.
Nor do I have any desire to extract anything from your
body.'

Bobby can sit alone for hours playing his own
imaginary games, but cannot easily play anyone else's
imaginary games because they are 'not real'. Imagine
(or use your theory of flexible mind and thought in an
imaginative way) that you have three pieces of string and
they are all criss-crossed and confused about what they
are doing. That's Bobby's triad – tangled up, complicated,
amazing.

My son is, fundamentally, adorable. I *would* say that
because I am his mother. I am not a fantastic disciplinarian,
admittedly, but one reason for that is because I find it so
damn hard to keep up with him. I do not make excuses
for my lack of ability in this area because at my post-
diagnosis therapy session (wow, was I in need of *that!*)
I was told that I could not be 'everything'. The woman
with the soft voice and sympathetic face said, 'You can't
be a mother, a father, a teacher, and a disciplinarian. *The*

best thing you can do for him is be his ally.' This is my mantra every day, and God help anyone who tries to make me believe otherwise.

With regard to health, Bobby has not done so badly in the medical sense. There were the usual bugs that he caught as a baby, colic and stuff, but nothing too scary until he was three years old. One morning he awoke with a rash, refused to be touched, went very stiff and was rushed to hospital with suspected meningitis.

Thank goodness that wasn't the diagnosis, but not so good was the lack of any idea of what was wrong other than an 'unidentified infection'. Having been discharged from hospital for a few hours, he then went on to perforate his eardrum (not deliberately) when the unidentified infection decided it wasn't getting enough attention and was found to be living it up in his inner ear. It was a messy experience as the infection burst through and the eardrum was quite traumatized for some time.

The other ear, just to be awkward and wishing to be independent from its symmetrical counterpart, got itself recognized as having hyperacusis. Bobby was then hearing too much of what he did not want to hear in one ear and hardly anything in the other ear (due to the perforated eardrum). When Bobby was accused of having selective deafness, this was actually genuine, rather than a case of him deliberately filtering things out.

There were also two troublesome teeth which had to be removed when Bobby was six. Taking lots of things into account, the wonderful dentist organized a 'special needs package' for the trip to hospital. Yes, it sounds rather like a specialized holiday, but this actually meant that Bobby would be first on the list and given a quiet area to wait before the operation, and that everything would be super-calm and organized. Ha, ha, ha.

Arriving at the hospital, Bobby walked into the main dental reception area to be greeted by the sights and sounds of hundreds of children all waiting to have their teeth pulled. He went through the door, took a look around and headed back out of the entrance. And then the testing of the fire alarm bell commenced and it continued to be tested every fifteen minutes for the next two hours.

Eventually, Bobby had had enough and stood banging on the glass of the door to get somebody's attention. It very much resembled a scene from *The Graduate*. At this point, a nurse noticed that he was causing difficulties and other patients were becoming distressed, so we were ushered into a side ward where we sat peacefully and quietly before the operation.

The teeth were pulled not long after and there was an anxious wait while Bobby took his time deciding when to wake from the anaesthetic. I was frantic, Granny was trying not to appear frantic – but not doing a very good job – and the nurse said, 'Gosh, he likes his sleep, doesn't he?' I laughed. No, actually, he doesn't, and that comment couldn't be amusing if you stuck a label on it saying, 'Look – I am an amusing comment. Please laugh at me'. 'Bobby likes his sleep' is like saying 'Jerry Springer is shy and withdrawn' or 'Dolly Parton has a boyish figure' or 'The Queen doesn't speak proper English'. But I don't suppose the nurse was to know about my son's sleeping habits, so I smiled and said, 'Yeah…'

Then there was a delightful moment when Bobby regained consciousness, sat up with dried blood around his lips, looked around with eyes the size of satellite dishes and said, 'Are we anywhere near Toys R Us?'

Other than the above, and moments when exhaustion completely takes over and incapacitates him for a few days, Bobby is reasonably healthy – apart from tummy problems, migraines and weak ankles from walking on his tiptoes for many years.

My very bouncy child likes to throw himself on to sofas or anything soft. If watching TV, he will run across the room and throw himself at one sofa before running back and throwing himself at another. This can go on for hours, backwards and forwards, while watching a TV programme and talking at the same time. It seems that this self-throwing activity actually helps him to talk because the words he says are coming out of his mouth with the same rhythm as his steps. This can make people feel quite nauseous, so I have found it is best to focus on one spot rather than try and follow him back and forth. It also wears a path in the carpet, so sometimes I change the furniture into different positions, but this is not really a good idea as Bobby, not surprisingly, does not like change.

'Why have you bought a new lampshade?'

'The other one was looking a bit worn.'

'Good grief! You have bought a new kitchen bin too!'

'Yes, because I needed a taller one. Just before you go into the bathroom, I need to tell you that…'

'Mum! What's with the new toilet seat? Why have you done that? Why have you replaced everything in the house?'

'I haven't – it's just those three things because they needed replacing.'

'No, they didn't! I can't believe you have done this to me! How mean!'

Bobby refused to speak to me for some time after this, and then cried, and then refused to use the bin, the toilet seat or to switch on the lamp which was flaunting its new shade.

Change to Bobby's environment or his routine has, inevitably, caused huge problems. He deals with it better now than he used to, but there are still times when we have to sit and go through the week's schedule over and over again.

'What day is the day after tomorrow, Mum?'

'Wednesday. Why?'

'What happens the day before?'

'The day before Wednesday?'

'No, the day before today.'

'You mean yesterday?'

'Yes! The day before today, which is the day before the day before the day before Wednesday.'

'That will be Sunday, so you tell me what we did the day before...I mean yesterday.'

'I suppose we did what we will do three days after the day after tomorrow.'

'That's right – we go swimming.'

'So, that'll be a Sunday, then. The day before Monday, which means back to school.'

Bobby especially loves to talk about the things he knows a lot about. For instance, he knows everything and anything about trains (and more recently cars, planes and World War Two as well). He knows quite a lot about space, and he knows even more about the workings of the combustion engine and the rusticles on the *Titanic*. 'Rusticles', from what I can understand, is a technical term that only like-minded *Titanic* fans will fully understand. Bobby hates little bits of his fingernails sticking out. He likes to see long hair on women, but a stray hair in the bath, sink, carpet, window-ledge or attached to the Hubble telescope will annoy the pants off him, and he can get quite abusive if the hair-disposal process is not as speedy as it could be. This used to be a major problem because I had *very* long hair. I didn't have it cut for the stray-hair reason, however – I *had* to cut it because he twisted part of it into a knot and I couldn't get it out again. Sadly, I couldn't go to a hair salon to have it cut professionally, as a previous visit concluded with my son tearing a chair to pieces and removing the foam padding.

He is not keen on visitors and will not even pretend to be hospitable. He doesn't like unfamiliar children and, come to think of it, he doesn't like familiar ones that much either. It is only fair to say that he does have a small group of friends who, over the years, he has learned to trust and depend on. Yes, friends, you know who you are. You are the ones who return home from school exhausted and with the words of Bobby ringing in your ears. You are the friends who spot a meltdown three hours before it happens, and you are the friends who deserve awards for dedication and bravery. You are also really lovely kids.

Occasionally, things go a bit wrong, but with lots of explaining, lots of social skills lessons with his teaching assistants (and lots of patience from his friends), he doesn't do too badly. One particular friend knows more about autism than I do, because he has taken the time to find out and his mum has been brilliant at explaining things to him. To have more mums like that in the world would be a good thing indeed! Some mums, however, don't get the whole 'autism' thing and think their child might catch it if they get too close. Small chance of that happening because Bobby would *never* allow them to get within a transmittable distance!

Bobby *can* have impeccable manners. Upon meeting an adult for the second or third time, he will have made his assessment of that person and categorized them into the 'chosen few' section or the 'trash can'. The *chosen few* are rewarded with manners and a deep and meaningful conversation about a Toyota Hilux or a Spitfire aircraft. The trash batch can forget it because it is never going to happen. The trash, the trash's partner and the trash's offspring are likely to be cursed for ever. The strange thing is, I have no idea how he analyzes these individuals and the criteria dividing the good from the bad, or the 'chosen' from the 'trash'. One thing is for sure: if you're trash, you will *know* you are trash. It will be so obvious to you that you will actually start to *feel* like trash.

Where was I?

Bobby can be very intelligent – when he wants to be and he is in the right mood. If the subject matter interests him, then he will digest and regurgitate information about it like a database and will remember facts for years to come. Sport is not a favourite subject, but he does love being in water, so swimming as a sport is allowed – as long as it is just him doing it and we don't talk too much about it and we don't watch anything related to it on TV. Oh – and he prefers it if no one else is in the pool at the same time, which can be difficult. Private garden pools in England are not so common and are usually status symbols of the more well-off. Dirty and unmaintained pools can be a symbol of fallen status (or swimming boredom). We, on the other hand, have a pond the size of a large dinner plate. Make of that what you will.

Bobby likes to be in control. A favourite statement is 'I don't tell you how to live *your* life'. The games he plays and the role plays he performs are all intricately orchestrated so that every comment and every move has been organized at least two hours in advance.

This makes playing board games very difficult, and so trying to get him to play one is tantamount to child cruelty and sometimes it isn't worth the high-pitched screech and dangerously low-flying objects. He likes predictability. Throwing dice is a joke.

If he is promised something, then the promise *has* to be delivered. Fatal accidents, serious illnesses and Armageddon are no excuse. The muscles in my back completely seized a few years ago, and although I did not expect any sympathy, I *did* expect to be exempt from our nightly rough and tumble game, 'Demolition Derby'. This involves us pretending to be cars, barging into each other and then me squashing him under me with all my weight. Sounds dangerous, I know.

I had *prematurely* granted myself this exemption as, when the usual game time arrived, I was reminded of my promise to play it at 6 p.m. every day, my selfishness and how I was the worst mother in the world. The truth is that I couldn't walk, breathe or even take myself to the bathroom, so rolling around the floor and squashing my son was not at the top of my agenda. But hey – that's bad mothers for you – always thinking of themselves instead of squashing their kids.

Bobby *really* likes to be squashed. The heavier the squasher, the better. If another child so much as brushes past him, then he is liable to erupt, but a heavy weight (I am not enormous, but I am certainly not petite) seems to let stress and strain ooze out of him. Yes – I make it sound as if there's a lot that oozes from the pores of Bobby. Maybe basic humanity and tolerance of other people can't get out because of all the other ooziness taking place.

Talking of humanity, there are a select few times when Bobby *can* show some sympathy and concern. It is usually completely out of proportion to the incident (or dead fly) that has caused it, and it can disturb him for many days and nights, but at least it is there. There are occasions when he cannot sleep because he is trying to think up ways to solve the problems of the world – all before dawn. You will have to wait to read the chapter on sleep problems to see how he gets on with *that* trivial little task.

It seems logical now to tell you that Bobby does not sleep well. He never has and it never seems to improve. Most evenings, it is me drifting in and out of sleep while Bobby lies at the side of me laughing, singing and humming the tune to *The Great Escape*. After a decade of this, I no longer know what I am like as a person when functioning at 100 per cent. Maybe I am efficient, maybe I am annoying. Maybe I remember to put the milk in the fridge rather than the washing machine. I am hoping that, one day, I may even remember my name and date of birth.

Eloquence is something that my boy possesses for the majority of the time. He can speak clearly and intelligently. He can also squawk like a parrot, shout at decibels not yet recorded and use words and noises that have never been invented. He will revert to baby language often and perfectly mimic various sounds from car engines to exploding bombs, and he instinctively *knows* when echolalia is not appropriate – and then do it anyway.

Animals are a priority. Bobby loves animals and a few years ago, while on holiday, he befriended a sheep whom he aptly named *Woolly*. He visited the sheep three times a day for ten days, and the sheep was very happy to respond affectionately to him. Leaving Woolly behind, when we were ready to return home, was such an emotional experience that I stood and cried with Bobby, in the middle of a field, in the middle of nowhere. I took a pair of scissors to the field that morning and we (wait for it, it's not going to be as bad as you think…) clipped off a bit of Woolly's fleece – which we still have in a tin. (Farmer – if you are reading this, then no animals were harmed in the fleece-snipping incident.)

'You know where you are with sheep. Woolly is one of my best friends ever and I can always rely on him.'

The *Titanic* is something Bobby is obsessed with. Other than many books and a complete *National Geographic* DVD box-set showing discovery submersibles, he lives for the year 2012 when he is hoping there will be a huge centenary exhibition somewhere in the world. Wherever it is, it is likely we will be attending, because he has now been counting down the days for five years. He isn't as fascinated with the *Titanic* movies, other than to argue with their technical content and what aspects they so annoyingly got wrong.

He is also concerned that, as 2012 will be the year that the UK hosts the Olympics, it may affect any proposed *Titanic* exhibition. It is causing sleepless nights that London, Liverpool and New York may all argue as to where the exhibition will be held. This is why my son has decided that the *Titanic* should never be raised – he fears the wreckage will be split in half and the bits separated between the UK and the USA. Although he thinks this is a very fair way of dividing up the salvage, he is actually considering the damaging effects that the oxygen in the air may cause to the ship and that any argument between nations would cause a delay. This would, therefore, leave the *Titanic* out in the oxygen for far too long and do unspeakable things to it.

The 'Happy Birthday' song is detested and he will neither sing it nor have it sung to him. He also hates me playing air guitar in the bathroom when he is enjoying an hour-long bath. I am unable to dance around the house, be overly dramatic, pull stupid faces or be generally light-hearted for the majority of the time. He doesn't like me singing either, unless the song is called 'Let's go out and buy lots of toys'. I do get the silly behaviour out of my system, though – I just wait until I am back in the office.

Toys are, in Bobby's world, the most important thing in life. As a child, this is only to be expected, but Bobby sees the act of *playing* as a constitutional right which should never be challenged or interfered with. It will not seem strange therefore, that Bobby does *not* like homework.

'A homework book? What on earth...! I work hard all day at school just so you can give me homework? God did not put me on this earth to work all day and all night. And how come I did really well in my spelling test last week and then get given more to do the following week?'

This statement was made to his teacher on the first day of his new school year when she presented him with a homework diary. She only wanted about 20 minutes' work a night from him, but this was clearly far too much to expect. When Bobby comes home from school, he will not change his clothes until his homework is done.

Changing out of his uniform symbolizes a change in activity from work to all-important play. This makes perfect sense to me and is *obviously* why I change into my PJs and sit eating chocolate biscuits when I return home from the office (where I have exhibited silly behaviour all day).

Accompanying ASD, Bobby also comes free of charge with a number of other semi-diagnoses, such as ADD, ADHD, PDD, ADHAADDDHDDA (or any other combination). Oh, don't forget EEE. It was decided, by those who know best, that one diagnosis would be better than 15 or so, as this would only serve to confuse people. Needless to say, my son exhibits his extra acronyms regularly and especially likes to refresh his ADHD at midnight. The only time he completely *stops* is when he is medically, physically and mentally exhausted and I have to carry him to bed. This happens every few months, and for the 18 or so hours he sleeps deeply, I will move around the house like a whirling dervish in an attempt to get as much housework and laundry (and personal grooming) done as possible. I have even managed a toilet break lasting more than 1.3 seconds during this time. What joy!

Although I work (honestly, I do get *some* work done) for 40 hours a week, transform into a Demolition Derby car every night, maintain a house, get little sleep and attempt to be the best mother in the world, Bobby only registers one particular ten-minute activity that he sees me do:

'My mum just sits and drinks coffee all day or talks on the phone. All day, every day, she just sits there – drinking coffee.'

He hates coffee with a passion. He hates the smell and the look of it, so I have to hide my all-day coffee-drinking sessions by being banished to the kitchen. He, on the other hand, has an obsession with cheese and ketchup sandwiches. Along with having them every single day for his school lunch, he also requests them for breakfast and supper. He does not have what you would call a very varied diet, other than the occasional tortilla wrap or toasty – which he will have stuffed with cheese and ketchup.

Sunshine is not one of his favourite things either. Or, to be more precise, warm weather. If it is sunny but with a slight cool breeze, then that is ideal. If the breeze turns into full-scale wind, then this is not so tolerable. If warm sunshine turns into hot weather, then Bobby will huff and puff as if he has spent a week in the Sahara Desert wearing a fur coat and ear muffs.

At the 'height of summer', even though we do not tend to have such a thing in England, an emergency kit is to hand at all times to prevent overheating. This kit will contain two pairs of sunglasses, a sunhat, thin and loose cotton clothes, a chilled drink and a bottle of cooling water spray. All will be applied before he ventures outdoors, and all will be reapplied at regular intervals throughout the day. He will then reapply everything before getting back into a hot car and will go through the whole performance a few more times on the trip home. And, throughout all of this, he will be huffing and puffing with increased volume as the day goes on.

I have tried to explain that the more huffing and puffing that is done, the hotter and more flustered he will make himself. In response to this, there are more huffs and puffs. Granny is another one who huffs and puffs for the same reason, and she doesn't take my advice either.

A day out in the summer with Granny and Grandson *together* is nothing but a huffing and puffing expedition which can get extremely annoying for those of us who don't do this.

If you still haven't had enough, here are a few more snippets you should know. Bobby:

- is very afraid of fire, and we have to sleep with a fire extinguisher in the corner of the bedroom and test the smoke alarms every night

- likes to visit my place of work so that he can leave obscure messages on the flip-chart – usually aimed at the Director. This is good as it deflects from *my* inappropriate behaviour

- will turn over the container or box of any new toy to see how many there are in the collection – and panic until he knows the whole set are still available for purchase

- adores cardboard boxes for sitting in, making into trains, Deloreans, space shuttles, World War Two bunkers or hiding places

- will disappear into a kitchen cupboard when upset or angry

- can anticipate a thunder storm from ten miles away and start to panic

- blames God for most things, but forgets to thank him for others

- thinks bullying is when someone has a difference of opinion

- believes Mrs H, his teaching assistant, is very inconsiderate and selfish when she is absent from school due to illness or holidays – and makes her very aware of this when she returns

- thinks Blu-tack (the poster putty stuff) is one of the best inventions of all time. He fiddles with it to relieve stress, makes things out of it to ease boredom, and attempts to sleep with it because it makes him feel safe

- assumes that when he leaves home for the day to visit family, I wave him off and sit all day in the same room until he returns (probably drinking coffee)

- calls the children in his class at school 'the amplifiers' because they are so loud

- likes to hold items of similar size and weight in both hands to help him feel balanced.

And last, but not least, Bobby believes that the small electric shock I received when I was pregnant caused the autism, as the result of an electrical current that found its way into my womb and proceeded to fry a part of his brain. I tell him that's not the case.

'Son, if the electric shock did anything, it sparked into life a part of your brain that many people never use. That's what makes you so special.'

Bobby is, in the nicest sense of the word, an oddity. Beautifully odd, annoyingly odd, amusingly odd and oddly odd. I love him with all his oddities and foibles, and would not try to change him for anything. I love the curiosity that he is.

Now, with all those lovely things to take into account, how can I stop a smile growing and how can I stifle a laugh? *I can't, so I don't.*

'The amplifiers' at Bobby's school

I *would* change his midnight hyperactivity, though. It would be lovely to go to bed without the repetitive mimicking of a police siren or air-raid warning at the side of me.

CHAPTER 2

BARKING AT PARENTS AND TODDLERS

'I'll have a collar on today, please. I am a dog now. If I have a collar on and walk like a dog, then people will know that I really am a dog.'

One morning, I awoke to find that my son had morphed into a dog. When I said my usual good-morning greeting, it was met with a brisk and sharp yap. It was a reasonable assumption that, at three years old, he was copying the family pet called Demi (as in Moore, but not remotely similar in looks) and would grow out of this as soon as his knees ached from walking on all fours and he tired of barking. Sadly, this was not the case and my son was a dog for many months. Luckily, his appearance had changed in no way whatsoever, but his behaviour was most definitely canine, and I began to think that a muzzle might become appropriate at some point in the near future.

It all began in the pre-diagnosis days, and I was told by the 'professionals' that because my son was an only child he was not developing social skills, and, as a mother, I *had* to do something about it. At the time, my response should have echoed my gut feeling – he chooses not to socialize because he doesn't actually *like* anybody. But, no. I was desperate to make (if not force) my child to act like other children, and so I nodded in agreement and did my motherly duty; I dragged him to every kindergarten and mother-and-toddler type of group I could, and forced the horror of preschool on the poor...dog.

When I was pregnant, I was most *definitely* going to have the perfect child. It was going to be so immaculate that I even considered trying for conception in a similarly perfect way. I suppose this would have been mistake number one, as when the next virgin mother is to be chosen, I may not be on the list of nominees.

Child was to be called Jessica (did you think for one minute that I was going to say 'Jesus'?) or Charlie, and child would be sweet and cherub-like. Child would love school, speak fluent French before the age of six months and would, with little effort, be invited to attend university at the age of eight. Oh yes, parents would seethe and gossip enviously about the perfect child who was immaculate in every way and the halo that glowed around it and its family. Mothers would contort their faces – no, their whole *bodies* – because of this most pristine example of childhood. (Do all mothers have this same odd and scary assumption, or should I assume – in an odd and scary way – that either I was utterly mad or it was due to an electric shock?)

But then it didn't quite happen that way, did it? I still ended up with 'perfect child' and I have learned to be grateful for that in a quizzical and amused sort of way, but I wasn't quite aware of this strange twist of fate in the early days and I thought our heavenly glowing auras had maybe got lost in the post. To be honest, I have come to the conclusion that they were never dispatched in the first place and something odd and scary at the aura factory stole them for itself.

The first day with Bobby as a dog went reasonably well – he still sat to the table to eat. Yes, he *did* eat out of a bowl, lapping up the food with his tongue (in a very skilled way, I must add), but I could live with this. After all, how hard could it be? I drew the line at old scraggy bones and letting him out on the garden for toileting.

It is fair to say that Demi was enjoying this new-found friend. Instead of Bobby pulling her tail, Bobby-Dog would scamper around the carpet with her and generally copy everything she did. Many hours were spent playing 'chase the squeaky ball' and 'see who can bark the loudest' when the postman arrived. Paper was chewed up, fluffy toys pulled to pieces and, generally, it was all good, harmless doggy fun.

Ironically, as a dog, Bobby could be quite calm, especially when he was being stroked and chewing something rubbery. He also curled up nicely in the dog basket with Demi and attempted to sleep on a beanbag. All in all, things could have been worse. And then things *did* get worse.

Putting a collar on him was a bit of a trauma. I decided against it for health and safety reasons: if Bobby had found himself hooked to a curtain pole, it would have been very hard to explain. I *was* expected to clip a leash to the edge of his sweatshirt, however. 'Come on, Doggy!' I would say joyfully as we wandered around the house, while he panted and looked up at me with big eyes. 'Good Doggy!' I would say, frowning to myself and wondering exactly how much psychological harm I could be inflicting upon him. The whole act was looking a little bit worrying, and I had all sorts of visions of me being the catalyst for his disturbed future relationships and fetishes.

Nonetheless, I learned to walk Bobby-Dog around the house while completing a whole host of other chores such as picking up toys, plumping the cushions, doing a bit of polishing. As housework goes, having a child on the end of a leash doesn't really hinder your progress *that* much.

Demi would follow behind, jumping and playing and tripping me up so that I fell down the stairs, but, hey, there are worse things to do on a Monday afternoon than fall down the stairs and narrowly avoid breaking your neck.

Answering the door to friends and neighbours was a bit more awkward and so it was generally avoided. Answering the door to neighbours and friends has *always* been something to be avoided because whether Bobby is a boy, dog or galloping wildebeest, it has often caused grief in one way or another due to his complete intolerance of people invading his space.

This, however, was nothing compared to the horror of taking my son – sorry, the dog – to the morning sessions of hell – otherwise known as the toddler groups, kindergartens and preschool sessions. From this point onwards I will refer to these sessions as 'torture', as this is the phrase that has been used for them ever since.

The first session of torture arrived, and as we walked into the waiting area, a billion eyes were fixed on me and Bobby. It was, realistically, more like 41 eyes, but it certainly felt like more. I realize that there is an odd number of eyes there, but my recollection is that there was a very *odd* feeling to the whole situation. I had, luckily, remembered to remove the leash and so Bobby-Dog was now like an escaped mad and wild animal with rabies. He scuttled into corners of the waiting area, sniffed at things that looked as if they had been there since Darwin discovered them, and gazed eagerly at people's ankles.

The next ten minutes seemed to go on for ever. Parents shuffled from one foot to the other in an exaggerated manner, as though they had something on their shoes and needed to be rid of it. The clock seemed to be ticking very loudly, while all 41 eyes were on me and the dog. I could hear the scraping of table and chair legs in the main room next door, the hushed words from one parent to another, other children giggling, little footsteps as the more eager ones tried to sneak their way into the room prematurely...and, crouched on the floor, the sound of my boy – tongue out, panting.

Another child approached him and my heart was suddenly in my mouth. (It is important to point out that one of my vital organs did not *literally* find its way into my communicating device, because when Bobby reads this, I would like to avoid two years' worth of nightmares which would be caused from visualizing something so horrible.)

With small child approaching, and heart not literally in my mouth but feeling like it, I had to wonder: Will he bark? Will he snap? Will he run for the door? Will he roll over and expect his tummy to be stroked? He waited quite calmly until the child got very close, then began a low grumbling snarl deep down in his throat. Everyone stood still, too scared to move, tumbleweed rolled past our legs in a rolling, tumbling fashion (not really, but it would have complemented the scene very nicely) and then it came: from the depths of the boy-dog's belly, one

Barking at parents and toddlers

huge bark. On a bark scale, this one would have been something to be *proud* of. Real dogs would have hung their heads in shame.

The whole room had been paused in silence as the 41 eyes, plus mine, had watched the situation in slow motion.

After the sudden and amplified bark, we had all lurched backwards, away from this rabid creature, and currently had our backs up against the wall. With nowhere else to look and nowhere to run, we stared at one another with horror in our eyes as the walls seemed to close in on us. But then I remembered: it was *my* son! So I had better do something about it!

Suddenly there was movement, and it wasn't the one odd eye rolling across the floor. The human children went into the main play room, although there wasn't so much giggling and excited anticipation any more. They all looked a bit subdued and wary now.

A grinning woman came out to welcome me and the dog to the group, and explained that, as a parent, I would be expected to go on the rota of helpers and stay for some future sessions. What joy. I would be able to spend a few hours watching human children playing nicely and learning social skills. I would watch them negotiate with each other about whose turn it was on the slide, help them sit and complete jigsaws and puzzles, listen to their basic conversational skills and smile lovingly at the little darlings who were painting pretty pictures for their parents.

In comparison, I would then keep an eye on my dog. I would watch him play skittles with the smallest children as he barged past them – unable to divert from the visual route of passage that he had made for himself. I would apologize profusely for the tears that the infants had been forced to cry, the paint spilled (thrown) on their pretty dresses, the bruises on their calves where my dog had whacked them with a spatula. Yes, joy indeed. (Someone remind me why I kept on going back.)

How I laugh at the memory. With hindsight, I should have acknowledged that a torture session would not be the best option. A kennel, or preferably *home*, would have been a much better and less stressful place to be. If not for the boy-dog, it would've been for *me*. After all, home is where the coffee is. I had, anyhow, missed my chance to escape, and now we were trapped with the grinning woman. Amnesty International would have been an appropriate organization to contact at this point. However...

> *'Hello there, young man, what's your name?'*
>
> *Bark!*
>
> *'Would you like to come and meet the other children?'*
>
> *Snarrrrrl.*
>
> *'Okay. Let's go and see if we can find you something to play with...'*
>
> *Yap!*
>
> *'I think Mummy should go now, and then you can settle in.'*
>
> *Bark! Yap! (Snarls and starts chasing his tail in distress.)*

Distantly watching this surreal conversation between teacher and dog take place, I decided that other parents are very amusing, especially those who do not have dogs for children. It seems that some people simply cannot hide the expressions on their faces when they are obviously disturbed and unnerved by the actions of a less than typical child. How boring. One mother had turned away and looked at the lovely view from a bricked-up window. One father began picking fluff from an area of his clothing that he should have been picking in the privacy of his own home. Two yummy-mummies, who were loudly discussing their villas in France, nearly trebled in size as they puffed up their already puffed-up chests and gaped like koi carp after taxidermy.

As for me, I began to feel as though I was shrinking into the cracks of the floorboards among the smell of playdough, paints, pee and PVA glue. I turned my back on the parents who were still firing confused and frightened glances at my child, and made a dash for the door. It was one of those doors that didn't really know whether it should be pushed or pulled, so obviously I drew even more attention to myself as I battled to get out.

While my son scuttled into the main room looking less like a happy puppy and more like a pit bull terrier, I, however, continued to argue with the door and floundered like a fly trying to escape the downward strike of a swatter. I could almost feel the hot breath of the parents behind me, waiting and watching to see if I was capable of opening a door, when, at last, I almost fell through it and then made my great escape to the car. (Why did nobody tell me that these torture places have security locks?) Then, as I sat, shaking like a leaf and with tears rolling down my cheeks, it suddenly occurred to me that:

- I had left my child-dog alone for the first time, in a place that smelled of things beginning with 'P'

- other parents were obviously not very nice people, and they did not like dogs in the same torture sessions as their own kids

- other parents did not like new parents, especially those who brought dogs and were incapable of opening doors

- there were obviously toys and activities to keep my dog occupied, but what on earth would happen at snack-time?

I had two and a half hours to entertain myself and beat myself up about being a pathetic mother before collecting him, and so, having cried a bit more and feeling incredibly upset, I telephoned Granny. (I may have slapped myself with a rolled-up newspaper a few times too, but I can't actually be sure.)

'He's gone. I feel sick.'

'He'll be fine, don't worry.'

'Yes, but he is still a dog, and he has gone in there barking.'

'Oh dear. Did he growl or snap at anyone?'

This conversation was one that would be repeated for many months to come, and each time there would be a discussion about how to try and speed up the dog phase that Bobby had got himself into. I tried, fruitlessly, the subtle approach:

'Hey, Bobby! How about not being a dog any more?'

'Why?'

'Because you're actually a child and it's getting a bit difficult when you are barking all the time.'

'Why?'

'Because you frighten the other children, and adults are looking at you in a strange way.'

'So?'

'Well, it's just a bit awkward sometimes.'

'And...?'

'Look. You really need to learn how to play and share things with other children. Maybe if they weren't scared of you, you could play together and make some friends?'

'I'll keep being a dog, then.' Bark, bark, yap, yap.

For the following months, the barking and snarling continued, and the ten minutes in the waiting room carried on being a trauma. When I think back, I do laugh at the very thought of it, but, back then, the barking, snarling and snapping consumed my whole life. What I wouldn't give to return for a day and offer a different response, such as 'What's *with* you people? Have you never tried mixing the DNA of a child and a dog before? What sort of Philistines are you?' With that, I would toss my flowing locks behind me and whisk my clear skin and floaty dress out of the pee-y waiting room and pretend my villa in France awaited me.

The subtle approach soon turned to hostility, and I found myself *demanding* that the barking stop. The car journeys to the torture sessions were dominated by conversations about it. We role-played barking scenarios and thought up alternatives. Obviously, acting like a child was a *ridiculous* concept, so I thought of more appropriate animals to see if I could help him practise being one of those instead.

'Perhaps you could be a monkey – that would be fun!'

'There's nothing to swing from. I am a dog.'

'A snake?'

'So you expect me to slither, do you? I'm a dog!'

'Hmm, good point. A fish?'

'Don't be ridiculous. You'll find that I am a dog.'

'A bird?'

'Can't fly.' (Yawns.)

'I think giraffes are quite nice.'

'And how do you expect me to fit in the car? I am a dog – look at me!'

I enlisted the help of Granny, as I have done on so many occasions. She decided to take her grandson-dog to the torture rooms herself and see if he would behave any differently for her. We had great hopes that this would break the cycle and that Bobby would be exorcized of his canine alter ego.

And so it came to pass that one morning I merrily waved both child-dog and Mother goodbye, let out a huge sigh of relief and returned home. Bobby-Dog was now in the capable hands of a no-mess, no-nonsense, no-dog-owning Granny. There was *no way* she was going to tolerate a dog, boy-dog, beast-child or any permutation of it. She would march Bobby into the torture room and she would, with the physical and emotional strength of an ox on steroids with an EEE mentality, deliver a child with a sound mind and human persona. This was the beginning of the end of the whole doggy debacle. I called her with confident anticipation in my voice:

'Hi, Mum. Any luck?'

'I'm afraid not. He barked at two children, growled at a baby and snapped at the teacher.'

'Oh.'

'I don't know what we are going to do.'

'No. Me neither.'

It would appear that Bobby-Dog had no intention of becoming a child for anyone, and if he had, it certainly wasn't for anyone I knew. Eventually, after far too much torture for any dog or its owner to endure, I went and spoke to the teacher – again.

Deep in conversation about development stages, achievement charts and social capabilities, the teacher decided that my dog was incapable of interacting with his peers and she could not cope any more. I am not sure if it was the barking or the other disruptive behaviour that made her look as though she had not slept for three years, but it was decided that an educational psychologist should be called upon to visit.

I remember quite clearly that the teacher always did look rather shell-shocked when I returned at 'collect-your-dog' time. Other than the appearance of lack of sleep, it would seem from her hair that she may have had an electric shock during the session. Perhaps electricity was becoming a problem in our town? She always seemed to be trembling slightly, breathing in a shallow way, and I could almost hear the palpitations in her chest. Perhaps the sessions were torture for her too?

There was one thing for sure: she had no idea what to do with a boisterous boy or a disruptive dog. It was time, I decided, to move on. I took my dog away from the torture rooms and never ever returned. We didn't stick around long enough for the educational psychologist to arrange an appointment, and anyhow, by then I had decided that it was mad-hair woman who needed a psychologist.

'Listen, Bobby, we won't be going there again.'

'Goo goo? Why?'

'Because we won't.'

'Ga ga. Good.'

'I don't think it is doing you any good and I think it is upsetting you.'

'Yes. Mama...mama.'

'I should not have taken you there in the first place. They don't understand you and they don't seem to want to try.'

'Hmm. Diaper! Ooooh!'

'Are you listening to me?'

'YES!! But you obviously weren't listening to me when I told you all that three hundred billion years ago, were you?'

It was some months later, but much less than three hundred billion years, while walking through some woods with Bobby (who had now discovered that being a dog was not all it had promised to be and had taken an interest in making baby noises) that the torture sessions were mentioned again.

In a sudden fit of anger, frustration and distress, Bobby let out all the dark feelings that he had been carrying around inside him for far too long. We stood, in that wood, and Bobby erupted with more force than Vesuvius having a seriously bad day, PMT, spots and no dress in sight. And no villa.

Bobby cried and I cried. Bobby held me tightly and I squashed him in return. Bobby screamed and I covered my ears. He shouted abuse and I shouted some more in encouragement. The culmination of this outburst was him telling me that the woman (with the electrically shocked hair) had pulled his arms behind his back and dragged him into a corner. I suddenly had an attack of contorted-face syndrome.

The outburst continued. He said he had banged his head on a coat peg because no one was listening to him. I said nothing because I was trying to stop myself from killing someone. He said that he had been called 'stupid', and I started physically restraining myself with my rucksack. He said that he had been left to go to the bathroom on his own and he was frightened. I was struggling to regain circulation in my arms. He kicked a tree, and I said, 'Be careful, you'll damage the bark.' (There was no pun intended.)

It was then that I decided that electric-shock woman had better be very, very careful, because once I had unrestrained myself from the rucksack I had tied myself up in, and the blood was flowing again, I was one contorted face away from carrying out some torture of my own.

In time, and with a few more disappointments, I eventually found a better preschool for Bobby to attend. It wasn't perfect, but none of the teachers seemed to have strange hair, and this one had a sensory area called the Magic Room where the kids could go if things got a 'bit too much' for them. Bobby found the Magic Room so fascinating that *everything* became 'too much' on a daily basis and he practically took up residence.

Nothing, however, is nearly perfect for long, and it was not many days before the educational psychologist was requested again and the home/school diary commenced. Each entry was pretty much the same as the previous one:

School entry: 'A bad day. He refused to draw a picture, kicked children under the table at snack time and choked on his food.'

My entry: 'Sorry. I think he is very tired and hasn't settled in yet.'

School entry: 'Another bad day. He spun around in circles all morning and made himself sick at the snack table.'

My entry: 'Sorry. I think he is very tired and hasn't settled in yet.'

School entry: 'Yet another bad day. He smacked a child on the head with an easel, forgot his own name, refused to go to the bathroom because the toilet hadn't been sprayed with disinfectant, and kicked a teacher on the shin.'

My entry: 'Sorry. He is definitely very, very tired and he does find it incredibly difficult to settle in. For a long, long time. Sorry. Again.'

It was nearly time for Bobby to start 'real' school, and, in spite of being advised to hold him back for a few months, I decided that this would not necessarily benefit him. The long-awaited educational psychologist had still not manifested itself, and the sooner my little preschooler got to know his new classmates and the longer he had to acclimatize, the better.

After three months of being in denial, I walked Bobby into his first session of school in September 2004. With hindsight, it was the best thing I did, but it was also the worst moment of my life. That boy, three times smaller than his schoolbag and half as heavy, did not bark. He did not cry, spin, flap his hands around or mention diapers, and he did not look back at me as I walked through the exit. He had, luckily, seen a piece of fabric with Thomas the Tank Engine on it, so I was no longer important.

The hours passed slowly and I cried. I rang the school to make sure he was okay. I cried some more. I ate a whole cake and checked the clock. Then I cried some more, drank lots of coffee and then felt very ill. Soon it was time to collect him, and I could not wait to see his little face – full of the joys of education and new friends! Bobby will have been a genius all day. He will have become more popular than anyone before him! He will have been the perfect example of good manners and good naturedness. (I am very good at setting myself up for disappointment.)

Bobby came out of his classroom, and I confidently beamed at him with a silly grin and cheeks aglow. He glared back at me with a furrowed brow and tightly pursed lips. He tried to move quickly, barging through the other children and parents, but the teacher caught my eye…'Could I have a quick word?'

And so it continued, but with one major difference. This time, someone was genuinely interested in my son's challenging behaviour. Someone knew that he wasn't just a badly behaved child with an attitude and a permanent frown. Someone had seen similar behaviour in other children. The word 'autism' was mentioned and no one flinched, cringed or took a sharp intake of breath. This truly was the beginning of a new journey.

'Mum? You know those torture sessions that you used to take me to when I was younger?'

'Yes?'

'Why did you do that?'

'I have absolutely no idea, sweetheart. Mummy must have been having a mad moment.'

'Yes. That's what I thought.'

'Do you like proper school any better?'

'No. What's for tea?

I wasn't worried at the response. I now had faith in an establishment which did not require Amnesty inspections and which seemed to treat me and Bobby as human beings (they were probably being slightly optimistic). So Bobby had said he didn't like school? A standard reply for millions of children, and how very, *very* 'normal'. I will tell you more about his opinions of school later, but, at the end of this chapter, I would like to leave you with a few light-hearted words of encouragement.

Don't think your whole world has come to an end if your child turns into an animal. It probably won't last for ever, and if it does, then just go with the flow. Trust your instincts when it comes to childcare establishments. If they look, smell or sound unsuitable, then they probably are. Use the same checklist for the people working there. Lastly, take notice of other parents with caution. You will get to know the ones you can trust – and the ones that are ignorant will probably continue to be so. *Their* problem – *not yours*. Just look at them as if they have two heads.

CHAPTER 3

TAPE MEASURES, STICKS AND STEALING ROCKS

'Have you got my tape measure? Where's the tape measure? Have the people we are visiting got a tape measure? Get *off* my tape measure! You're treading on it!'

Welcome back. If you are still with me, you will, by now, probably rightly assume that it is *me* who needs therapy rather than my son. I have been flicking through my notes and recalling the days when Bobby required certain objects almost to be surgically attached to him.

Although a comfort blanket of sorts is a regular security measure for young children, the desired object or obsession is often more unusual or exaggerated for children with autism. It's that EEE thing again. Why have a nice fleecy blanket when you could have a rubber band, a rusty nail or a piece of copper pipe?

The placement of body parts has also been a contributing factor to our less than usual lifestyle. There have been times, for example, when the palm of Bobby's hand has rested on my cheek and has flatly refused to budge. Many a journey has been driven with my eyes having to work overtime because I have been unable to move my head.

My eyes are quite large, as are his, but when they are pushed to the extremities of their sockets, they can take on the appearance of two golf balls in a tumble dryer. Putting aside the safety aspects of driving a vehicle with only two golf balls for assistance, imagine how ridiculous it can look.

The palm of Bobby's hand still regularly takes up position on my cheek. Sometimes it appears above me in bed. It reaches over in a perfect arc and then drops right into position – usually like a dead weight, with the sound of a wet fish slapping against the hide of a damp horse. Obviously, your powers of deduction will work out that Bobby chooses my bed above and beyond any other. I will attempt my justification of this later. I am experienced in my defence of this particular habit of his, as I have spent nearly a decade perfecting it for the benefit of the 'professionals' out there.

At three o'clock in the morning, and with the hand hovering above me, I can do little more than await its impact. If I wake myself up enough to catch the hand first, I can guide it into position and secure a safe and painless landing. More often than not, I am far from awake until the sting of the hand resonates around my head.

The hand itself is not an unpleasant fixture, and although it has caused great difficulty when attached to my cheek, I much prefer that to the days when it decided to start slapping me. Bobby himself did not really have control of the hand and it would lash out at any unsuspecting moment. The hand was akin to an independent being, living an autonomous life. Hand would flap, Hand would slap, Hand would book itself a vacation and go AWOL on occasion. Conveniently, Hand could usually be found at the end of a confused, dizzy and disorientated arm.

Hand now has a very close friend called the Other Hand. Together they happily slap anything in sight, particularly their owner's own cheeks, and together they can drum the perfect rhythm of many a tune. Worryingly, Hand and the Other Hand also have a habit of drumming on people's buttocks. The buttocks usually belong to me, but no one's buttocks are *completely* exempt.

Palm of Hand on my cheek *could* be quite pleasant at times. I feel it necessary to point out that I am referring to the cheeks on my *face* at this moment. Slapping, flapping Hand could be quite painful. The nightmare came when happy, slappy, flappy Hand changed to Forehead – and slapping was substituted by an isolated incident of knocking me out and breaking my nose. This was not even *remotely* amusing at the time, although as my nose had been broken before by a particularly evil and low flying parrot, the second break cosmetically corrected the first one. So, with hindsight, things could have been worse and at least I no longer had to consider paying for surgery. An added benefit is that I can now laugh at the incident and forget the pain – a bit like childbirth.

It was early one morning, around 5 a.m. to be precise, when Bobby decided tape measures were very interesting things. Not to measure with, not to learn centimetres or inches, but to drag in a perfectly straight line behind

him. Why had he chosen a tape measure when he had
so many toys to pull around? Why do these obsessions
always manifest themselves at hours of the day that don't
really exist for other people? Why, oh *why*, was I even
contemplating dragging-items at 5 a.m. on a Friday
morning? Because, obviously, there was no option.

Quite often there *is* no option because I know all too
well that if there's something to be discussed, then Bobby
is going to discuss it – whether it is a perfectly acceptable
time of day or whether a tornado is bearing down on us.
As the dawn chorus chirped happily at 5 a.m. on that
Friday morning, the tape-measure obsession was born
and, by 5.10 a.m., it was in full swing. Literally. It swung
around the room, it swung around his head and it swung
too close to me and slapped me across the face.

I blame my mother. As a 'crafty' type of woman – you
know the sort: wool, fabric, knitting needles and crochet
hooks all over the place – she often had tape measures
idling around the house like pet snakes. I had better not
mention 'slithering' because it got me nowhere the last
time I suggested it. In fact, she probably had so many
that, end to end, she could measure from her street to the
end of the earth and back. Bobby's aunt once suggested
that Granny had created so many crafty items in her life
that she had probably crocheted the very house in which
she lived.

So, from that morning onwards, wherever Bobby
went, a tape measure would be sure to follow. Preferably
a white one, although any colour would do if there was a
shortage. A creased tape measure or one slightly frayed at
the edges was not so good. Well, it wouldn't lie perfectly
flat, would it? And if it doesn't lie perfectly flat, then
there's no *way* that tape measure is going to be dragged
in a perfect line.

When Bobby went to the bathroom, the tape measure went too. If we visited a friend, then the tape measure came too. If we visited family, then not only would the tape measure join us, but we would telephone ahead to make sure there was a spare one just in case it got lost in transit. Bobby would search through people's belongings, eager to find tape measures of any description. A great-aunt provided three. Granny must have checked every corner of the crocheted house as *she* discovered quite a mountainous collection – some dating back to the 1940s (the rest dating back to the ice age).

'Do you have a tape measure, Aunty?'

'I should have one somewhere. Why?'

'Because I need one.'

'It looks as if you have a few already.'

'I need a spare.'

'You have a spare one in your pocket and another spare one in your mum's bag.'

'I need a spare spare just in case the spare gets lost.'

'Okay, shall I see if I can find you one?'

'Yes, please. And a spare one would be good.'

The tape-measure thing was quite harmless. There was little risk of Bobby accidentally wrapping the tape around his neck, because he would have been anxious not to ruin the nice straight line it made. On many lonely evenings, however, it would be me who sat with a few hundred tape measures, attempting to untangle them before Bobby awoke the following morning to find a spaghetti-like concoction.

Come to think of it, the tape measure was a symbol of a more serious and sinister fascination with straight lines. There were trains and train tracks, of course, the lining up of toy cars, pencils and books. There was, and still is, the obsession of organizing family members into a very straight line – single file – when out on a walk.

'Get back in line, Mum!'

'But I want to talk to your granny.'

'Why?'

'Because I need to tell her something, but she is in front of me and I can't see her face.'

'Then talk to the back of her head.'

If anyone is brave enough to move out of line, then beware. The procession will be brought to a halt and the leader will come to put you firmly back in your place. Needless to say, it is *Bobby's* place to be at the front. And, no, talking is not advised, because it draws attention to oneself and everything is likely to come to a halt again.

Perhaps when out walking with the family in our regimental row, we could spice up the outing by incorporating another obsession and slap the buttocks of the family member in front. We already look ludicrous, so why not take it to a whole new level?

Things are not so bad these days, because if we *do* go out for a family walk, we know what is expected of us and automatically file into place as soon as we leave the crocheted house. Yes, we get stared at, but at least there's no barking involved and I am sure it brings much amusement to onlookers: 'Oh look, honey – there goes that family that walks in a straight line and never speaks to each other. Hold the lunch – let's wait and see how they negotiate that tight corner…'

There were many times when the tape-measure and single-file-walking obsessions were conjoined, and this was particularly difficult as it increased the length of our human procession by another four feet and six inches. With lots of practice, however, our meandering group was able to cross roads, walk over bridges, almost tackle tight corners and even move around our homes in a similar fashion. We were the perfect linear family and *proud* to be straight.

This straight walking continued throughout Bobby's first few years at school. Along with the continuation of a train obsession which started the moment Bobby was born – yes, he was born chuff-chuffing his way into the maternity delivery suite and arrived nearly two weeks late (typical of a train in the UK). Bobby would expect other children to trail behind him on the playground and *he* would be the engine at the front.

Whether a good or bad day had been had at school often depended on whether other children had joined his train and whether they had been compliant passengers or not. The novelty for many children lasted long enough to provide a few good days, but eventually the children found alternative means of getting across the playground (such as regular walking) and their interest waned.

The highlight for Bobby of one particular school year was when all the teachers, including the head (that's the head*teacher*, not a head that had become detached from someone's body) joined his train for the final day of term. This was, to Bobby, the best thing that could have happened on a school day, because his train had been endorsed and the trip enjoyed by the most important people in the building. It was a day he will never forget.

The tape measures and the train processions were a little less burdensome than a later obsession with rocks and stones. Between the ages of four and – actually, it's still going on – Bobby liked to collect stones, pebbles and rocks. Nothing unusual in that really – many children like to collect stones. Most children, however, do not fill their school bags with boulders and remove whole sections of the playground in order to bring them home.

'Your school bag is heavy. You must have a lot of books and homework.'

'I just have a few pebbles.'

'How many pebbles, exactly?'

'Not really pebbles…more like stones.'

'Well, you must have collected a lot of stones today.'

'Not really stones…more like rocks.'

(I open the bag to find a huge lump of concrete.)

'Hmm. Not really rocks, Mum… It's nice though, isn't it?'

I was running out of room for the pebbles and stones (and ideas for what to do with lumps of concrete).

Granddad once took Bobby down a cave on a guided tour and was intrigued to see him slowly bending up and down. When they returned home, Granddad found that his heavily weighed-down grandson's pockets had been filled with rocks from the cave, and the weight of these was causing his trousers to fall down.

The geology obsession had to be embraced, so we now have a garden complete with a pebbled area, rock garden and a few concrete sculptures. (We pretend it's modern art.) Bedroom shelves display a selection of beach pebbles and crystals, drystone walls and hard lumps of tar. Some things are unidentifiable and I would prefer them to stay that way.

Although the rocks caused me some concern, mainly due to their size, I much preferred these to what I found one day in his sandwich box.

'There is grass in your sandwich box Bobby...what for?'

'Don't touch it! The contents are very precious.'

'But I have to clean it out and get your lunch ready for tomorrow.'

'No! Don't touch it!'

'Could we put the precious contents somewhere else? I will make sure it is somewhere safe.'

'No! They will die!'

(I calmly step away from the sandwich box.) 'Okay, could you tell me exactly what is in the sandwich box?'

'You can peep.'

(I peep in the sandwich box, heart pounding.) 'SNAILS?!'

It would appear that, while at school, Bobby had decided his new mission would be to rescue the wildlife and bring it home. At lunchtime, he had stumbled across a few snails, put them in his pockets and then transferred them into his sandwich box ready for the journey to their new home.

'Well, Mum, would you want me to leave them there? Would you want them to get eaten by birds or crushed by those horrible children?'

'No...but they could get eaten by birds here...'

*'Hardly. Not when we are going to keep them in the kitchen.
And there are no horrible children in our house.'*

(I contemplated a sensitive reply to this ironic comment.)

Now, sticks are a different matter altogether. Tape
measures were reasonably easy to discipline and control,
rocks were too heavy to argue with, snails were happy
in their sandwich box, but sticks – phew, they really are
something else.

The perfect stick needs to be completely straight,
completely smooth and completely submissive. The
perfect stick must not break, include any sticky-out bits or
be either too short or too tall. God help anyone who has
a more perfect stick than Bobby, because the offending
person will be struck with force with his offending stick
(as Granddad knows all too well).

At the preschool of the electrified woman, there was
great concern that every time Bobby went out to play
outside, the first thing he would do was start a stick search
party. Personally, I didn't see what the big deal was, but
then I was told he was wielding sticks like batons and
swinging them around in an attempt to take out as many
children as he possibly could. Surely, boys will be boys?

My pretend laid-back attitude towards the 12 children
who were struck down was prematurely cut short, as it
was explained to me that the woman with the live current
running through her had been taken hostage with the
wooden weapon and had been held at stick-point,
outdoors, for quite some time. It was raining (rather
dangerous for *her* in particular, what with water and live
currents not being too friendly with each other) and cold,
and all the other children had been safely evacuated.
Well, then – no harm done. At least the stick did not have

bolt-ons, which is something that came to be another problematic issue.

In yet another wood, on yet another linear walk, Granddad made the mistake of finding the *perfect* stick. But this stick was like no other – as well as being perfect in every way, it came with an end attachment called 'a whaspy bit'. The whaspy bit was to be used for plucking up leaves from the ground and flicking them behind one's shoulder. Granddad was very happy with this. Grandson was definitely *not*.

'Granddad, can we swap sticks?'

'No. I like my whaspy bit.'

'But I haven't got a whaspy bit.'

'But I am using my whaspy bit.' (Proceeds to pluck up leaves *and flick over his shoulder in a conceited manner.*)

'That's not fair! Give me your stick. I need a whaspy bit.'

'No. Go and find your own whaspy bit.'

This particular incident shaped the stick incidents of the future, and Granddad does not take offence when we suggest that he may have a very slight spectrum of his own. From that point onwards, no stick was ever good enough and there seemed to be a countrywide whaspy-bit shortage. Whatever stick was found for Bobby (and a stick is a prerequisite for most walks), they were denied, declined and heartlessly rejected. Note: low self-esteem in sticks is becoming more prevalent, but no one is sure whether it is due to better diagnostics or something more controversial.

The whole walk would then be a time bomb while I shuffled in the undergrowth and climbed up trees. The first stick would break, and Bobby would stamp up and down, blaming the tree from which the stick had come. The next stick would have soil on it (you can't really blame it), and that would make his hand dirty. More tantrums and throwing himself about would ensue. The fiftieth stick would still have bark on it, which made it rough, and the two-hundred-and-forty-seventh stick would look *too* wooden. There is nothing worse than a stick that is too wooden. The stickless boy would sob uncontrollably and blame the world for being such an unjust and evil place. He would glare at passers-by as though they had deliberately placed the reject sticks there themselves.

'Mum! What is he *looking at?'*

'Please keep your voice down.'

'What are you staring at?!'

'Please stop being so rude to people.'

'He is looking at me as though I am mad! Imbecile!'

'Yes, well…'

'Fine. Fine! FINE!! I am mad, yes, look everyone, mad, mad, mad! What a bunch of imbeciles!'

Not so long ago, Bobby and I enjoyed a sunny afternoon sitting near a river. I found three eligible stick candidates and the successful applicant had graduated in whaspiness. Eager to feed the ducks, lumps of bread were attached to the whaspy bolt-on and the stick was held above the water like a fishing rod. What an invention – the first whaspy duck-feeding fishing-rod utensil™. The ducks, however, looked confused and disturbed. One looked positively traumatized and was never seen again.

'Come on, ducks. Come and get your food.'

(Ducks swim around aimlessly.)

'Come on…come on… Here's some nice bread for you.'

(Ducks not interested.)

'Oh, come on! I have got bread for you!'

(Ducks subtly look in a different direction.)

(Stands up and shouts) 'Look! Bread! Come and eat it!'

(Ducks start to talk among themselves.)

'Oh, for God's sake! Just take the bread!'

Tears began to form in Bobby's eyes, frustration took hold and the whaspy bit quivered under the weight of the now soggy bread. Bobby did not quite know what to do as the ducks had clearly not understood what was expected of them, and this was *not* good. In an eager attempt to escape the scene, Bobby hastily turned. And slipped. And fell into the river.

It took me an hour to convince Bobby that the ducks were quacking at the disturbance and not laughing at *him* in a sadistic way. I'm not so sure myself. Bobby's shoes, in the meantime, were placed in the centre of a hot oven and dried out nicely. I didn't check them for sponginess and a light golden brown colour, but it was one of my better baking attempts.

Now the strange thing is that all rejected and broken sticks have to come home with us. I don't know why this is so, but we have a lovely stick display at the side of the concrete, opposite the pebbles and near to the plate-sized pond.

Nothing has really changed with regard to sticks, stones and broken bones (although my nose has, luckily, retained its shape). Things are still expected to be straight, and whaspy bits still cause grief. There is still a collection of odd rock-type things in the house and garden (actually, I found something in a paint tin today that looked like a piece of moon rock), and train tracks are still built in the house to a straight specification whenever walls and window ledges will allow.

Incidents involving things like lines, sticks and soggy pieces of bread point towards a trait of Bobby's which quite often causes madness and mayhem. If he sets out on a project and works very hard at it, there will be a perfect plan of what to do and what the result should be. If 99 per cent of the plan works out well, then that is not sufficient to say it has been successful. That all-important missing 1 per cent will mean the project is a complete and utter failure and a tantrum of some sort will be justified. He certainly does not get this theory from me, as I don't consider myself to be too much of a perfectionist. If a project of mine manages to reach 51 per cent completion, among the many distractions and lack of sleep, then as far as I am concerned, it's been a great success. If you notice that this book finishes with a very abrupt ending, that'll be why.

'Argh! That's it! I may as well just kill myself!'

'It's okay, Bobby. Let's have a look and see what has happened.'

(Between sobs) 'I was making a jet-propelled car and it had to have extra exhausts, and the exhausts are not the same height or shape and they won't stick on! And now I have wasted two bits of tin-foil because the exhausts will have to come off and I will have to start again! Forget it! Just forget it!' (More crying.)

'Okay. Well, the exhausts look the same size to me. There must only be about a millimetre difference between them.'

'*Exactly! They are not the same size, then, are they? Stupid!*'

'*Let's take them off and do some new ones, then.*'

'*No! No! Just forget it. Just go away, and I will throw it in the bin. I hate life. I might as well just die. Why is my life so horrible? Why is nothing ever right?*'

'*I think that's a bit over the top.*'

'*Fine! You go and waste more foil, then. Do what you like, I have had enough of life. Just forget it. My whole day has been ruined. My whole life has been ruined. I hate life, I hate today and I am stupid. I am so stupid that I can't even get two bloody bits of foil to be the right size. Why was I born?!*'

'*Would you like something to eat?*'

'*Cheese sandwich, please.*'

If ever you are in doubt about obsessions and collections, then remember that it could always be worse. I will have to write very carefully now because whatever obscure obsession I mention, one of you is likely to jump off your chair and say that your child has it. Okay…I am back to treading on eggshells… Well, let's say, for instance, very hypothetically, that your child has an obsession with collecting alkaline batteries. This is much better than an obsession with alkaline batteries being hammered open with Granny's false teeth and the contents being used to smear over your eyeballs while watching your favourite TV channel. I think I am pretty safe with that one, but please get in touch if not.

Embrace obsessions and collections as much as you can, unless they are seriously harmful to your child or anyone else. If your daughter cannot leave the house without a pump-action bottle full of water to squirt at everything, so what? Just as long as she isn't near anybody electrified, then who cares what people think? If your son decides that dragging a piece of string with an old knob from your bedroom cupboard and a magnet on it is the way to go, then just bear in mind that the knob may come in handy at some point. If he starts propelling it around his head and fracturing skulls, only then is it time to intervene. Don't take it off him – just ask the skulls to go somewhere else.

Lastly, if some narrow-minded individual looks perplexed or disturbed that your 13-year-old child is chewing a piece of wool, humming to herself, holding a bunch of chives in both hands and walking backwards while avoiding cracks in the pavement, then state that Madonna was seen doing exactly the same thing in *Vanity Fair* last month. Perspectives will suddenly (and drastically) change. And then you can laugh – *at the fickle absurdity of 'normal' people.*

CHAPTER 4

TROLLEY WARS AND BATTLES WITH FRUIT

'I am not going shopping. There is no way I am going shopping. I hate it, it's boring and it makes me really mad. People who go shopping must be mad or something, because it is a stupid thing to do. If you make me, don't expect me to be good. And don't expect to get me through the door.'

Taking Bobby to a supermarket is not my idea of fun. I know he hates it, he knows he hates it, and I know that he knows that I know he hates it. Sometimes, though, through no fault of my own, my food-shopping trips (which I try to schedule in when Bobby is otherwise engaged) become out of sync with what's in the fridge. When I notice that the fridge is hosting just half a pineapple, one clove of garlic and a stray pea, then it is unfortunate but inevitable that I am going to have to go and shop – with Bobby.

I plan to arrive as soon as the shop opens so that it is quieter, and I always take something small to keep him entertained, such as a piece of concrete or something squidgy that oozes in different directions (I seem to have a fascination with oozing), but nothing works. A full-sized model of the *Titanic* would definitely work, but, just like a giraffe, it wouldn't fit into the car.

The moment arrives and the shop opens. We enter the foyer with trepidation and I let Bobby push the shopping cart as it has wheels – this should keep him happy for long enough for me to dash around the aisles and grab things like a mad woman. One particular day, however, the cart had other ideas. It wasn't so much that he had a desire to cause mayhem; no, it was definitely the fault of the cart.

Things were going well until the shop went into full swing. Cash registers started beeping, lights were flashing, people were talking, announcements about the latest offers were being made, and busy shop assistants were wheeling giant cages around. Bobby was not amused by this hive of activity, and as I tried to speed up, this only served to cause more distress.

Grabbing things that I wouldn't usually grab (but nothing to cause any offence to anyone and certainly no body parts), I weaved in and out of displays and tried to assist Bobby in his attempts to keep the trolley under control. That's a laugh in itself really. Keeping Bobby under control is one challenge I haven't yet mastered, but Bobby with wheels requires a five-day training course at least.

Bobby started to do odd things with the trolley. I tried to be quick and efficient, prodding plums and squeezing melons (in a non-offensive way). I avoid the kiwi, just in case I encourage echolalia of the kiwi kind, and I steer

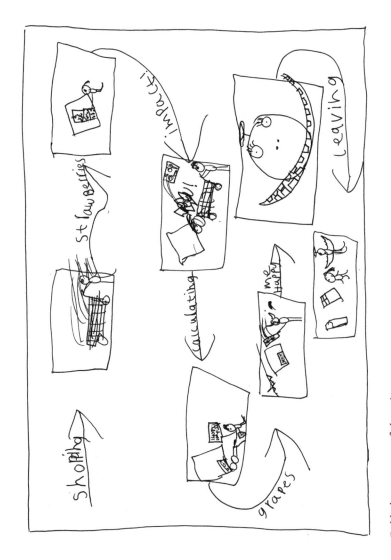

Bobby's story map of shopping

away from bananas – because Bobby would be likely to tell the nearest person, at length, of his allergy to them.

Another sideways glance and I was sure that the trolley was veering out of control. Bobby seemed to have got it in a spin, quite literally, and it was making its way towards a huge display of packaged strawberries. My son was standing on the back of it and seemed unaware that his mode of transportation has lost all sense of direction and was careering towards a perfectly docile pile of fruit. I think I closed my eyes, but when I eventually opened them, I saw it all happen – round and round the cart went, and the out-of-control driver started to look dizzy and disorientated.

Meanwhile, back on Planet Earth, at the side of the strawberry display, bending over to study each packet with great concentration, stood an innocent shopper. She was unaware of the runaway cart and in her own little strawberry world, until it ploughed straight into her backside and knocked her flying into the unassuming pile of fruit. She landed face down and spread-eagled.

At that moment, I died for five seconds. Bobby went into a daze and I am *positive* that he was calculating the amount of carnage he had caused by recalling the angle that the trolley had hit the first strawberry and the estimated speed at the point of impact.

Other shoppers stood and looked and watched, making disapproving noises (like when you have something stuck between your teeth and try clicking and clucking like a hen to try and get it out). I was still deliberating whether the pearly gates of heaven were a safer option and if I had done enough good deeds in my life to be let in, or whether I should get myself back to the crime scene.

Among all of this clicking, clucking and deliberating, I then remembered that there was still an injured party on the floor of the supermarket covered in strawberries and she still wasn't moving. So, pretty quickly, I returned to the little face of a very worried and scared-looking boy. He had turned the colour of an olive. It would have been a green olive because anything red would have indicated embarrassment and there didn't seem to be any of *that* on display from *him*. Nonetheless, he did look rather bemused and quite ill.

Suddenly, I remembered my manners, walked towards the horizontal strawberry woman and bent down to talk to her. I asked her if she was okay, but there was no answer, although I did see a flicker of movement within the pile. I began to move the offending cart out of her way and then bent down again to offer her my hand for support. Shaking her head in disbelief, I asked her again if she was okay. She continued to shake her head, and then her shoulders and neck, and then the rest of her body.

Apologizing profusely to the shaking strawberry shopper, I encouraged Bobby to say something apologetic.

'Look what has happened!'

(Starts to look around the shop to see if he could see what was happening.)

'Here! Look! Here! Look what has happened to this poor lady!'

(Looks at woman with his olive-green complexion and eyes so sunken that they were on the back of his head.)

'I think you ought to say something to this poor lady...'

(Looks at me with a frown) *'What would you like me to say?'*

Once again, in a very British way, I acquired my posh voice and offered my most sincere regrets to the woman, who, by this time, was walking out of the door, still shaking. The other staring shoppers punctuated their disgust with a sigh, a couple of clucks and a shake of their heads, and then dispersed among the pineapples.

Many hours later, and when Bobby's colour had returned to his cheeks, I began to explain to him the requirements of good cart-handling and how he should make himself aware of other people in the space around him. He did not listen much because he was face down on a table, spinning himself around, but he did ask one very interesting question.

'You know how the lady was looking at the strawberries a lot? And you know how she was looking at every detail of them? Well, if they were so important to her, then why did she leave the shop and not buy any?'

I thought it a fruitless exercise to explain that maybe the strawberries were not so important to her after the degradation of being sprawled across a supermarket floor, so I didn't bother. I just looked as confused as he did, and pretended to share his concern at the lack of a purchase.

That was not the only time that Bobby found himself in a difficult position in the vicinity of fresh produce. Another badly scheduled emergency shopping trip caused more distress for the consumers at our local supermarket.

Knowing from the outset that I could expect trouble, I explained to Bobby that we would be very quick at making a purchase, and that it was important for us to buy a present and deliver it to the recipient on time. This seemed to be understood and he helped to choose some gift wrap which was on a long cardboard tube.

'Can I stand behind you because I don't want to get squashed in the queue?'

'Yes, but stand just there near the grapes where I can see you and hold the gift wrap. When I call you, bring the gift wrap to me and then I can pay for it.'

'Okay. I am here, look. Near the grapes. Holding the gift wrap. Waiting for you to call me.'

(After a short time) 'Okay, I am ready for the... What are you doing?'

He had been trying to hook up the bags of grapes with the roll of gift wrap, and it hadn't really worked out. So, in his frustration, he was now thrashing the gift wrap around like a samurai sword and beating the grapes to within an inch of their lives.

I continued to call him, but Bobby was far too engrossed in punishing the grapes for refusing to be hooked. I apologized to the cashier and marched towards him, still trying to get his attention. He could not hear me for the sound of grapes hitting various people and articles around the shop.

An escapee grape flew from its bag and hit me on the ear. A few more followed suit and saw their chance for freedom, jumping from their bags and rolling under shelves and people's shoes, which wasn't a very sensible thing to do if they wanted to escape unblemished.

'Stop! What on earth are you doing?'

'Trying to sort out these damn grapes!'

'But why are you hitting them with a roll of gift wrap?' (There is no text font called 'High Pitched and Frantic', so bear in mind that I was at least an octave higher than usual.)

'I. Am. Trying. To. Get. Them. With. The. Hook!'

'They. Are. Not. Supposed. To. HOOK!'

'Then why do the bags have hooking handles on them?!'

(A bit quieter and now not talking through my teeth) 'Because the handles are there to make it easier for people to hold their bag of grapes.'

'Oh, I see. Are you ready to pay for the gift wrap now?'

We made our way back to the cashier, who was politely pretending that kids beat the bags of grapes regularly, and paid for our goods. I did not buy any grapes, as I knew what condition they would be in.

The response from other customers in the queue was mixed. Some looked horrified, some looked as though they were stifling grins and some didn't quite know how to look. As is usually the case after one of these events, I took Bobby by the hand and walked from the shop as though nothing had happened. Out he skipped with the gift wrap, quite happy that his work there was done.

Getting into the car, I took a long, deep breath and let it out as slowly as I could. We *appeared* cool, calm and collected, which was more than I could say for the gift wrap. The truth is, I felt exactly the same as the paper – frayed, creased, crushed and worn out. I wasn't yellow with cartoon pictures of farmyard animals on me, though. At least that was good news.

Many, many years before, back in the days when Bobby still liked to ride in his stroller and before he could talk (and therefore offend anybody), he liked to hold out his arm to the side and see how many things he could knock off a shelf in one go. I have seen many other children do this before, so although I used to get annoyed, I was not overly concerned. It started with a few items before his arm began to ache, and then his arm became stronger and he was capable of more destruction. We were lucky that nothing breakable was ever at arm height.

Then, eager to improve his knocking-off capabilities, Bobby worked out how to twist his ankle to the side and remove the contents of bottom shelves while I continued pushing the stroller down the aisles, unaware of the trail of products behind me.

At a similar age, Bobby was still drinking from baby bottles, much to the disgust of other parents whose children had progressed on to china teacups. While being strolled around, Bobby learned (I have no idea how) to shake the bottle and hold the teat in such a way that he could spray a milk fountain and cover anything and anyone close by.

For some time, I fed Bobby as nature intended, but, though happy to help him latch on, I was incapable of unlatching him and used to walk along pushing an empty pram while holding him to my chest. He was a very hungry baby. Although breastfeeding is still rightly promoted as nothing to be ashamed of – in public or in private – there was something a little disconcerting about a mother trying to walk with an empty pram, a pained expression and a child dangling from her chest. So that is why, in public, we had reverted to the bottle method.

I will not confess to Bobby's age when I was finally able to stop buying new teats, as I will feel the need for more justification and it's getting late. Let's just say, I had to pretend to him that there was a teat shortage and there was *no way* I was going to able to find any within the next three months as they were having to be imported from China.

Admittedly, I had recently discovered that it was actually the rubbery teat that Bobby liked chewing on as opposed to the contents of the bottle. I have seen many children with autism who have various attractive chewing attachments such as colourful ribbons, soft spongy malleable sticks, rubber rings and soothers specifically made for the purpose, so I considered giving Bobby a rubber car tyre and then thought it may look a bit over the top.

I needn't have concerned myself, as Bobby decided for many years that chewing a corner of his sweater or T-shirt was just fine and was not at all put off by the big, damp patches on his clothes. He then progressed to sucking his school tie, which, after much discouragement, has now also stopped.

But back to the shopping. Hardware stores and garden centres are not exempt from Bobby's list of places where 'incidents' can happen.

One spring, I thought it would be nice if Bobby had his own little patch of garden and was encouraged to tend to it during the year. He was quite excited at the prospect of this and we went to the shops to buy flowers, shrubs and seeds. Obviously the colour, feel and shape of the plants was important to him and so he took his time and wandered around.

After a while, it appeared that he had not made any choices, but what I did notice was the path of petals behind us where he had casually plucked the petals from the plants and dropped them on the floor.

'What are you doing?'

'Dropping petals on the floor.' (My fault for asking a stupid question.)

'But you are pulling off the flowers and leaving them on the floor!'

'Yes. That's what I just said.'

'But you can't do that. People might want to buy those flowers.'

'But how will we find our way back out of the shop?'

'Because I know the way out of the shop.'

'But I don't. So I am leaving the petals on the floor so I can find my way back out.'

'If you do that, you will go back the way you have come, and go out of the entrance instead of the exit.'

'Then I won't throw them behind me.'

'Good boy. That's a good idea.'

'I will throw them in front of me.'

I thought that this was probably a strange twist on the tale of Hansel and Gretel and so I said no more. I did, however, walk at his side, kicking petals and flower heads out of view.

A few days after we'd planted the seeds, he spotted some weeds and was ecstatic because he believed his seeds had grown into something. The weeds were nowhere near where the seeds had been planted, but he was convinced and I felt I shouldn't argue with him. It did mean that for the rest of the summer I had to leave the weeds where they were. When the real seeds finally did grow into something interesting, Bobby believed that these were weeds trying to ruin his display of plants and proceeded to pull them up.

I hoped he wouldn't ask to go and buy more seeds as it seemed a waste of money when we could grow a multitude of weeds for free. But he did ask, and I did buy, and I was clever enough to put them in a propagator so he saw the results very quickly. After a few months, we then had to cope with plant death. Bobby could not have been more traumatized if the whole of his family had been struck down with the plague.

I recently died again when Bobby ran off in front of me and down the toy aisle but, at the time, I didn't know that is where he had gone. He flew out of sight within the few seconds that it had taken to check my wallet was in my bag.

Frantically running up and down the aisles, scanning each area and praying to God that he would reappear, I had just about lost all hope and was ready to call security. My sense of urgency and flying around was obviously contagious, as other shoppers began to do the same for no reason whatsoever. They didn't know that a boy was missing and they didn't seem to be in any sort of rush beforehand, but now they were shopping like tomorrow was never going to happen.

Just then, I saw the peak of a baseball cap very quickly disappear behind the cardboard cut-out of a large chicken. I'm not sure if the chicken was advertising the new release of a DVD, but it certainly wasn't advertising *chicken* – that's for sure. Well, unless chickens always wear helmets and fly biplanes.

Remember the scene in the original *Halloween* movie? It was just like that – every time I looked in the direction of the cut-out, the baseball cap disappeared.

'What are you doing?' (I ask that question a lot.) 'I thought I had lost you!'

(Talking through clenched teeth and without moving his lips) 'I am a piece of cardboard. Shhh…don't let people see you talking to me because they will think you are weird.'

'Yes, they will. But why are you a piece of cardboard?'

'I am trying to look like a cardboard chicken.'

'Why?'

'Why not? I don't tell you how to live your life.'

The cardboard chickens stood for a while longer and then the one disguised as Bobby decided to move. While I had been waiting for him, the peak of the baseball cap had popped in and out a few more times and the cardboard cut-out now looked as if it was staring directly at me. I stared back. I had, however, been standing there staring at the chicken for quite some time while Bobby had been a piece of cardboard, so I think the staff were beginning to wonder what I was doing. They could see me staring at a cardboard chicken, but they couldn't see Bobby *pretending* to be a cardboard chicken. So – not surprisingly – the staff looked concerned for my welfare and almost sympathetic.

So that's supermarkets and garden centres. Hardware shops are easy to tell you about – solar lights. That's about it. If the shop sells solar lights (what a great tongue-twister!), then we can forget paint, wood, hammers and nails because we are going home with *nothing* but solar lights. Do we need solar lights? No. Could we think up any reason to make use of solar lights? No. Do we live in a dimly lit area and fall over our pathways every night? No.

I know – you are wondering what do we do with the solar lights. Aha…well, what we do is charge them up when it's sunny (it may sound obvious, but the sun only shines here between 12 noon and 6 p.m. for about two weeks every year) and then we light up the pile of sticks and concrete in the garden at night. Strangely enough, the solar lights are also shaped like rocks, so the illuminated rock and stick garden surely could be the envy of all our neighbours.

Restaurants and cafes are a different matter. The mere words fill me with anxiety and dread. The mere *mention* of them fills Bobby with much worse – vomit. There are a number of reasons why Bobby hates eating establishments.

- They are usually busy, because people tend to want to eat at the same times – strangely, mealtimes.

- The tables and chairs are usually spaced with just two centimetres between them, so you can't sit down if you want to.

- Because they are busy, and you can't sit down, there is lots of scraping of chair legs – Bobby's ears practically *bleed*.

- People eat food in cafes and restaurants, and sometimes the staff don't get to clear it up before the next person (who has to be a size triple-zero to slide between tables) sits down.

- You have to wait. And wait. And wait a bit more. This is why people are size triple-zero – because they never get to eat.

Imagine a hot day on a day trip (so Bobby is in an unfamiliar place wearing two pairs of sunglasses and, on that particular day, two baseball caps with the peaks facing different directions so that he looks like a cross between Stevie Wonder and Dumbo) and I have forgotten his food box. We have to eat because, first, we will die if we don't, and, second, it's mealtime and that's what people do. I explain this to Bobby and he goes as rigid as a cardboard chicken. There is no forgiveness and, yet again, I am Beelzebub and have done this deliberately just so that I can ruin his day. I persevere and we walk towards the restaurant/cafe (it was kind of a hybrid), me quite loose and floppy, Bobby very stiff. Nightmare of all nightmares: there is a queue. The cardboard boy starts to loosen up enough to start throwing his arms about and he begins to vent his frustration by insulting the size triple-zeros. I don't worry about this as they are not big enough to fight back. Thinking I can divert his attention elsewhere, I suggest Bobby peeps outside to see if there are any benches free so that we can sit away from everybody else.

'No. No benches.'

'You haven't even looked yet.'

'There are NO benches.'

'I will get us something that we can take out with us and we will sit somewhere else.'

'There is nowhere else.'

'We are in the middle of about four acres of gardens – we will find somewhere. Don't worry.'

'There is nowhere *else! There are billions of people out there and nowhere to sit.'*

I stand my ground and pay for the food while Bobby begins to spin and flap his arms around. I make a quick exit and there, in very clear view, are five free benches. Now, either the people who had been using them had moved very quickly – all at the same time – or Bobby had not been able to see the free seats because of the mass of shade he had covered himself in. I am very surprised that he does not attach himself to a meandering cloud in the style of the fashion icon, Eeyore.

'Look – we can sit here.'

'Argh!'

'It's only a wasp – I will get rid of it.' (A wasp was buzzing around a bit of food that someone had left on the table.)

'Arghhhhhh!!!'

'Stand there, and I will get rid of the wasp.'

'It's not the wasp, you imbecile! It's the...(gags a few times) food!' (gags a bit more.)

I ferret around in my bag (a description that is very accurate, having been the owner of ferrets in another life and knowing what they look like when in a bag) and try to find the antibacterial wipes. Antibacterial wipes are something that we take *everywhere* as they are needed on many occasions: cleaning public lavatories before Bobby will use them, wiping his hands should a molecule of anything sticky touch them, and as an emergency cooling measure should we run out of the three packs of cooling wipes that we keep in the car (along with the cooling spray).

As I continued to do a fantastic impression of a ferret in a bag, I obviously did not get to the wipes quickly enough as Bobby was running up and down the seating area gaining the attention of the size triple-zeros and the hybrid cafe's staff. A woman walked passed and very helpfully said, 'For goodness' sake, it's only a wasp!' Yeah, I think to myself, very helpful. Thanks for that, lady, you have made things so much easier. Bobby was not so subtle: 'It's *not* the wasp! It's the damn, disgusting, vile, sickening food in this hell-hole of a dump! Somebody just get me out of here!' I was almost hoping that he would say, 'It's not the wasp, you sour-faced woman. It's the sight of your flaky knees in those figure-hugging shorts that you are clearly *not* size-zero enough to wear! Now go and get yourself a dress!'

Hearing the commotion, an annoyingly calm waiter swaggered to the table with a cloth and cleaned up the food with an exaggerated sweep of his right hand. He glared at me, glared at Bobby, and swaggered back inside with the type of attitude that only an annoyingly calm waiter can carry off. I didn't get chance to thank the man, as I was rescuing my ferrety hand from my bag in order to chase Bobby, who had now sprinted half the length of the four-acre gardens to somewhere unknown. I found him sitting under a tree, sobbing, with a wasp buzzing around his twin peaks. He could not bring himself to look at me as he was disgusted with my behaviour. Apparently.

'I found your antibacterial wipes...' (*I handed him one as a peace offering.*)

'How dare *you take me somewhere like that? How* dare *you put me through it?'*

'I was trying to be quick and I knew you would need something to eat. The table is clean now.'

(Looks at me and rolls his tear-stained eyes.)

'I am really sorry, but I thought if I was quick enough...'

'Don't even talk to me. Don't even look at me. You have ruined my day.'

'Sorry. I...'

'You're talking.'

Attempt hand signals to say, 'Shall we go back to the car now and go home?'

'We will have to sit in the car and eat the food.'

Looks back over the two acres to the bench and sees annoyingly
calm waiter removing our food and taking it away. Contemplate
self-flagellation. Try to think of a hand-signal that means,
'Errrr...I don't quite know how to say this, but...'

Looking on the bright side, it had been a sunny day so the
solar lights had charged up and the concrete was glowing
wonderfully when we returned home. No falling over on
the well-lit path for *us* that night.

I usually remember to keep food with me so that we
do not have to endure similar experiences, but Bobby
once decided to surprise me.

Having gone to great lengths to organize a room-
service breakfast at an unavoidable overnight stay in a
hotel one year, Bobby uncharacteristically decided to go
to the restaurant instead and sit in a very well-behaved
manner. The restaurant was reasonably quiet, pristinely
clean and, other than the morning coffee smells, Bobby
seemed quite at home. There was an ulterior motive to
his placid attitude.

The continental breakfast selection was on a circular
display in the middle of the dining area. This meant Bobby
could walk around it in circles, picking up croissants on
each cycle and stuffing them into a strategically placed
napkin. This was, he later told me, so that we did not
have to queue at any busy, dirty restaurants later in the
day.

Recently, supermarket fear has also been solved. We
now go late at night when the aisles are quite empty
and Bobby can speed up and down them in a cart with
reckless abandon and the wind blowing in his hair. Let's
be honest, it *is* one of the more interesting activities to
do in a shop. Try it one day and you'll realize that life
isn't about dawdling among the detergents. Life on a

supermarket cart and living with a child with autism can be viewed in the same way: *seize the moment and enjoy the ride.*

CHAPTER 5

HOLIDAY HORRORS AND DISASTROUS DAYS OUT

'I don't want to call anywhere on the way. We are taking the direct route, aren't we? I just want to see where we are staying and then we can do something else. I don't want to call and do anything else until I have seen where we are staying. Then we could do something else – as long as we take the direct route to get there and the direct route back to the place where we are staying – just as long as I can see that place first.'

You will find that this chapter is quite lengthy, so could I advise that you make yourself a drink and get yourself comfortable? It is lengthier because, first, more incidents occur when away from home or on an outing, second, Bobby is currently resting due to a sudden onset of hay fever and heat exhaustion caused by a freakily warm early summer's day (he is currently wearing very little but he does have his right sock on), and, third, I have accidentally drunk a few cups of strong caffeinated coffee which means I am now typing at the speed of light while on the ceiling.

Planning a holiday, vacation, day trip or any other small retreat from mundane life is a mission on a similar scale to planning a crossing of the Sahara Desert on a paddle steamer. For a trip lasting longer than a few days, the assistance of Granny and Granddad is often required as this means my son is surrounded by an additional two responsible adults who can track his every move, rather than just me – one bordering-on-the-responsible adult attempting and failing to keep some sort of order to the proceedings. I have gone it alone a few times, but I usually return home with an urgent requirement for respite care and a long-term stay at the local asylum.

Because of the two and a half responsible adults who are willing to embark on such an adventure (in the loosest sense of the word), there are a number of things that must be taken into account prior to making any reservations:

- Reserving accommodation out of school holiday periods so as to avoid overload of holidaying children.

- Coordinating holiday-leave for three adults all working in different places, and agreeing on the same week (which is out of the school holiday period).

- Does the potential accommodation allow dogs? We no longer own a dog, but we have to find out first and then reserve somewhere that does *not* allow dogs. This is to limit the risk of any dog hairs being found.

- Is the accommodation spacious and close to somewhere safe, quiet, as uninhabited as possible, with trees and preferably water? This is not so Bobby can entertain himself and joyfully run around outdoors like the children on advertisements. No, it is so that a single adult can take him out for a short while so that the other two can stand down for half an hour.

- And, not quite finally, as there are a dozen mini-criteria that have to be taken into account, but *nearly* finally... Is the accommodation accessible via a direct route with as little chance of delays or queues as possible, and can it be reached with the minimum chance of stopping anywhere else en route?

Once all of the above have been approved, then a reservation is made, usually between nine and twelve months in advance. This is to ensure that everything can be as organized as possible prior to the trip. The dates are recorded on the calendar and we can begin the countdown.

Packing is great fun. I usually pack as few clothes as possible so that I can utilize the space for essential accessories: a train track and trains, toy cars, paper and pens, Blu-tack, cuddly toys (a minimum of one but usually around twelve), a soft blanket, plenty of things to eat and drink, earplugs (for Bobby, but often more needed by the adults), sunglasses, sunhats, spare sunglasses, spare sunhats, cooling spray, wipes (yes, you had already guessed *those* items, hadn't you?), medical kit for hand luggage, extra

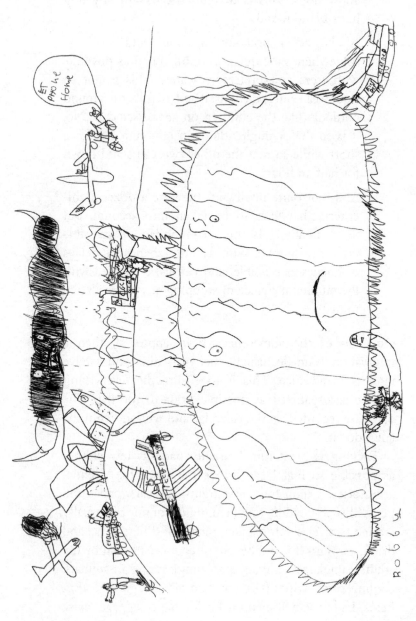

Holiday horrors – melting brain

medical kit (containing more medical items than the first) and extra-strong burst-resistant balloons (not inflated).

Balloons are wonderful things to have when all else fails, as they can be played with for hours. A balloon is more predictable than a ball because it is much more laid-back and it doesn't rush around erratically getting overcome with too much stimulation; it just takes its time and floats around as if it has all the time in the world to get to its destination. Bobby likes this as it gives him plenty of time to position himself ready to take a swipe at it the next time it descends.

'Where is my train track?'

'It's in the red suitcase.'

'Where is the red suitcase?'

'It's on the bed.'

'Where is the bed?'

'In there...' (*Points to the bedroom while the adults dash around trying to unpack because we have only just arrived at the accommodation. Slight delay as the train track is meticulously connected.*)

'I have done my train track.' (*Yes. Right in the middle of the main walkway of the room, causing the adults to trip over.*) *'Where are my trains?'*

Everyone looked at each other knowingly as the trains for the track had been left at home by mistake, and nobody knew what to say or do for fear that they might be cast out into the street. One and a half adults rushed to the nearest shop in an attempt to find trains. After all, the adults have only had *a year* to get organized, haven't they?

'What am I supposed to do now?!' The track found itself at the end of Bobby's foot before joining the balloon in the air. A track is not as laid-back as a balloon, and a track does not feel the same as a balloon when it hits you on the head. This is a sad fact of life.

Bobby and his entourage visited a seaside resort a few summers ago and he had set his mind firmly on purchasing a die-cast model of a traction engine. The entourage promised that a visit to the model shop had been planned during the week, and he ate, drank, slept and breathed the thought of his die-cast traction engine. I am sure this is a thought that *many* of us live and breathe every day, and, to him, it was *everything*.

The day arrived and anticipation hung heavy in the air. *So* heavy that the weight of it was resting firmly on the shoulders of the entourage, and a pleasant feeling it was most definitely *not*. So heavy was the burden that my height had reduced by three feet and my elbows were dragging on the floor and bleeding. Not to worry – I had the portable medical kit in my rucksack.

We all entered the model shop, one responsible adult at each side of Bobby and me bringing up the rear. The One to the right (Granddad) wasn't much use as he zoomed off at a tangent having spotted something interesting. The One to the left (Granny) studied the face of Bobby as it was exhibiting a peculiar grimace. I was still bringing up the rear like a sheepdog (that is, a dog that rounds up sheep rather than a morphed hybrid similar to a boy-dog) and so couldn't see the grimace which was clearly expressing its own alarm call: *Too Much! Overload! Get me out! Beep! Beep! Beep! Sirens!* So, I merrily started talking in an animated and dramatic manner which, allegedly, is something I do quite often.

'Oh look at all the models! I am sure we will find something for you in here!'

Bobby slowly swayed towards the glass cabinet which was packed full of more die-cast traction engines than a die-cast traction engine factory working overtime for the Die-cast Traction Engine Appreciation Society. I continued, 'Look! Look at all those traction engines!' I wasn't helping the situation but, as I was still at the rear, I couldn't see his grimace change to a vacant expression, grey pallor and beads of sweat on his forehead. So I continued once more, 'Wow! I have never seen so many traction engines! Look at that one! And that one there, look!'

If it had been me, looking at me, then I would've had to slap myself for being so ludicrously annoying and animated.

Bobby remained silent, other than the occasional word which was incomprehensible and small squeak-like noises, but, in a sudden outburst of common sense, the One at the left took him by the hand and led him out of the shop. The One who had previously been to the right tagged along with a confused demeanour, and I followed up at the back, as this seemed to be my acquired position for the day. (Being at the rear is quite a sought-after position as it means your buttocks can't be slapped.)

Outside the shop, Bobby was firmly sat down by Granny who was no longer the One to the left as she had taken control of the situation and was now the One in central position. He was given fluids by Granny, and I regressed to my ferreting behaviour as I searched for lavender oil and Bach's Rescue Remedy. It was my birthday that day, I have just remembered, but no one ever said that ferreting on your birthday was a crime, so I continued.

As my poor child was clearly in a dazed and distressed state, as well as overheating and practically steaming from the ears, I sprayed him in the face with the cool-spray while shoving lavender oil under his nose and trying to get Rescue Remedy drops under his tongue. Granny pushed me aside and gave me the 'For God's sake! Give him some space!' look. So, appropriately, I stepped aside and gave him some space. I am not sure if God actually benefited from that particular manoeuvre in any way, but I was not in a position to argue with the formidable Granny who seemed to be the only person in control.

Once I had put my brain into gear, I fetched Bobby an ice cream in the hope that it would cool him down. He reluctantly tried a bit, but seemed listless, weak and not in an ice-cream mood, so I ate it myself. It was then collectively agreed that we should all return to the car and travel back to our accommodation.

Bobby sat in the car saying very little as the rest of us performed a dissection of the incident by way of a debrief. It was a unanimous conclusion that he had been completely overloaded by the sheer quantity of merchandise in the shop, the colours, the sounds and the smells of the very things that he loved so much – die-cast models.

'Are you okay?'

'No.'

'How do you feel?'

'Blank.'

'Do you have any aches or pains?'

'Yes.'

'Where?'

'All over.'

'Can you tell me what the aches and pains are like?'

'Like I am going to be sick.'

'Do you think you are going to be sick?'

'Yes. I am going to be sick now.'

Sadly, Granddad's brand new car did not stop in time and, as promised, vomit arrived. Upon returning to stable ground, we helped carry the sick child who could not hold himself up and could not keep any fluids down. An hour later, the sick child and entourage were in the local accident and emergency hospital where the physician in attendance confirmed a case of die-cast model overload. We had been lucky that England was in the middle of a World Cup soccer match and so the hospital was very quiet.

Very dehydrated and weak, we carried Bobby off and laid him down for a rare sleep totalling eighteen hours. The remaining three of us wished me a happy birthday and then discussed how to get a die-cast traction engine without going back to the shop. The traction engine did materialize eventually, but it took a three-mile walk by the One on the left and the One on the right the following day.

Luckily, Bobby fully recovered and was now a boat. Yes, he was now *sailing* around the apartment on a bedside table which was on castors, mimicking maritime-like announcements while skidding across the floor. This continued for the following four days, and any attempted conversations were interrupted by the swish of a bedside table gliding past us at speed. The noise was awful and I considered taking the earplugs to the people in the apartment downstairs, but at least he was well again, even if he *was* a boat.

> *'Would you like to go for a walk?'*
>
> *'This is the* Esk Belle II, *please return to your seats.' (Zooms past to the right.)*
>
> *'Cheese sandwich? I had better top up your drink too.'*
>
> *'Approaching the harbour now.* Esk Belle II *is now approaching the harbour.' (Swishes to the left.)*
>
> *'I will put a few potato chips on the side for you.'*
>
> *'Welcome to the* Esk Belle II. *I am your captain today.' (Skids the length of the apartment and docks at the front door.)*

Anything with wheels is of huge interest. It doesn't have to be a train or a car or a die-cast traction engine. It can sometimes be a suitcase on wheels.

When Bobby was very small, about two or three years old, he had a mini-suitcase on wheels. It was taken on every holiday for two reasons: first, it contained the train track (and trains when I remembered to pack them) and, second, he could pull it behind him wherever he went. After dinner each evening, we would go for a walk around the block, and the wheelie case would come with us. As he got older, this activity continued, and eventually he explained why he liked doing it:

> *'When I pull the case behind me, it follows me in a straight line. And if you listen to the wheels, they sound like a train on a track going clickety clack, clickety clack. And if I can hear*

the sound of the train going over the track, then I can't hear anything else.'

One thing that didn't have any wheels was a certain piece of cardboard that caused a stir on a beach somewhere. This particular piece of cardboard wasn't as visually interesting as the cardboard chicken – it was about the size of a magazine and around an inch thick. I do not recall where the card had come from, but it had fast become a highly desired object, and Bobby had found that his bottom fitted on to it quite nicely. For a few hours, the card was used to sit on and slide down a long ramp which led down to the sand. Everyone breathed a sigh of relief as he happily slid down the ramp hundreds of times, squealing with delight.

Granny, Granddad and I had been sitting like the Three Wise Monkeys throughout this time. I was neither speaking nor seeing evil and the other two were hearing none of it either. But then we were summoned to try out the cardboard for ourselves and we took it in turns to squeeze our somewhat larger bottoms on to it.

One bottom, however, must have been slightly bigger and heavier than the others (although nobody would admit this) because the card began to tear. At the sight of this, Bobby's distress manifested itself in pulsating screaming that lasted for a continuous twenty minutes. Now, I quite understand the need to scream at the sight of one's *own* bottom, and I do it every evening when I get out of the shower, but it was the tear that had caused the outburst rather than anybody's bulbous butt.

I made a number of attempts to stop the excruciating noise, including hugging him very tightly, stroking him gently, distracting him, talking softly to him and screaming along with him (but louder). Nothing worked.

By this time, the few people present on the beach (luckily, we had positioned ourselves some distance away from any other life form, human or otherwise) began to move further away, craning their necks to see where the noise was coming from. Bobby began to sob intermittently between screams – which was very clever because it is difficult to sob and scream. Granny and Granddad were beginning to collect belongings and shake the beach towels so that a quick getaway could be achieved as soon as possible. I gave up trying to calm the situation and sat swaying to the rhythm.

Eventually, the screaming stopped and I hugged my son tightly. The beach had cleared (cue the tumbleweed) and everything returned to normality, although my ears were hurting a bit. Granddad was on his way back to the car with our belongings, and Granny was staring at me, shell-shocked. 'Well,' she said, 'I have never seen *that* one before.'

Returning home, we found a new piece of card, but it was not appreciated or wanted, because Bobby had resumed position on the bedside table and was too busy sliding past us at however many knots the *Esk Belle II* is capable of.

There have been many incidents that have been *not so funny*, including the time he nearly fell off the edge of a cliff when a Harrier jump jet flew over low in the sky and he did not get his hands over his ears before the noise startled him. Not at *all* funny. Then there was the time he was doing his usual method of walking – *hop–skip–jump–stumble* – on a pavement outside a transport museum and fell off into the path of an oncoming tram. Really *not* amusing (although I had the medical kit in the rucksack and so the bleeding knees were easily patched up). Now you know why I always have a medical kit and a rucksack. Maybe it would be a safer option to put Bobby in the rucksack and walk hand in hand with the medical kit.

We went on a pleasure-boat trip once and I enjoyed a nice cup of tea while Bobby walked around in a large circle for the full ninety minutes. We went down a cavern on a guided tour one day and he shouted '*Boring!*' so loudly that it echoed for what seemed like a lifetime (as it *would* do in a cavern). He didn't actually think it was boring – he was really rather enjoying it – but he liked the sound that the word 'boring' made and had an urge to shout it at that particular moment.

It is, though, Bobby's fascination with and attraction to animals that has been obvious during most of our trips, and as one of our more regular holiday destinations is like a giant nature reserve, he could not be happier. We made the mistake of taking Granny one summer. Well, Granddad came too, and it wasn't exactly a *mistake*, but it was poor Granny who was held a prisoner in the villa for many hours.

Bobby had somehow learned how to communicate with swans and had attracted such a huge crowd of friendly ones that they refused to leave. The villa was situated next to a lake, so the posse of swans grew in number by the minute, and as Bobby happily strolled among them telling stories and enjoying their company, Granny was unaware that the patio doors were wide open. She sat calmly reading a magazine, unaware of the horrors that awaited her – until my offspring and I left her unattended and went for a walk.

Upon returning, poor Granny was shut in the villa. She had left some keys on the patio table outside and was desperate to retrieve them, but the swans (who were not as friendly with Granny) were refusing to let her out.

While Bobby and I had been enjoying our stroll, and Granddad was off having a sailing lesson on the lake (and falling in), the swans had begun to enter the building, and the petrified Granny had shut the patio doors to prevent a full-on invasion. So there she was, stuck. Upon our return, Bobby promptly reopened the doors, told Granny not to be so silly and let them all roam free.

'Hello, swannies. I am back.'

'Could you shut the doors, please?'

'No – look at the swans, they are all coming to see you.'

'Yes, but could you shut the doors, please. They are frightening me.'

'Don't be silly, Granny. They just want to come in and say hello.'

'I don't want to say hello. Shut the doors – THEY ARE COMING!'

(Bobby shut the doors with Granny on the inside and him on the outside. Socializing with the swans continued.)

Granny mouthed through the glass doors, 'And could you get me my keys, please...'

One particular day, which should have been a very important occasion in Bobby's life, was his aunt's wedding day. This being his one and only aunt and this being a wedding that was two years in the making, it was decided in advance that he might be able to deal with the responsibility of being pageboy. As the months went by and the date got closer, the family became unsure as to whether this would be the case.

Now, Bobby loves his aunt very much. First, because she makes ridiculous noises to make him laugh, and, second, because she can sulk and throw a tantrum in a similar way to him – so they understand each other very well and he sees her unpredictability as very predictable. He also educated her on the benefits of articulated lorries once, which she enjoyed immensely, and so she was added to the list of acceptable people in his life.

Luckily, the soon-to-be-uncle was also granted the highly acclaimed status of 'approved person'. Not because he was marrying the aunt, but because he often managed, somehow, to play the same game with the same noises and in the same way for hours and hours and hours, according to the instructions that he had been given.

The day of the wedding rehearsal came, and Bobby entered the church with trepidation. Halfway down the aisle, he decided that the underneath of the vicar's cassock was a more appealing place to be, and so he placed himself there while everybody else tried to continue the rehearsal.

It was difficult. I was trying to pretend to straighten the veil of an imaginary wedding dress, which is difficult enough, but to do it while my son was staring at me from underneath the vicar was near-on impossible. Cross-legged and clearly unimpressed, he began to make noises with intermittent splatterings of the not-so-appropriate word 'hell'.

'Dearly beloved…'

'Eeek, eeek, beep, beep, hell!'

'We are gathered here today…'

'Hell, hell, hell. Yawn, yawn. Cuckoo!' (Checks imaginary wristwatch.)

'Let's practise the opening prayer, shall we?'

*'Hmmm. Hell. Let's do that. La la la.' (Reads imaginary
newspaper.)*

*'Perhaps it would be helpful if someone could take the little
boy to the back of the church for a short while so that we can
continue?'*

'Hmmm. OUT of the church would be better.'

So it was sensibly decided, after vast consultation with
cassock-child, that his role might be a 'bit too much
for him', as the practice only had around eight people
present and the real thing would host around a hundred.
Although disappointed, a sigh of relief was exhaled by
many. On the day itself, however, Bobby dressed up in the
suit that had been ordered for him, attended the evening
reception, took a few photographs, collected his gift and
promptly left half an hour later. He declared that the only
part he was interested in was seeing his aunt's dress and
checking out the car she had been chauffeured in.

I have no doubt that if his aunt had been an owl, a
sheep or a boa-constrictor, and the wedding had been
scheduled to take place in a zoo, there would have been
no problem. But despite the fact that both she and the
groom were very loved, the whole event was far too much
for him to contend with, and rather than risk another trip
up the cassock, he had appropriately bowed out.

'Did you enjoy the short time you spent at the wedding?'

'The car was really nice. It was a Bentley.'

'She looked very pretty, didn't she?'

'Did you see the fairy on the hood?'

'So what did you think of her dress?'

'The leather interior was amazing.'

'Yep. It was amazing.'

'She looked like a fairy.'

'Who? Your aunt?'

'No – the figure on the hood.'

'Oh. You are still talking about the car.'

'My aunt looked like a princess.'

Sometimes it is the little things that are said, when least expected, that really take my breath away. Saying his aunt 'looked like a princess' was one of those moments. This highlights another magical thing about autism and an annoying thing about everybody else. People tend to scatter compliments around like cheap confetti. We all do it and we do it for the right reasons – to make people happy and to make them feel valued. But consider a compliment given by a person with autism – it means much more because it will undoubtedly be given with the most genuine of intentions. And it will be the truth.

On the subject of truth, a holiday to the British Lake District was a very welcome retreat. The cottage was for sale, but no potential buyers were planned to visit during that particular week as it was the holidays and we were looking forward to welcoming in the New Year in the beautiful scenic surroundings. We had decorated the rooms, assembled a miniature Christmas tree and planned a party tea for the two of us. Idyllic.

As we all know, however, the best-laid plans of mice and men (I have no idea what that means, but it is something to do with a poem by Robert Burns and nothing to do with mice-architects or vermin problems) do not always work out.

On the first day, a couple knocked at the door and said they had come to stay in the holiday cottage. The couple were human beings, not mice with plans and a good command of the English language, and Bobby looked them up and down, and then slowly up again, finally resting his eyes firmly on their faces. I explained there must be some mistake, but rather than leaving, they almost began to justify their desire for a weekend break. I couldn't quite understand why they were telling me this, but I nodded in agreement and then apologized for refusing to leave. Why? *Why* did I do that? That's another strange thing we 'normal' people do – we apologize for things that we shouldn't be sorry for and for events over which we have had no control.

During the conversation, I had used my left arm as a barrier so that Bobby could not get too close to the couple. They didn't look dangerous in any way, but in the background I could hear him muttering comments like 'Yeah. Well. Tough because we are here' and 'Hmm…a likely story. Oh well, deary, deary me, there's no room for you here so off you go…'

He found the incident quite unsettling as we had not expected any visitors at all, but he also had a suspicious look on his face and it was just asking to be questioned.

'Okay, I can see you want to tell me something, so I am all ears.'

'No, you are not all ears and that is a stupid thing to say.'

'Go for it. You have my undivided attention.'

'That's silly as well because you can't divide something that you can't see.'

'Just tell me what you are thinking.'

'I am thinking about those stupid people.'

'They weren't stupid. They were probably just looking forward to a weekend of hill-walking and sightseeing, and now they have to find somewhere else to stay.'

'Aha. That's what you think.'

'Yes. Why, what are you thinking?'

'Tell me, Mum. Did they look as if they were dressed for hill-walking?'

Too busy apologizing for my very existence during my conversation with the couple, I had not paid much attention to the fact that the female was wearing a leopard-skin coat, stilettos and lots of make-up. And they had little luggage: just overnight bags. My son had obviously worked out their intentions more quickly and efficiently than me, which was slightly worrying, until he said, *'I* know what they were going to do. Nothing but shopping and buying lipstick. How awful!'

The following day we heard keys rattling in the lock and it was rather scary at the time. I told Bobby to stay in the room and shut the door while I went to see what was happening, a broom in my hand. I thought the broom would come in handy if it was a burglar, although a burglar would not have keys, and with a broom as an offensive weapon, I could've only swept him to death. Not to worry – it was only the real-estate agent. Bobby heard the confused conversation and joined me. A potential buyer had decided they would like to visit at short notice.

'This gentleman needs to show a lady around the cottage, Bobby. We are going to stay nice and quiet so they can have a walk around.'

'Are we? Well, you might be, but I am going to carry on as normal. And don't let them near my Lego.'

'Nobody is going to touch your Lego.'

'Touch it?! They can't even look at it!'

'They will completely avoid your Lego.'

'Shame they can't avoid coming here. It's damn inconsiderate.'

We sat reading a book until the agent and the potential buyer began to make their way back to the door. But then she decided she would like to interrogate me.

'Sorry, I am not the owner, but I will do my best to answer your questions.' (Yes, once again I had apologized for something I did not actually regret, and Bobby looked at me with pity as if to say, 'My poor, dear mother. She is so pathetic.')

'Is the central heating easy to use?' she said.

'Yes, we just turn on a switch and it kind of, well, it just... works,' I replied before being cut short by Bobby.

'Nope. It's very difficult and we have to follow a very long list of instructions.'

The lady looked at him as though he should not have a voice and continued with, 'Do the dogs next door make a lot of noise?'

'No,' I replied, 'we only hear them when they are disturbed.'

'Yes!' said Bobby. 'They were barking all last night and the noise is unbearable because they are very large dogs.'

'Do you like visiting here?' she said.

(I wanted to reply, 'No. I just come for the fun of it so I can have a miserable time being disturbed by people like you and have a dog barking all night. Why?')

I actually said, *'Yes.'*

Bobby concluded the conversation with, 'We like it very much because we are not usually disturbed. I don't think you would like it, though. You didn't touch my Lego, did you? Anyway, goodbye.'

The lady did not buy the cottage and I think she had guessed that Bobby did not want it to be sold. Our trip away had not gone according to plan at all. On the third day our car broke down. It was minus six degrees, the morning of New Year's Eve, and our car would not start. The recovery vehicle arrived. The mechanic managed to start the engine and he suggested that we immediately pack our bags, get into the car and get ourselves back home before it died again. So, within half an hour we were on our way home on the three-hour trip.

'So, Mum. We drive three hours to the Lake District for a New Year's Eve party, we unpack, decorate the cottage, put up with surprise visitors, have to call out a mechanic, and now we are on the way back home. It's cold, it's foggy, the roads are busy and I'm starving.'

'I'm sorry, sweetheart. I know it hasn't worked out so well this time, but at least we can get home and we aren't stranded. We can get the car properly mended in a few days.'

'That's not the problem. I am just really angry that I had to move my Lego. What if it gets damaged on the way home?'

As I write this, we have just returned from a trip to a quiet Scottish island, and I have very fond memories of a perfect vacation – sunshine (not too warm), sea, beautiful beaches (with no people on them), one tiny main road (with very few cars on it), lots of nature and very little noise pollution. Bobby was at his best while enjoying the peaceful surroundings and not having to socialize too much. The trip had been planned a month earlier than our usual annual vacation dates due to the holiday cottage only being available for limited periods.

Incidentally, Bobby tells me that he gets no vitamin D from sunlight. Apparently, he gets vitamin G. Vitamin G is 'Grim', and that he why he is unhappy when it is too sunny.

As the trip involved a six-hour drive and a one-hour ferry trip, it was important (essential) that the entourage came too. We hired a larger vehicle for maximum comfort, and the tinted rear windows were so gratefully accepted by my little travelling companion that he settled into the journey immediately. The car also had lots of little storage compartments in the inside roof which, although of great interest to him, caused quite a lot of problems for the passengers. On any one day, the compartments would be filled with stones, plants, shells and toys (plus a little Lego pirate which he insisted came with us on every trip).

The greatest use of the compartments, however, and the many light switches and air-conditioning controls, was for Bobby to pretend he was a pilot. Each trip was accompanied by a full on-board safety check which we all had to abide by, and the Pilot would talk us through every gadget manoeuvre he made. Far from getting angry when the small compartment doors kept flying open, he thought this hilarious and incorporated it into his new role. The gadgets, and the continual announcements from the Pilot, did cause the rest of us to mishear each other rather a lot, such as this conversation on the way home.

'Does anyone need a toilet break?'

'Testing all controls...'

'Sorry?'

'I said, does anyone need a toilet break?'

'The rain's too heavy to get out of the car.'

'Please remain in your seats. Beep beep.'

'Yes – looks like a cloudburst.'

'Sorry? Did you say the tyre's burst?'

'Forget it. Does anyone need to stop or not?'

'Please fasten your safety belts. We are experiencing turbulence.'

On the same island, we were elevated to the position of 'Imaginatives'. An Imaginative sits on the beach thinking up things for Bobby to create out of sand. We were very good at it, except when we got carried away and had a normal conversation between ourselves. At that point, we were reminded of our status (elevated from 'normal people' but not important enough to be an equal) and we were told to sort out our brains and get some imagining done. So we did, for around three hours.

Returning home was a bit of a shock to the system, as suddenly the noise of traffic and lack of sandy beaches caused both me and him to get Scottish-island withdrawal symptoms. Bobby, however, seemed to be dealing with it slightly better than me. There were two reasons for this – first, he now only had one week to complete at school before the end of term, and, second…

'What month is it?'

'May.'

'What month is the next month?'

'Let's work it out. It goes April, May and then…'

'June?'

'That's right. Why?'

'Great! We always go on holiday in June!'

'We do. But this year we went in May, so we went a month early.'

'So we are not going on holiday next month?'

'No.' (Starting to quiver.)

'Well, that's just great, isn't it?! You have just ruined everything! And the school sports day is in June and that means I won't escape it by being away on holiday! I might as well just run away now!'

'Don't run away. You will miss our next holiday if you run away.'

'When is it? Next June? Or are you going to mess it all up again and plan it for May? Whoever thought that a holiday in May was a good idea?'

'It was us. The Imaginatives.'

'You're all fired.'

As is usually the case, holidays end with an urgent need to plan another – just to get over the one before. The preference would be to have one in June because it would appear that anybody with even half a brain cell would not dream of a holiday in May. But then what do *I* know? I am only an unemployed Imaginative, and one that didn't think to point out this momentous change to routine prior to allowing myself to enjoy it. Note to self: book holidays for *June*, remember trains for train track, get a new job and *accept that routines are not there to inconvenience you – they actually help!*

CHAPTER 6

SLEEPING IS *NOT* AN OPTION

'What's the point of sleep? It just interrupts time that would be better spent on playing, and how am I supposed to know what is happening if I am asleep? Anything could happen and I wouldn't know, and that could be very dangerous indeed.'

Seeing as this chapter is all about sleep, it is 11.30 p.m. and my brain is losing the will to live, I shall continue in the format of a bedtime story. I have now adopted a soft and gentle voice as one mysteriously does when reading a bedtime story...

'Why do you talk all quietly and soft when you are reading to me at bedtime? Do you have a sore throat or something?'

Once upon a time, there was a little boy called Bobby and he did not like sleep. No matter what his mother did to help him on his way to the land of nod, it was not appreciated and it did not work.

When the little boy was only a few years old, the unhelpful and inconsiderate Mr Sandman had a bit of a nervous breakdown, and instead of sprinkling his magical dust into the child's eyes, he made nasty and naughty night terrors come and cause the child to thrash about and bang his head on the wall. The poor little boy did not like waking up with bumps on his head and so he decided not to go to sleep – ever again.

One day, the child's mother was looking somewhat haggard, and so he said to her, 'Mummy, what are those saggy bits of skin under your eyes and why are they darker than the rest of you?' The mother hugged her little boy close to her and said, 'It is because I get no sleep, little one, and therefore my eye-bags sag and I take on the appearance of a used plastic carrier bag.'

'Oh,' said the boy, 'why are you getting no sleep? And why do you *want* to sleep anyway?'

The mother smiled in her comforting and contented way and, without moving her lips, because she was suppressing an inner urge to wail like a banshee, said, 'Because I am awake all night looking after you, my honey-bunny-sweetie-pie, and if I don't sleep soon, I will surely fade away into oblivion.' (Or words to that effect.)

Many years went by and the child did not learn to love sleep any more than before. The mother had not faded away completely but she had become a more pastel-coloured version of her former vibrant self.

'Mummy,' said the boy, 'I do not wish to sleep as it is not dark.'

The mother chuckled delightfully and said, 'Of course it is not dark, my precious little lamb, as it is the fair season of summer and the sun shines brightly until late at night.' (This was a lie, because it wasn't between 12 noon and 6 p.m. with a Z in the month.)

Later in the year, the little bundle of joy said, 'Mummy, I do not want to go to sleep as it is very dark and I am afraid.'

The mother smiled affectionately and said, 'Of course it is very dark, my angelic sweet cherub, it is winter and the sun must go to bed and recharge its bright rays.' (Which we never get the benefit of, and Vitamin G is unpopular anyway.)

The boy and the mother continued their bedtime talks for many years to come and yet still he did not succumb to the delights of sleep. The mother became more and more tired, and the child continued to question the reason for sleep and the justification for such a waste of time. The older he became, the more he would avoid it.

'Mum,' said the child, 'I am unable to sleep as there is so much suffering in the world.'

'Yes,' replied the mother, 'but there is little you can do about it at midnight on a Tuesday.'

'You don't understand,' retorted the boy. 'How am I supposed to sleep when there are abandoned animals in the world and people are treading on spiders?'

'That is very considerate of you, my dear, and maybe we could talk about this tomorrow?'

'When is tomorrow, and what is the day after today?' he questioned with wide eyes and warm cheeks.

'Well, officially, tomorrow begins a few seconds after midnight and the day after today is Wednesday.'

'This is good news you bring me!' said the child exuberantly, 'as it must *surely* now be past midnight and we can discuss the matter because it is Wednesday.'

Hugging her son closely to her fluffy brown oversized man's bathrobe which made her look like a bear, the mother sighed and discussed suffering in the big, wide world until at last the sleepy child was overcome by exhaustion, keeled over and banged his head on the headboard. And so the little boy awoke again and said, 'Mum, what happened, and what do we do about the spiders?'

The years went by and the child still trotted from his bedroom to the mother's as soon as she walked up the stairs to bed. The child sleepwalked and was found in a wardrobe one night and in a washing basket the next. He eventually became too large for his mother to carry him back into his own room. The poor mother found that the only way she (or he) could get any sleep was to leave him be in her bed.

One fine summer's evening, the mother showed her son a beautiful sunset. 'The sun is going to sleep and now *you* must too,' she said, gently but firmly shuffling him from the window to the bed. The mother blacked out the windows and turned the nightlight away from him so that a deep, dark red glow filled the edges of the room. The mother read lovingly to the child and pronounced each word of a calming poem as softly as cotton wool.

'Shhhh…now you must allow yourself to drift to sleep,' she whispered, walking backwards out of the room. 'Shhhh…' she said as she hit her ankle on the bedroom door.

The child lay on his side, staring into the peaceful dark red abyss at the side of him and then, in a quiet and monotone voice said, 'How can I sleep when the last remaining survivor of the *Titanic* has died today at the age of 97?'

The mother sighed her signature sigh and replied, 'My child, she has probably gone to the big ship in the sky where she will forever be in peace. Hush now and go to sleep.'

'That makes me feel no better whatsoever. Good*night*!' replied the angry, sleepy child.

As the mother wearily made her way downstairs to the oh-so-familiar kitchen sink, she heard a rat-a-tat-tat from a room above. She looked this way and that, that way and this, this way, that way, the other way and that way again. Had that cheeky little mouse returned to her humble home, and was it time to bring out the humane traps again? Was a stranger lurking in a corner? Was her child in danger, and should she growl like a bear in a bathrobe to frighten off the unidentified creature that stalked her abode?

The mother crept ever so slowly up the creaky stairs and, holding an old cast-iron cooking pot, she leaped into the room where her child was sleeping. Correction – *should* have been sleeping. For there was the delightful boy-child hammering the palms of his hands on the bedside table and drumming the tune of *Ghostbusters*.

'My child!' declared the mother in an exasperated way. 'Why do you drum so?'

'Practising. Am going to ask Santa for some drums. You can go back downstairs. Just leave me to it.'

Eventually, the short nights of summer (and the refuse-bag blackouts) were replaced with the chillier evenings of autumn, when the mother's son could not sleep for fear that bonfires made of leaves would set the house alight and that hedgehogs might not escape them before it was too late.

Autumn again changed to winter, in a mysteriously predictable fashion, and the little child could not sleep because he could not choose which soft toys to take to bed, as he didn't want to upset any of the others. Winter made the little boy's feet cold and so he put on a sock in a delightfully quirky way.

The mother, late one night, sat nodding by the fire and contemplated meaningless things because she was too tired to contemplate anything else.

'Mum?' called the child.

'Yes?' replied the mother.

'I have had a nasty dream.'

'You haven't been to sleep yet, dear,' stated the mother.

'Then I have had a nasty thought,' came the reply.

'What was the nasty thought, my love?' questioned the mother.

'The house may catch fire and the fire truck will get stuck in a traffic jam and not get to us on time and all my toys will get burned.'

'Relax, my love. The fire station is less than half a mile away and they would arrive within minutes.'

'How many minutes?'

'Not many.'

'How many?' the boy persisted.

'A couple,' the mother said bluntly.

'Two minutes, then.'

'Two or three, yes.'

'Is it two or three? A couple is two, so is it two or three? Make up your mind.'

'Two minutes,' said the mother. 'They would be here in two minutes. Now you go to sleep and Mummy will keep guard. The smoke alarms would wake us up and I would call the fire truck and the firefighters would get us out very safely and put the fire out. So you have no need to worry,' the mother declared very confidently with a metaphorical full stop at the end.

'All my toys could burn in two minutes,' cried the child. '*Two minutes* is not good enough.'

'Go. To. Sleep!' said the mother, who crawled into a dark corner and began to rock hysterically.

Half an hour later, the mother returned to the room to ensure that her little one was asleep and no longer worrying about the potential materialistic damage that a blaze could cause in their modest home on the outskirts of a small town. Her son lay in bed very still, breathing deeply and silently and staring up at the ceiling with his fingers holding open his eyelids.

'Please go to sleep tonight, my dearest one,' said the mother. 'I am very tired and must get some sleep myself.'

'Well, you should be in bed if you are tired,' said the sensible and logical child.

'I should indeed, my little delight, but I have a few jobs to do and must do them before sunrise.'

'Then you must only do the important ones.'

The mother muttered an inane monologue under her breath. It went something like, 'Everything is important because you have left me barely enough time to breathe let alone do less-than-important jobs! Why, oh why, can you not just go to sleep, you beastly child? Why must you insist on making me run up and down the stairs a hundred times a night? Correction – *drag* myself up the stairs approximately *ten* times per night. And actually, you don't *make* me do this – I just choose to because of the mindless fool I am! Why am I such a mindless fool? And why, in God's name, am I wearing the biggest bathrobe ever made?'

'Yes, sweetheart,' said the mother, 'I will just do the important jobs like cleaning out the goldfish bowl, as the fish has not seen the light of day since 1973 and the Hanging Gardens of Babylon are growing on the inside of the glass.'

And then, quite suddenly, everything went very quiet. The mother sat on the sofa, slid off on to the floor, and kept sliding across the rug until she looked like a nonchalant sloth. She opened the newspaper that she had been carrying under her arm for days, unable to get ten spare minutes to read the thing.

'HAVE WE FOUND KEY TO AUTISM?' shouted the front page. The mother didn't know! She panicked! 'Have we?' she thought. A 'MOMENTUS ACHIEVEMENT' it gushed. 'Stop shouting!' the mother complained to the newspaper. 'You will wake up the restful child!' She returned to the corner where she rocked some more as she realized that talking to a newspaper signalled the end of any sanity.

It would appear it's all down to genes. Oh yes, flaws in proteins and cell adhesion molecules and mutations in genes involved in brain interconnections. That's what it's all about. Of course, the mother always knew that – it's just that she never told anybody. She did not understand a word of it, actually, but suspected that, somewhere along the way, some maverick genes rebelled, turned into something else, screwed up all the protein-like stuff and something else happened after that.

The mother wondered if those genes belonged to her. She wondered if they could mutate into anything else later in life like Transformers.

The mother continued her one-woman debate. 'Refrigerator parenting' does not cause autism, she stated to herself, as she wanted to make it quite clear that she had never put her son anywhere near a refrigerator. He wouldn't fit in it because it was too full of cheese.

Eventually, she peeled her body off the floor and crept up the stairs (now looking like a sloth doing t'ai chi) and popped just one stray eye around the bedroom door. The child was sleeping soundly. The mother exhaled in a staccato style because she was rather stressed. And then, in the dead of the night, shrouded by peace and tranquillity and only disturbed by the hooting of an owl and the nearest main road, the tension oozed (yes, obviously *oozing* has to be involved) from her body. Until...

'Ha! Only joking! Is it time to get up yet? I thought I might have chance to watch *The Great Escape* DVD before school. What's for breakfast? Shall I tell you about my dream? Why is it still dark?'

The child did a huge stretch and plodded down the stairs. The mother did a huge groan and slid down them behind him.

And they all lived happily ever after.

The moral of the story according to the mother is: if you suffer from lack of sleep, act like a sloth and don't even attempt to do the important jobs, and then your body will perfectly match your baggy eyes. You will, in effect, end up like a crumpled old carrier bag.

The moral of the story according to the child is: don't sleep. It's overrated. Think how many years of your life you waste by sleeping – time that you could spend *playing*.

If I could write one of Carol Gray's marvellous Social Stories™ to help get both mother and child some sleep, it would read something like this:

> *Sometimes people need to sleep. Sleep is good because it helps me to stay healthy. Sleeping each night can help me feel better*

each daytime. Sometimes I don't want to go to sleep. This can make my mother very irritable, grumpy and ugly. Sometimes I do not want to sleep for years. This can make my mother feel so miserable and exhausted that she nods off while on the toilet and says obscure things that make no sense, like 'Which amount is the dish cheese at sundown?' This is not *okay. Getting some sleep will help my mother get some rest too. This would be good. This would be very okay. This may help my mother be a reasonable and popular person. I will try to like going to sleep. But I would rather play.*

CHAPTER 7

THE 'A' WORD IS *NOT* AUTISM

No, no, my friend. The 'A' word is 'achievement'. I do not believe that you or I think there is a single person on the autistic spectrum who does not *achieve* in some way. There is a very small percentage of talented individuals with superior musical abilities or incredible artistic skills, for example. I happen to know a woman with autism who can hammer random blocks of wood like no one has ever hammered wood before. There are also children like ours who are superior at singing the *Hallelujah Chorus* in an operatic style very early on a Sunday morning, and have been called 'artistic' by confused people who do not know the difference. They really should get out more; they would learn a lot, wouldn't they?

I have met people on the spectrum who can speak better than most television presenters. Even those who rely on sign language communicate more effectively than most television presenters. While the rest of us are worrying about whether the colour of our toenails matches our dentures, there will be a child out there categorizing his collection of barcodes, receipts or gas masks, which is more beneficial and actually achieves much more than our own follies.

There are many children and adults with autism who have communication and mobility difficulties, yet, with help and support, every smile and every reaction they give us is an achievement. I have no doubt in my mind, or heart, that my child and yours achieve and are talented in their own special way, and that we celebrate this with such gusto that we would put the Millennium celebrations to shame. Show me a child who *doesn't* achieve things and I will personally collect every copy of this book, roll them all up and proceed to thrash grapes with them.

What about us? You and me? We *believe* in our children, try to understand them, support them and alter our lives to accommodate them and *their* needs. The 'A' word, achievement, does not only apply to our children, because being a parent of a child on the spectrum, and doing everything we can to stand by them – and *stand up for them* – is an achievement that we too should be proud of.

'Today I have accomplished some independent work which was a great success and I have now attained one of my goals. By telling you this, I have accomplished another goal which is "to talk about myself and my abilities in a positive way."'

Bobby has been taught how to acknowledge his achievements by me, his family and his teachers. This act of acknowledgement forms part of his IEP (Individual Education Plan), SSSEN (Support Service for Special Educational Needs Medium-Term Plan to Support School Individual Education Plan) and his WBMDTFBAHAIHSET (What Bobby Must Do To Feel

Better About Himself And Improve His Self-Esteem
Target).

While the rest of us mere mortals are analyzing the
advantages and disadvantages of a fondue set and reading
'Ten tips for the perfect scented drawer liner', there are
thousands of individuals on the spectrum trying to work
us out. What motivates us? Why do we get hung up
on such trivial little issues? If we have two heads, we
should have two brains, so why don't we at least use *one*
of them?

It is an achievement that anyone with autism manages
to understand us at all. We may be on different planets,
but I truly believe it is the neurotypicals who lost their
minds with the invention of the wheel and drove ourselves
off to Planet Kiwi. Who, with the benefit of *two* brains,
invented the painful, masochistic and evil act which is
commonly known as 'waxing'? You're never going to
convince me that the inventor was sane – or anything
other than bald.

In the past, Bobby was allowed to leave school for
one afternoon each week to join a group of children at
a local mental health clinic. (All were girls, boys, dogs
and cardboard chickens on the spectrum.) I thought
this would be brilliant and he would meet like-minded
children and make some friends. What possessed me?
Why did I think that children on the spectrum would
be clones who walked around in straight lines and spoke
to each other in robotic language? The only things they
had in common were various obsessions and the desire
to jump on a beanbag – all at the same time. Bobby was,
however, the only one trying to escape by keeping his
back to the wall and sliding down it, along the corridors,
until he reached the exit.

'Don't ever take me there again! Why did you ever take me there?'

'It's a way of getting to know other children in a safe environment, children who have autism.'

'Safe environment? Other children? What are you talking about?! I would rather be at school!'

'I thought it might help you understand more about other children and more about autism — how it affects people and stuff.'

'What a stupid idea! I know how it affects me — it's me that has it!'

'The other children were nice, though, weren't they?'

'No. They were all odd.'

'Do you want to go back again next week?'

'I would rather die. Take me back again and I will escape — and this time the safe environment's security doors won't stop me. Please call at the newspaper shop on the way home. I need to look at a magazine with cars in it as I am very distressed.'

The above experiment taught me that children on the spectrum are *not* the same — they are as delightfully different as their individual achievements. We shouldn't dismiss the thoughts, views and opinions of other people just because they may be different. We should embrace diversity, listen and *hear* what is being said to us. Sometimes it can be hard to get to the crux of a story among all the verbal details, but there can be knowledge, wisdom and profundity at the end of it. And sometimes, there is no end to a conversation at all:

'I like outer space you know, Mum.'

'I know you do. What do you like about it?'

'It's peaceful and quiet. What do you like about it?'

'I like how it's mysterious and magical.'

'Mysterious? Not quite. There is a space station up there, you know.'

'Yes, but space is a big place, so it's still quite mysterious.'

'It's not just big, it's massive.'

'Exactly. So because we will never see it all, it's mysterious.'

'I don't quite get why you think it's mysterious. Explain.'

'It's mysterious because we don't know a lot about it.'

'No. Well, perhaps we ought to sort out Planet Earth before we go finding out more about space. Anyway, what do you mean by magical?'

'I think space is magical because it's…mysterious?'

'Well, it isn't mysterious because we have just agreed that. And there's no magic going on in space. You don't really know what you think, do you, Mum?'

'I thought I did, but now I'm not so sure. What do you think?'

'I think I like space because it's peaceful and quiet. What do you like about space?'

'I don't know. You had better tell me what I like about space.'
(Repeat until fades…)

I shall finish this book in the same spirit in which I started it: it is up to *us* to support our community of people with autism and the community to which we belong. We need to stand together and challenge the preconceptions *now and always*. Naivety and ignorance cause other people to lack understanding and – for them, for us and for everyone who lives with autism – it has to stop.

In 2009, the UK saw the landmark *Autism Bill* passed through Parliament and become the Autism Act, which will give legal rights to everyone with autism, ensuring ongoing health and social care support. Way to go! This is the sort of achievement that we – yes, *us* – make happen, and it paves the way for a smoother trip through that tunnel, lighting another candle along the way. It's amazing what we can achieve when we put our hearts and souls into the most worthy of causes – our kids.

In the meantime, as well as campaigning for big things, we can continue to recognize (and get extremely excited about) every tiny little achievement we witness:

> My darling son, for standing on a stage for 45 minutes, while the child behind you flicked your wool and cardboard ears when you were a sheep in the 2005 nativity play, and not retaliating, *I stand up and applaud you.*

> For learning to play the bass notes of *Yellow Submarine* on the guitar and playing it relentlessly for eight months, and for giving your toy soldiers individual physical examinations and therapy sessions (just in case they had suffered psychological harm) when another child had crammed them into the Batmobile, *I stand up and admire your persistence and dedication.*

> For eventually accepting, after nine years, that learning to write would be a good thing, and completing a journal with detailed entries of the injustices of life, why your mother has no sense of direction and that she should be referred to as an 'ape', *I stand up and praise you* (but don't necessarily agree with you).

For saying 'Yes, yes, I KNOW!' to people who are boring you with information that you logged in your brain while still in the womb, when most of us would stand there and continue to be bored for a further three hours, *I stand up and envy you.*

For making me take care of my appearance, choosing my outfits, encouraging me to be more appreciative of cheese, teaching me about things like the history of the Dinky car and...rusticles, and making me grow up enough to realize that acting like a child is an essential and enjoyable part of life, *I stand up and thank you* for the education I clearly missed out on at school.

For giving me the opportunity to prove my determination, strength, patience, stubbornness and stamina in this mad, mad world, *I stand up with all my physical and emotional presence and face that world* with the main aim of supporting you and the phenomenon that is 'autism' – with more ferocity than my growling bathrobe on a bad day.

For making me endure a roller coaster of emotions since the day you were born, making me laugh so much that I cry, making me cry so much that I laugh, and for turning every day into a comedy, *I stand up and laugh...and cry and get slightly hysterical.*

For every person who has been touched by autism and has gone on to contribute to the care, awareness-raising and support of those who need it, *I stand up alongside you and share mutual respect and admiration.*

To all those people who experience similar incidents to mine on a regular basis, we can exchange knowing glances and give each other the 'yep – I know how you feel' smile. It's a fantastic medicine for the worst of events! And to those of you who witness such events, please continue to be patient – we are trying *really* hard not to panic when our children decide that you might look better in a pile of strawberries.

We love it when you smile, nod and *laugh*, but we do understand that may be difficult if you are horizontal on a floor. Please accept our apologies, and help us neutralize the tension with a chuckle or two as we tend to your wounds, offer a helping hand. You may be slightly degraded, unconscious or temporarily incapacitated, but you (and any onlookers) *do have permission to laugh*.

Dear readers, please join me in standing up. Standing up together – with smiles, determination and unity – will get us through the most trying of times and create a force to be reckoned with. *Let us stand up and stand proud – of our children and of ourselves.*

Thank you for being a wonderful audience; it has been an absolute pleasure. I hope we meet again some day.

My son and I have now left the building – backwards and in a straight line (probably in the wrong direction), humming, holding a bunch of chives in each hand, an alkaline battery up my nose and a barcode stuck to my butt. Here's to the quirky side of life...

'Be who you are and say what you feel: because those who mind don't matter and those who matter don't mind'

– Bennett Cerf